BAPTISTS IN CANADA

BAPTISTS IN CANADA

Search for Identity
Amidst Diversity

Edited by

JAROLD K. ZEMAN

G.R. WELCH COMPANY, LIMITED
Burlington, Ontario, Canada

ISBN: 0-919532-37-3

Published by: G. R. Welch Company, Limited
             960 Gateway
             Burlington, Ontario
             L7L 5K7 Canada

Printed in Canada

Contents

Preface   vii

PART ONE: INFLUENCES AND IDENTITY

1 *Identity and Mission*   1
   Samuel J. Mikolaski

2 *British Influence in the Nineteenth Century*   21
   Robert S. Wilson

3 *Witness in French Canada*   45
   W. Nelson Thomson

4 *They Speak in Other Tongues: Witness Among*   67
   Immigrants
   Jarold K. Zeman

5 *North American (German) Baptists*   87
   Edward B. Link

   Editor's Note   104

PART TWO: PUBLIC LIFE AND SOCIAL
RESPONSIBILITY

6 *Baptists and Human Rights, 1837-1867*   107
   Paul R. Dekar

7 *A View of Some Canadian Headlines, 1860-1912*   137
   W. Gordon Carder

8 *THE CANADIAN BAPTIST and the Social Gospel*   147
   Movement, 1879-1914
   John S. Moir

9 *Baptists and Radical Politics in Western Canada,*   161
   1920-1950
   Walter E. Ellis

10 *World Relief, Development and Inter-Church Aid*   183
   R. Fred Bullen

*PART THREE: THEOLOGICAL TRENDS AND
CONFLICTS*
   11 *The Modernist Impulse at McMaster University,*   193
      1887-1927
      Clark H. Pinnock

   12 *Another Perspective on T.T. Shields and Fundamen-* 209
      talism
      Leslie K. Tarr

   13 *Baptist Leadership: Autocratic or Democratic?*   225
      John B. Richards

   14 *The Struggle for a United Evangelical Baptist*   237
      Fellowship, 1953-1965
      Kenneth R. Davis

   15 *National Survey of Baptist Ministers*   267
      James A. Beverley

Appendix One: Contributors   279
Appendix Two: Symposium Papers Published   281
   Elsewhere

Preface

For several generations, Baptists have been regarded as one of the "mainline" Protestant denominations in Canada. Yet their geographical distribution has been very uneven. In some areas, such as parts of Nova Scotia and New Brunswick, they constitute the largest Protestant communion. At the same time, in many rural areas of the Prairies, or in Newfoundland, they are virtually unknown.

In contrast to the United States where Baptists have surpassed in numerical strength all other Protestant churches (over 30 million members) Baptists have remained a small minority on the Canadian religious scene (about 200,000 members). Nonetheless, through the two centuries of their organized life, they have made notable contributions to Canada's spiritual, cultural and political life.

In their insistence on the right of every individual to interpret the Bible and to seek the will of God for himself or herself; in their emphasis on local church autonomy, and in their distrust of centralized denominational structures, Baptists have displayed a greater variety of beliefs and practices than any other major Protestant group. Such diversity must be expected, and treasured as the legitimate expression of the "free church" tradition.

However, a closer scrutiny of the heterogeneous trends and seemingly irreconcilable positions — which at times resulted in denominational divisions — will bring to light an underlying common identity of basic convictions. The first and last chapters of this book confirm such analysis.

The essays collected here reflect "the search for common identity amidst diversity" among Baptists in Canada, in the past and today. The papers were originally prepared for presentation at the International Symposium, "Baptists in Canada 1760-1980," held at Acadia University, Wolfville, Nova Scotia, on October 15 to 18, 1979. More than thirty scholars and many more interested persons from across Canada and the United States took part in the unique event. For the first time in this century, spokesmen from all major Baptist groups in Canada — and from the related denominations in the United States — met to interpret selected aspects of the Canadian Baptist tradition.

The symposium was sponsored by Acadia Divinity College as part of its annual Hayward Lectures series. The Social Sciences and Humanities Research Council of Canada provided a grant. Further assistance was received from the Baptist Federation of Canada, the Baptist Historical Committee of the United Baptist Convention of the Atlantic Provinces, and from the United Baptist Women's Missionary Union of the Atlantic Provinces. The undersigned served as symposium coordinator.

No topics were assigned. The symposium participants were free to submit research proposals on any subject related to the Canadian Baptist tradition. The final programme displayed a surprising degree of concentration on several crucial themes such as those expressed in the three sectional headings of the book: Influences and Identity; Public Life and Social Responsibility, and Theological Trends and Conflicts. The topics and authors of the other nineteen symposium papers, being published elsewhere, are listed in Appendix II.

A definitive history of the Baptists of Canada is yet to be written. The task will require exceptional maturity of scholarship and of judgment in interpretation. It is our hope that this volume, together with the other published essays from the symposium, will provide an incentive to further studies and thus bring us closer to the goal.

The production of this book, *Baptists in Canada*, has been underwritten, in part, from the Hayward Lectures fund at Acadia Divinity College. Several persons who wish to remain anonymous contributed to the costs of publication and thus substantially reduced the retail price of the book.

One could hardly wish for a more appropriate time to release this volume than the spring of 1980. In July, several thousand Baptists from all around the world are expected to gather in Toronto for the 14th Baptist.World Congress. May this book help them as they seek to understand Baptist life in Canada.

Spring, 1980   Jarold K. Zeman

Part One

Influences and Identity

1

Identity and Mission

Samuel J. Mikolaski

Identity: Canadian and Baptist

The sense of identity and mission of Baptists in Canada during the early years of this century appears to us today to have been almost idyllic. Witness the excellent statement of Dr. J. L. Gilmour as he describes Baptist life and faith in a general encyclopaedia on Canada in 1914:

> The Baptist people seek to found all their doctrine and procedure on Biblical teaching and practice, and they refuse to bind or be bound by creeds; they make the individual local church self-governing, and independent; they insist on credible evidence of regeneration as a prerequisite to church membership; they have two kinds of church officers — pastors and deacons; they have always stood for the separation of church and state, believing in a free church in a free state; they believe in government, and teach the duties of loyalty and good citizenship; they have always opposed persecution by the state for religious beliefs; they do not believe in state support for religious work; they hold that the ordinances should be "outward and visible signs of an inward and spiritual grace," which grace can reside only in those who have intelligently and personally received it; and they maintain that baptism should be by immersion. . .In polity the Baptists hold to independence and voluntaryism, so that any encroachment on the autonomy of the individual church is met with prompt and decisive opposition.[1]

Baptist life in Canada seems to have been remarkably coherent and stable: the growth pattern relative to population trends was acceptable. The public role of Baptists in Canadian life, though small, was visible and influential. Baptist unity was a growing, even received, dogma. Whatever disunity emerged was within the bounds of confessional Christianity. Cultural identity was unshaken due to the dominance of the British charter group. Nationhood aspiration and ideals burgeoned. Canadian identity was something concrete to aspire to and to lay hold upon. Theological instincts as to Baptist beliefs and church practices were clear. The lines between classical evangelical Protestantism and sacerdotal Catholicism and Anglicanism were clear, and Baptists were thought of as hand-maidens of the Canadian Protestant scene. The excellent joint hymnary of the United Church and Canadian Baptists which served Baptists so well for so long was a product of that mood.

Of course, things were not so simple. Nevertheless, compared with today they were much more coherent and stable. One can now reverse many of the foregoing points as indicators of changed Baptist circumstances in our time.

The substance of religious identity should not be confused with its accoutrement nor with peripheral activities of special interest groups. Identity is best reflected in a powerful current that sets the direction and pace of a religious tradition. In this sense it has a clear theology, is deeply religious and is powerfully motivated to mission.

The recent publication of a new Canadian Baptist hymnary is significant, but will be cosmetic unless the deeper elements of identity which it is supposed to reflect are present. The cessation of the joint agreement between the United Church of Canada and Canadian Baptists on the production of Sunday School materials is also important. But is it more than a defensive move if the Baptists do not produce more Christian education materials of their own as positive expressions of their identity and mission?

Charismatic renewal influences have been only marginally influential on Baptist life in Canada and have not altered either fundamental Baptist theological perspectives, churchmanship, or spirituality. Indeed, the changes that are taking place among those who call themselves charismatics are far more extensive and radical than any change they have wrought upon Baptist life in this country. The same applies to other renewal groups that have sprung up in recent years. Their relation to evangelical life in general and to Baptist life in particular is more as effect than as cause.

Baptist identity in Canada was forged from its British Baptist and British Free Church antecedents, with little historical awareness of the parallel Anabaptist tradition. In Canada, Baptists were thought of as part of the mainstream of Protestant life: liaison with this tradition meant the English Free Church tradition (Scottish and English Presbyterian, English Methodist, and English Congregational) rather than the European Reformation tradition which was more evidently the case in the United States. As a theological symbol and religious antecedent, the European Reformation and its Reformed tradition have never had the impact in Canada that they have elsewhere in the Protestant world. Thus, when the Canadian Protestant tradition moved massively into the theological liberal camp, and at the same time into international ecumenical ranks, Canadian Baptists remained checkmated and puzzled for a generation or more. This was not because they were frustrated in seeking their identity in ecumenical dialogue, but because they no longer sensed the confessional and religious link with the Free Church tradition that had in the past nourished the invisible tie between Baptists in Canada and their non-Catholic brethren. It is thus wrong to say that Canadian Baptists sought their identity in the ecumenical movement, though some Baptist leaders may have.

Dr. Gilmour's statement also reflects a coherent and stable view of government and of the state. It conveys a sense of dedication by Baptists to good citizenship. To be a good Baptist meant, as well, to be a good Canadian. I can attest to this as I recall the atmosphere of my childhood and youth in Ontario in the years before and after World War II.

As part of the work for this essay I visited Toronto for a round table discussion with a group of Baptist leaders on the subject of identity and mission. Their impressions parallel my own. In comparison with the upbringing of the middle-aged and older generation of Canadians, we seem in this generation to have lost the patriotism and emotion of our emblematic moments, and we increasingly suffer the public trivialization of our language and traditions. Public events are less occasions for commemoration and reflection and more for personal enjoyment and gratification.[2]

The meaning of Canadian identity is today elusive and problematic. Some of our sociologists question the appropriateness of the term "Canadian Society," and whether there is a Canadian identity. Factors that bear on this are many and complex: Was Canada's genius as a nation a counter-revolutionary spirit, as the United Empire Loyalist tradition suggests?[3] And does this spirit continue to be a significant force in Canadian society? Or, is Canadianism centred in a counter-nationalist mood, especially vis-a-vis the United States?[4]

There has occurred a strong emotional detachment from British ties, and a significant decrease in the prominence of the British charter group and its traditions, paralleled by increasing American cultural influence. Despite the emphasis on the cultural mosaic, Canada's growth is due more to natural increase than to immigration. There has been a displacement of class and status as criteria of citizenship in favour of definition in relation to the state (as in a number of modern industrial societies). Expanding economic organization aims at a modern integrated society, which generates conflicts about one's personal share of the economic pie rather than about political, societal and cultural ideology. There is increased population mobility. Regional economic and political aspiration has arisen in a new, strident way: Is Canada's economy one or many?[5] Should Canada have a weaker federal system, or a stronger one as some outside observers say?[6]

Fraternity is the corollary of cultural cohesion and national identity. Fraternity is essential to significant religious growth—certainly to regional or national renewal. I mean not only religious but also societal fraternity. Religious leaders have failed adequately to grasp this point: that societal granularism is as injurious to the Christian mission as is religious granularism. In light of this, consider the view of Calgary sociologist, Harry H..Hiller, on the state of Canadian society:

> It is clear that Canadian society does not consist of a homogeneous group of people with manifestly similar backgrounds who have lived together in the territory for a long

period of time. In fact, just the opposite is true. The society has been constantly changing and has never attained a period of social stability and calm in which coherence and a common tradition could emerge naturally and throughout the society.[7]

The critical importance of this — Canadian cohesion and identity—should not be lost sight of in any discussion about Baptist mission. Identity shapes mission and mission shapes identity. There cannot be effective, nationwide mission without regional and national fraternity. Social cohesion has diminished in Canada in my lifetime.

The integration of a society is more a spiritual, social and cultural reality — an issue of social and cultural ideology and of faith — than of politics, jurisprudence and consent. In Canada like interests of language, custom, belief and history have not generated a strong national consciousness of identity, except in Quebec. Unlike interests tend to divide the regions rather than to rally them around a common cause. Federal policies aimed at enforcing biculturalism and multiculturalism have simply skirted the sympathies necessary to develop a societal consciousness and cultural homogeneity. Political expedients have exacerbated the problems rather than fostered enduring spiritual bonds.[8]

It is unlikely that a Christian religious awakening can occur within national borders that lack social coherence. At least I know of no such case in history. This may be in part why national awakenings have occurred in Britain and in the United States but not in Canada, with the exception of the Atlantic provinces in the late eighteenth and early nineteenth centuries where there was present a strong regional cultural awareness and identity. Societal fraternity is a precondition to regional and national religious awakening.

Baptists and Emerging Trends

Evangelicals, including Baptists, are not transcultural. We are not a generalized, socially neutral international group as some Canadian evangelicals suppose. We think not only as evangelicals and as Baptists, but as Canadian Baptists who are evangelical. Our culture and trends within our society affect, and sometimes afflict, our conception of mission and the effectiveness of our ministry.

First, signs of unrest are discernable in the population about Christianity and the churches. Many Catholics disagree with the moral teaching of their church, yet remain loyal Catholics and show keen interest in biblical studies. Many people feel that churches and clergy are losing their spiritual character and that they need to be more open to renewal. There is growing distaste for mores strictures, each in their own way among Catholics and evangelical Protestants, though not necessarily a distaste for moral discipline. Interestingly, such liberalization of attitudes has not stimulated a resurgence of liberal churches and liberal theology. Conservation of fundamental Christian beliefs and respect for authentic Christian religious experience seem to be of profound concern to many. Many believe that church leaders and theologians of major denominations are out of touch with the faith of the people. There is an incipient faith, but without religious experience, among the unchurched which is heightened in periods of crisis, change and uncertainty and which offers outstanding opportunities for evangelism.[9]

Second, radical unrest is shaking the evangelical establishment of the northern United States, which inevitably affects Canadians because this is the major source that nourishes Canadian evangelicals. A new, young evangelical religious left is coming in from the cold and is invading the traditional evangelical churches. Demanded is concern for social justice and third world justice, disarmament, greater personal flexibility as to mores (a better word in this case than "freedom"), increased diversity of the evangelical cause even on the ways faith is expressed in the authority of Scripture, examination of the impact of affluence on the life-style of evangelicals, reach-out to minorities, reach-out to Christians of other major communions, and broader ranges of biblical interpretation that will furnish alternatives to slavish literalist viewpoints. These are but a few of their concerns. North American evangelicalism — a powerful religious force — is now being reshaped in the United States and Canada.

Third, new forms of political, economic and military radicalism have invaded the world church community. I shall not speak here of the furor caused by the World Council of Churches financial support for African development, some of which ended up being used for the military activities of certain African revolutionary groups. Edward Norman in his Reith

Lectures on the BBC during the autumn and winter of 1978 drew loud protest for his critique of ecumenical support of leftist and Marxist causes in South America and Africa, and of the undigested economic and political clichés that are widely accepted among left-thinking Christian leaders.

Let me concentrate on the Canadian scene. Last May Peter Brimelow, columnist for the *Financial Post* (May 19, 1979), analysed a broadsheet circulated jointly by leadership of the Anglican, Roman Catholic and United Churches on the federal election. The attitudes to election issues were significantly left-wing. Beyond such generalizations as the demand for more effective redistribution of income, the report advocated economic isolation for Canada (especially as to international trade in food and energy); economic sanctions against several countries; more open immigration even for radicals, and self-determination for northern native people. It drew conclusions such as that self-reliance in food via subsistence farming as against industrialized agriculture would solve world hunger; that multinational corporations are perverse; that competition exploits and generates repression, and that Canada should not refurbish its defence forces. The list of omissions from the sheet is long and noteworthy, including: the plight of the South-East Asia boat people; the persecution of Christians and Jews by communist, revolutionary and reactionary regimes; the growing international body of prisoners of conscience; the intense arms race among the communist countries, and the monolithic character of Marxist and Moslem states.

These examples indicate increased radical activity on the part of religious leaders and increased puzzlement by Christians as to the role of the churches in such matters.

Historically, Baptists have been radicals. They originated through the sacrifices of the Radical Reformation. However, in North America during the past fifty years they have become identified with the cultural, political and economic establishment. Should we therefore take the advice of today's religious and social radicals? Should our former spiritual and theological radicalism now shift into cultural, political and economic radicalism? There are certainly many individual elements of contemporary radical protest that no thinking Christian can evade (such as the socially detaching and careless affluence of today's elite lay and clerical evangelicalism). Nevertheless, I call into question the theory behind some contemporary radicalism, and some priorities. I urge that we renew our commitment to elements of the primitive radicalism that produced us.

Baptist radicalism is supremely person-preserving. The freedom of the individual and of the individual conscience, based on a philosophy of man that derives from the biblical doctrine of creation, is central to Baptist faith. The extension of this premise is that Baptists are, as well, radically antimonolithic and are pluralist socially, politically and religiously. Baptist radicalism today should show itself in extreme skepticism about uniform utopian schemes, whether of the right or of the left.

New forms of monolithic uniformity plague the world not only politically, but culturally, religiously and in economics. The alleged utopian hedonist societies advocated by some today are as optionless and monolithic as their classical, medieval and modern totalitarian counterparts were.[10] An important difference is that we are at a greater disadvantage than our forefathers and our situation is potentially more horrific than theirs. Whereas ancient and medieval closed systems allowed man to be man even if degraded and enslaved, the modern monoliths have the power scientifically and technologically to refashion man biologically, psychologically and socially to match their theoretical image of him.[11]

Baptists need to voice again their defence of diversity. In this they will keep company with many humanitarians who have not succumbed to utopian schemes.[12] The first lesson of modern man should be that the study of human behaviour can never be an exact science; that history can never be organized in the way in which biology or physics or mathematics can be organized. Thus, those theories and schemes which claim that the study of man and society can be an exact science, and who claim that total planning for a society is not only possible but necessary, are simply incompatible with the mental assumptions by which we live and act. Baptist radicalism must reassert the uniqueness and infinite value of the individual against new forms of historical, psychological and social determinism. Better poverty-stricken, starving and free than preprogrammed, gorged and happy.

The implications of Baptist radicalism for society are of great consequence. These principles nourished the political and religious structure of the new society that formed in the United States and Canada in contrast to the European models. They entailed rejection of the medieval ideal that a monolithic culture (the spiritual and temporal as two sides of a single coin) is prerequisite to social stability, as well as to political and theological integrity. The progress of the Believers' Church tradition in Canada with its voluntarist emphasis and pluralist social and religious outlook calls for the reorientation and reeducation of the public mind. In this Baptists must take the lead. We are strategically placed to do so.

Baptist pluralism impinges directly on questions of Canadian identity and the functions of the social contract. Pluralism cannot work without fraternity, and fraternity requires equality and liberty for its operating framework. Without these, contemporary forms of radicalism will become more oppressive than what they claim to cure.

A sense of national identity can be reactivated within the Canadian cooperative political and cultural structure. Canada's current malaise is due in part to a delayed reaction to the challenge that created the American national spirit. We have been dramatically cut off emotionally and culturally since World War II from our British charter group past. Britain herself has turned to Europe. While we are a mosaic, we did up until my generation share a common past with the cultural and political traditions of the dominant British charter group in Canada. We are now increasingly a people, as the Americans have been, who do not share a common past, but who do share a common future. The eschatological motif of our forefathers — the hope of the kingdom to come — must rekindle within us a new urgency to enter into a deliberate compact with the future.

Baptist Faith and Baptist Mission

A glowing opportunity confronts Baptists in Canada in our time. This calls for a new sense of who we are and what our mission is in Canadian life. Baptists need a renewed sense of their historical roots, of the apostolic character of their Christianity, of their faith and polity, and of the greatness of God — the God of righteousness and love who searches the hearts of men.

Baptists in Canada should set about to call the nation to God. Their task is nothing short of national evangelism and their mandate is the Great Commission of the crucified, risen and ascended Lord.

New Mind-Set

This new post-World War II Canadian mosaic calls for massive new effort and deep dedication by Baptists to overcome the social and economic stratification that characterizes Canadian religious life, including the evangelical tradition.[13] Our track record in ethnic ministries has been excellent but it needs urgently to be better in relation to the solitudes created by culture and class. Baptists in Canada are not primarily a Canadian cultural expression, but must profess a faith and practice a life-style that will infuse and transform cultures. The goal of the Gospel is to unite all men in Christ, in whom barriers of race, language and culture are overcome (Ephesians 2:11-16; Galatians 3:26-28). Let us strive therefore in a new way for greater interregional cooperation, a less establishmentarian frame of mind, less withdrawal and defensiveness, and more identification with the traditions of the Believers' Church ideals and the commission to evangelize the world.

The most public issue to confront us as a nation in recent years is multiculturalism. Nevertheless, another somewhat muted issue, that of class, is probably of equal if not greater critical importance religiously. Baptists in Canada must recover their place among the working class people of Canada. Let us be in the forefront of a new wave of people-appreciation, of whatever culture, status or class. Let the multitudes move our spirits to compassion.

A corollary is the need to reactivate the Baptist art of private and public criticism, combined with a cooperative spirit. Baptists in Canada have come through deep waters since the 1920s. We rightly fear the demagogue. We rightly deplore the catastrophic and fratricidal battles that have divided us and blunted what could have been explosive growth during the past two generations. Nevertheless, we must redevelop the art of criticism targeted to results and deep loyalty to each other as well as to Scripture and our Lord. We need more trust and less edginess and a larger sense that we all stand under the judgment of mission. We need as much orientation to results as we now have to activity.

This cannot be accomplished without leadership. Historically, a nice play can be discerned between leadership being produced and leadership being thrown up. We do need urgently a new mood in theological education that embraces a partnership between theological educators, pastors and the people. Important to this is the post-seminary development of able leadership. But the schools cannot educate what they do not get. Pastors and dedicated lay Christians are the key to recruitment and development of leadership. Thriving church programs — especially rural and small town ones — invariably throw up new generations of leadership who are subsequently able to encompass the new challenge of changing times. We must understand, however, that competent growth-leadership is often abrasive — or appears so. It has always been this way. Certainly the prophetic ministry in Scripture was almost invariably thought to be abrasive. We need to develop and accept leaders who, while loyal to the denominational cause and to us all, have the art to discern trends and the moral courage and drive to compel attention to strategic issues.

For example, is it really true that Baptists in Canada declined numerically between 1977 and 1978 as reported by the *Baptist World?*[14] What are we going to do about it? Or do we take a ho-hum attitude and carry on as usual?

In a mid-election campaign editorial on the Canadian scene the editors of the *Financial Post* (May 5, 1979, p. 6) wrote, "The leader who admits there is something wrong in the way we go about our economic affairs and has the mettle to propose excellence as the test, hard work as the means and equitable prosperity as the end merits a lot of attention. Too demanding? No." Can we frame a parallel demand for Baptist witness and ministry in Canada in our time? Let us pledge ourselves to rigorous program effectiveness analysis, measured against Christ's mission mandate and the growing Canadian population.

Kerygmatic Clarity

The vast majority of visible evangelicals in Canada are of the Believers' Church tradition. Baptists are the backbone — historically and numerically — of that tradition in Canada. They have the opportunity to reaffirm their Free Church heritage through a clear statement of the Gospel and enthusiastic proclamation, practice and living out of the Gospel. A critical issue in Canadian evangelicalism is the truncation of the Gospel — while personal faith is emphasized, baptism and church membership are thought to be optional.

Agreement as to essential characteristics of evangelical faith is widespread. This includes: faith in the uniqueness, authenticity and authority of the Bible as God's saving word to men; belief in Jesus Christ as Lord and Christ, in grace, and redemption through Christ's cross; and personal faith in Christ as Saviour.

Baptist faith impinges upon criticisms that many modern radicals have made of recent evangelicalism in two important respects. First, Baptists have always stressed discipleship and character formation. Not that others have not; only that traditionally "behave" has been the corollary of "believe" in Baptist evangelicalism. The resulting stewardship is seen to embrace the whole of life including personal habits, life-style, relationships, and the handling of the created order. All of this is conceived to be under the cross and under the Holy Spirit. Second, such faith and discipleship are seen to be inconceivable if private and granular. According to Baptist understanding of Scripture, granular faith is a truncation of the Gospel. The life in Christ makes secret, invisible Christianity impossible. This was a strategic issue in Anabaptist restitutionist theology. For Baptists, following New Testament practice, faith entails public confession in baptism, identification with the people of God in the believing fellowship of the church and obedient discipleship combined with sacrificial ministry. Thus the discipline of discipleship comprises not a set of rules or mores, but the call to forsake all and follow Christ and, nevertheless, to claim all for Christ.

No other priority can surpass the evangelistic one in our time. This is a simple and direct mandate, but not at all simple-minded. To relegate to the periphery that which is central, or to make what is central one among equal priorities, is neither theologically sound nor strategically astute. Clarity of message is essential to the Baptist mission and task. At the risk of being repetitive, I restate the following from my paper at Winnipeg last year as to our mission:

To preach the word of love and grace and redemption. To call men to repentance and faith in the Lord Jesus Christ. To baptize them without delay, upon the profession of their faith, which in the New Testament is the door into the church and into ministry. Conversion, baptism, reception of the Spirit, and membership are one event in the New Testament and in the post-apostolic church. Further, the task is to lead believers to develop the life in the Spirit which they have received, the life of obedient discipleship, and to teach them the biblical necessity of the local church of believers. This simple pattern needs to be repeated over and over again.[15]

People Concern

People concern today must wed compassion to keen sociological insight. We minister to need. To profile groups and communities in our society calls for a different set of assumptions than, say, secular social planning, but the growing importance of statistical population data and sociological research for the work of the church needs to be understood and acted upon.[16] No pastor, no association, no convention can now do without such information in order to achieve specific local program effectiveness. And if some pastors or leaders are successfully implementing growth-oriented ministries it is because they intuitively, if not formally, have sensed strategic areas of need and have tailored programs to meet those needs.

As an example, consider the changes that are taking place in the structure of Canadian households, classified by age of head, as these trends affect religious work.[17] A household is a family or a single individual living alone. In 1951, 40 percent of the population twenty years of age and over were classified as household heads. By 1979 this ratio had increased to 49 percent. Significant increases have occurred in the youngest age groups. That of ages twenty-five to thirty-four has increased from about 25 to 47 percent and that of ages twenty to twenty-four has doubled (from about 12 to about 25 percent). Today, young people leave home to set up on their own, and often they get married, at an earlier age. Correspondingly, marriage breakdown and divorce have rapidly increased.

Similarly, there is a significant rise in headship rates among the sixty-five and over age group as well (a rise from about 52 to about 58 percent). Formerly, many of these would have lived with their children. Now, not only changing extended-family patterns, but also improved pension payments, mean that more older people maintain their own separate households.

The implications of such data for ministry are great. First, they quantify reasons for the increase in loneliness in our society (which correspondingly affects the suicide rate), but as well they point to reasons for financial hardship, loss of practice in developing and maintaining extended family and primary personal relations (which contributes to marriage breakdowns), and loss of contact with religiously-oriented groupings in favour of the secular, impersonal social context.

Here is evidence of the strategic function of the local church as a koinonia and teaching center. Just as in the generations of the early church during the first three centuries, so today the increased depersonalization of modern man affords to us a marvellous opportunity. We cannot win people to the Lord impersonally. We must as much win them to ourselves as to the Lord. We must open our lives to them. That is a strategic function of the Body of Christ. Conversion isolates people unless the Body of Christ becomes surrogate family to them. Is this not the intent of the New Testament?

In an age of decreased sensitivity to suffering and increasing brutality, as well as of increased economic pressure due to inflation, Baptists must care about people. Our churches should renew their sense of community and become radically egalitarian. Here emotional and social security should be found. In an age of increased impersonal behavioural control, the local church needs to be supremely person-centred and person-preserving.

Committed Churchmanship

Baptists have been so consistently identified with Protestantism in Canada that their distinctive ecclesiology and views on discipleship have been blurred. This occurs precisely at points where the Radical Reformers declared that the Reformation cries of "Scripture alone" and "Grace alone," though key issues, diverted attention from the Reformation being a halfway house. Baptists and Anabaptists resisted Protestant monolithic uniformity as much as they resisted Catholic monolithic uniformity. Canadian establishment-minded religious attitudes perpetuate the situation.[18] The modern dress of religious attitudes serves simply to obscure deeper questions, whether from the religious right or left. Baptists in Canada must make up their minds whether they will remain in the camp of their forefathers and take the lead in the modern Believers' Church movement, or whether they prefer the status accorded the mainstream Protestant and Catholic traditions. I do not believe that Baptists in this country can have it both ways and survive as authentic representatives of their own heritage.

Contemporary Baptist beliefs and ideas parallel those outlined by Dr. Gilmour, with which I began this essay. Some of them are: the belief that Christian faith and practice must be biblically based; noncreedal association which is nevertheless strongly confessional in theology; the principle that each local church is self-governing, but also that each church cherishes and cooperates with churches of like faith in associations and conventions; church membership based upon credible evidence of regeneration and baptism by immersion; the duties of discipleship and good citizenship; separation of church and state, and rejection of state money for religious work.

Fundamental to Baptist faith is the view that the church is a local body of believing people. It is a fellowship of those who have personally professed faith in Jesus Christ the Lord and have been baptized by immersion. Thus, Baptist understanding of the church makes it socially, religiously and politically discontinuous with the rest of Christian-oriented society. Discontinuity claims honour for the rights of the individual.

Baptist concern for freedom of conscience and the freedom of the individual spring from an understanding of the biblical doctrine of creation and grace. This view is supremely anti-reductionist and is person-preserving. It contrasts with modern reductionist and behaviourist trends which undercut, inhibit, and in some cases eliminate spirituality and freedom.

New opportunities are open to Baptists in Canada to express their dedication to pluralism, to regionalism, to self-determination, to the priesthood of the believer, and to the ministry into which baptism places each Christian. Nationally, the cultural mosaic is increasingly a problem. It should be seen by us as a great opportunity. Baptists can make of diversity an ally. Personal commitment, the conventicle, the autonomy of the local assembly, respect for the individual, and appreciation for the cultural values of others are traditional Baptist convictions and methods which are of great current value.

Other attacks on churchmanship are more subtle. Distortions of the doctrine of the invisible church provide an excuse for many evangelicals to flee local church responsibility. Where spiritual inertia enervates churches, transchurch movements appear to be attractive alternatives, though in the long run no method is as fruitful and efficient as the local church. Parachurch organizations are espoused by others; however, their self-perpetuating boards develop a dynastic character and they tend to be culturally exclusive. Church union has been the avocation of many, especially of clergy, notes the British sociologist, Dr. Brian Jones, but such movements have the dull sound of modern industrial takeovers rather than of spiritual power. The results we achieve are only as good as the assumptions contained in the model. Simplicity and lay duplicability dictate the terms of growth, as all major revivals and church growth movements have shown historically. Spirit-inspired worship, effective Bible teaching ministries, fellowship that generates primary personal relationships, loving concern that embraces people along with their problems — all of these are traditional forms of Baptist ministry. They are still the key to new growth for a new day.

Spiritual Grace

As evangelicals, Baptists in Canada are ideologically committed. Commitment to theological and spiritual principles is essential to convincing ministry. Paradoxically, such conviction can draw the worst out of people as well as the best. Humility befits Baptists.

Those of the "permissive generation" of the 1940s and 1950s have become the working husbands and wives of the present acquisitive and need-satisfaction oriented generation. This is the generation of the instant cure, instant gratification, instant fulfillment, and instant genius. North Americans have become morbidly self-loving, cut off from communion with the past and feeling little responsibility for the future. How can we minister to the conflicting and rapidly changing moods of our time?

First comes repentance. But is repentance consistent with a strong self-image? And image today is everything. Of course we thank God for the faithfulness of pastors, lay leaders, and ministering members. A great deal has been accomplished. But I cannot recall that the devastations of our spirit during the past half century have called forth from us nationwide public declaration of our failures and public commitment to new attitudes and new goals. Baptists in Canada need to look to themselves.

Anyone who has lived through Baptist events of the past half century in Canada knows full well of what I speak. Some have been strident, self-righteous, unloving, given to controversy, schismatic, and even fratricidal in spirit. We still continue to be suspicious, unbrotherly and defensive in inter-Baptist relationships. Pride in holding to the truth has at times made us look ridiculous. Class consciousness inhibits a wider-ranging witness and ministry.

Let us renew our commitment under the covenant of grace. We do not merit God's grace, nor are we lords of it. As the objects of Christ's mercies, what have we that we have not received? The gifts of grace, the qualities of life in Christ, should surely enhance our growth in Christ. They should build our relationships with others in Christ's body for the harmonious development of the body. We are saved as individuals, but not to individualism. There are no granular Christians in the New Testament. When God redeems us, He is concerned not only that the goodness in us springs from good motives, but also that our lives take on a beautiful form. Let the beauty of the holiness of God be our image in modern Canadian society. The life in Christ is its own vindication and witness.

> Let your light so shine before men, that they may see your good works and give glory to your Father who is in heaven (Matthew 5:16 RSV)

Let us move into a new era of cooperation. Let us generate a new mission-mood to reach Canadians for Christ. Let our loving concern be patterned after that of Christ's self-giving. Let us put the cross to centre in our lives.

> If any man would come after me, let him deny himself, and take up his cross and follow me. (Mark 8:34 RSV).

1   Identity and Mission, S. J. Mikolaski

1. J. L. Gilmour, "Baptists in Canada", *Canada and Its Provinces,* eds. Adam Shortt and Arthur G. Doughty, Volume XI (Toronto: Glasgow, Brook and Company, 1914), pp. 346-348.

2. Witness Caravan Week in Toronto. Its form inevitably stresses ethnicity rather than Canadian identity (reported in the *New York Times,* March 11, 1979). The July 1, 1978, issue of the *London Free Press* included a special feature section entitled "What Is a Canadian?"

3. S. M. Lipset, *Revolution and Counter Revolution: Change and Persistence in Social Structures,* rev. ed. (New York: Basic Books, 1968).

4. I. L. Horowitz, "The Hemispheric Connection: A Critique and Corrective to the Entrepreneural Thesis of Development with Special Emphasis on the Canadian Case", *Queen's Quarterly* 80 (1973): 354.

5. *New York Times,* February 4, 1979.

6. *Financial Post,* February 17, 1979 (written by an American analyst).

7. H. H. Hiller, *Canadian Society: A Sociological Analysis* (Scarborough, Ontario: Prentice-Hall of Canada Ltd., 1977), p. 37.

8. *The Financial Post* published a special fourteen-page Federal Election issue on May 5, 1979. The features included written statements by ten prominent Canadians. They universally called for leadership, coherent loyalty and a cause, and they concentrated questions on substantive issues of the social contract and its purpose for Canadians.

9. Current surveys of religious opinions in Canada are not available. Recent attempts have been made in the U.S. to gauge attitudes. Princeton Research Center (a division of the Gallup Poll) reported in the *New York Times,* June 25, 1978 that 89% of the churched and 64% of the unchurched believed that Jesus Christ is the Son of God. Only 6% of the churched and only 21% of the unchurched believed that he was simply a religious leader. Some 43% of the churched and 24% of the unchurched said they had had a religious experience. Many observers note that while church structures and leadership are losing ground, there is a powerful undercurrent among constituencies to conserve fundamental elements of the faith. Cf. *Evangelical Newsletter,* Vol. 5, No. 18, September 8, 1978.

10. Note, for example, the landmark studies of the closed social systems of Plato, Hegel and Marx by Karl Popper, *The Open Society and Its Enemies,* 2 vols. (London: Routledge and Kegan Paul, 1966).

11. There is in principle no difference between Pavlovian doctrine (which the Russians employ in conditioning men) and Skinnerian doctrine (which our own behaviourists employ to create their North American utopian counterpart).

12. Consider the essays by Isaiah Berlin, *Four Essays on Liberty* (Oxford,

1966). His latest defence of pluralism is *Against the Current. Essays in the History of Ideas,* ed. Henry Hardy (London: Hogarth, 1979).

13. See S. J. Mikolaski, "The Believers' Church in Canada: Present," in *The Believers' Church in Canada,* ed. J. K. Zeman and W. Klaassen (Brantford-Winnipeg: Baptist Federation of Canada and Mennonite Central Committee of Canada, 1979), pp. 41-53; and S. J. Mikolaski's essay on developing multicultural ministries and fellowship in Canada in the *Enterprise* (Toronto, Spring 1979), pp. 25-28. Note also the data concerning Baptist growth patterns in Canada in two articles by the same author, "Peeking Over the Baptist Horizon" in *The Canadian Baptist,* May and June 1979. Recent sociological studies should be noted, including: *Introduction to Canadian Society: Sociological Analysis,* ed. G. N. Ramu and S. D. Johnson (Toronto: Macmillan of Canada, 1976). This important symposium includes an essay by Harry H. Hiller of the University of Calgary (and a Baptist) entitled, "The Sociology of Religion in Canada" (pp. 349-400) to which is appended an excellent bibliography. See also *Religion in Canadian Society,* ed. Stewart Crysdale and Les Wheatcroft (Toronto: Macmillan of Canada, 1976). Special mention should be made of the work of S. D. Clark, *Church and Sect in Canada* (Toronto: University of Toronto Press, 1948).

14. *The Baptist World,* February 1979. The figures were compiled by the Baptist World Alliance. They require more detailed analysis and interpretation.

15. *The Believers' Church in Canada,* p. 49.

16. Statistics Canada publish detailed population statistics, demographic characteristics (such as ethnic concentrations and use of mother tongue), and detailed data on the religious composition of Canada's population, including age and economic factors. In addition, many Canadian companies and business groups have commissioned studies of national and regional population trends and characteristics.

17. The data are drawn from a study by Clarence Barber, *Financial Post,* July 14, 1979.

18. Modern religious establishment attitudes derive from a coherent set of long-established principles. These have become embedded in the religious consciousness of the Western nations. They derive from the Constantinian fusion of the temporal and the spiritual, of the secular and religious power, in the *Corpus Christianum.* Pluralism is hard to grasp. The concept of unity, whether religious or political seems, to some, to preclude diversity. Baptists are among those who continue to champion pluralism on biblical grounds.

2

British Influence in the Nineteenth Century

Robert S. Wilson

The nineteenth century was a period of great expansion for both the British Empire and British Baptists. During the century the empire made major acquisitions around the globe and Baptists as administrators, soldiers, settlers and missionaries followed in the train. At home, the Baptists experienced unparalleled growth in both numbers and influence as they touched almost every phase of the nation's life.

The question under consideration here is to what extent the British Baptists influenced their denominational counterparts in Canada. Since the colonies were British, they shared common institutions and ideals with their brethren in the mother country and because they were Baptists there were common areas in polity and theology. Areas such as education, church-state relations, theology, missions and denominational structures all show direct British influence on the Canadian scene.

Baptist beginnings in the Maritimes date back to the pre-Loyalist settlers. In the Canadas, Baptists made their presence felt as a result of the "great awakening" which caused American Baptist missionaries to become concerned about the Loyalists and American settlers in Upper Canada.[1] Stuart Ivison and Fred Rosser tell of six American missionary societies that sponsored preaching tours in the Canadas.[2] Even there,

there was British Baptist influence, for one of those early missionaries was the Englishman, the Rev. John Upfold, who in
1816 was sent by the Hamilton Missionary Society to the
Niagara Peninsula. He remained as pastor at Clinton for nine
years before returning to the United States.[3]

At about the same time there were several British pastors in
the Maritimes, such as the Rev. Thomas Griffin who came to
Germain Street Church in Saint John.[4] A deacon at Germain
Street, Thomas Lockey, had been a member of Griffin's Kid-
derminster church while another member of the same congregation, David Nutter, accompanied his pastor to the New World.[5]
Germain Street Church thereafter often looked to Britain for
pastoral leadership.[6]

Large-scale British influence in Canada began with the coming of Scottish Baptists. In 1814, one of these, Alexander
Crawford, moved from Nova Scotia to Prince Edward Island to
initiate the first consistent Baptist witness in that colony. From
his efforts several congregations grew and a lasting Baptist work
took root.[7] After numerous contacts with the Regular Baptists
in New Brunswick and Nova Scotia, and after extended debates
over the administration of ordinances by laymen and controversy about marriage to unbelievers, the Prince Edward Island
Baptists joined the Nova Scotia Association in 1833.[8] It should
be noted that Alexander Crawford was a product of the
Haldane Revivals in Scotland and was one of those who were
immersed when the Haldanes became Baptists in 1805.[9]

The Scottish tradition had an even more pronounced influence in the Ottawa Valley with the arrival of Gaelic-speaking
Scots in 1816. The Breadalbane Church, established in 1817,
was the first of a number that were to make up the Eastern
Association in the Canadas.[10] These Baptists also came out of
the Haldane movement, and brought with them their sense of
independency as well as lack of concern about ordination as a
prerequisite for ministry.[11] The ordinances were administered
by lay people, and preachers were selected from the congregation.[12] Thus, as Ivison put it, "the main stream of influence
flowed not from the United States, but from the Highlands of
Scotland.[13] It was through the Scottish Baptists that direct
British involvement was to come.[14]

In the rural frontier setting, the Baptists with their lay leadership and revivalist preaching by itinerant evangelists were ideally fitted for growth. The problem was that while the revivalist preaching brought many into the church, the congregations did not always survive after the preacher moved on.[15] The Scots of the Ottawa Valley became concerned that leaders of the churches were poorly trained, and they naturally turned toward Britain for aid. Education, therefore, was to be the area which saw the greatest direct involvement by British Baptists in Canada.[16]

In 1819, John Edwards came from Scotland to Clarence in the Ottawa Valley.[17] An active Baptist, he developed new fields of ministry during the next ten years. In 1829 he visited Scotland and England to stir up Baptist interest in Canada and to encourage men to come to the New World to provide leadership for the churches.[18] John Gilmour came to Toronto, and then moved to Montreal. William Fraser came to the Ottawa Valley.[19] As men like Edwards, Gilmour, and the Rev. Newton Bosworth traveled and preached, they became convinced that trained pastoral leadership was a necessity.[20] They also felt it was impractical to bring missionaries from Britain in sufficient numbers, so they decided to train young men in Canada.[21] Since resources were limited, they turned to Britain for financial aid and academic leadership.

In 1834 William Fraser wrote to Britain and told of the need for trained and dedicated workers.[22] In 1835 John Gilmour wrote to the *London Baptist Magazine.* He urged that more interest be taken in the Canadian situation and introduced the idea of an academy.[23] In the same year, while the anti-slavery agitation was at its height, English Baptists sent F.A. Cox and James Haley to the triennial American Convention. From there the two men traveled to Canada where they found, to their surprise, "nearly a hundred Baptist Churches."[24] This directed English attention to the New World for Cox reported that the lack of education for the preachers was "a seriously weakening factor."[25] British Baptists thus became aware of both the Baptist expansion in British North America and the need for an educated ministry.

The English had been struggling with the problem of education for themselves and so were particularly sensitive to Canadian needs at this point. Because English Baptists were excluded from endowed schools and universities, they began to found their own training schools.[26] Several societies such as the Northern Education Society (1803) and the Welsh and English Education Society (1807) were founded to provide a trained ministry.[27] Horton Academy was founded in 1804 and the Baptist Academical Institution of Stepney was founded by London Baptists in 1810.[28] Cox, who visited Canada in 1835, was a joint secretary of the board at the establishment of the University of London in 1825.[29]

Since the usual way to meet a problem in the early nineteenth century was to form a society, the Baptists in England began to consider one to aid education in Canada.

The Ottawa Valley Association was formed in 1836 and began at once to give attention to founding a college.[30] John Gilmour traveled to Britain to seek assistance. In a letter to the *London Baptist Magazine* in January, 1837 he said:

> Another helpful sign of the times in Canada is the number of youths recently turning to God, many of them young men of promising talent, deep piety and fervent zeal, athirst for knowledge, inured to hardship, and for whom Canada, with all its difficulties, has its charms. Had a seminary been established years ago, we could have found suitable men to enjoy its benefits. God has now given us men, we want the institution and partial support. We propose to educate twenty students and to aid in the support of ten missionaries, and we need for this work a sum not exceeding £760 per annum.[31]

There were also letters from Edwards telling of the work and needs in Canada.[32] *The Christian Messenger* gave an account of a January 15, 1837 meeting of Baptists interested in Canada at the London Tavern. Dr. F.A. Cox moved and W.B. Gurney seconded:

> That this meeting, viewing the present circumstances of the Canadas with reference to the means of religious instruction, and the extensive openings which those colonies present for evangelical labours, consider it highly desirable that a Society should be formed for the purpose of aiding missionary operations in that country in connection with the Baptist denomination.[33]

The Rev. J.J. Davis moved and the Rev. C. Stovel seconded:

> That the name of the society shall be The Baptist Canadian Missionary Society. And that the following shall be the plan and con-

struction thereof: That the object of the Society shall be, the moral and religious cultivation of the Canadas, by aiding the establishment and support of a Collegiate Institution for the education of pious young men for the Christian ministry, and the employment of missionaries in those provinces, and such other means as may be deemed suitable.[34]

Donations of £475 were made at the meeting with another £88 4s pledged.[35]

Gilmour returned to Canada in March of 1837 with about £1,500 toward an educational institution.[36] He then toured Upper Canada seeking support. He found out that Edward Rees had gone to England on a similar mission for a proposed college at Beamsville.[37] The British Baptists advised that they get together on the project.

Jacob Beam offered a farm property worth $5,000 at Beamsville but it was turned down because there was no building.[38] A society was formed to match the one in London. It undertook to establish the Canadian Baptist College in Montreal and to provide support for missionaries in Upper Canada.[39] The college opened in 1838 and Dr. Benjamin Davis, the first Ph.D. on any Canadian faculty, was sent from England to be the first principal.[40] He remained until 1844 when he returned to England.

The college was under suspicion because of the Davis position on open communion and therefore few students and little money came from the west.[41] John Mockett Cramp was then sent to Montreal to replace Davis, and remained at the college until it closed in 1849.[42]

The college became the focus of the contrasting ideas of British-trained pastors and American revivalist techniques that worked so well on the frontier.[43] At a Baptist Colonial Missionary Society meeting in London on May 30, 1841, the Rev. W. Grosser expressed the English view very well when he said it was "a known fact that in Canada there were many Baptist churches and associations which were ignorant of everything pertaining to even common literature and whose theological knowledge was very defective."[44] The curriculum of the college illustrates this cultural emphasis. Greek, Hebrew, Latin, Aramaic, Syriac, and German were taught but no French, even though the institution was situated in Montreal.[45] They sought to place an English academic institution in Canada which did not meet Canadian needs and so was out of place.[46] There were conscious efforts to defend this position as illustrated by the 1841 statement in the college's third annual report:

> To prevent all mistake, we again repeat that we do not design to make a trade of theology. The object is to enable young men of approved piety to cultivate their minds and acquire such knowledge as will, by God's blessing, render their gifts of more service to the church and the world. It is not our aim to make the students classical scholars, but to render them conversant with Biblical and Theological Literature, in the hope that they may thereby become better able "rightly to divide the word of truth" and to defend and propagate "the faith once delivered to the saints."[47]

When the suspicions over the open communion stance of the faculty at the college was added to the general economic decline of 1848 and 49 the college simply could not continue to exist.[48]

Pastoral training was also a matter of major concern in the Maritimes and Baptists there looked to Britain for aid. In 1839 the name of the Baptist Canadian Missionary Society in London was changed to the Baptist Colonial Missionary Society as a result of a request for aid by the Fredericton Seminary.[49]

Both the Fredericton Seminary and the two schools at Horton were in operation by then with the impetus coming from Anglicans who had become Baptists. W.T. Whitley's statement about Britain applied to Canada as well when he said that the people with the greatest cultural influence in the early nineteenth century became Baptists by conviction from some other setting.[50] One such Baptist, F.W. Miles, principal of the Fredericton Seminary, went to England in 1839 to seek aid. He returned with £415 in donations for the library, and accompanied by a Miss Bennett who then became principal of the female department.[51] When Miles retired, the Baptist Colonial Missionary Society sent the Rev. Charles Spurden to replace him.[52]

Nova Scotia Baptists also made several appeals for financial aid to Britain on behalf of Horton Academy and Acadia College. In 1835, 1844, 1849, and 1874, there were appeals, and each time questions were asked about government grants to institutions.[53] In 1845 the Baptist Colonial Missionary Society paid £500 toward the salary of the professor of theology, E.A. Crawley.[54] Because of the strong feeling in Britain against state aid to denominational schools, the appeals of 1844 and 1849 fell short of expectations.[55]

A good illustration of the differences between the Baptists on both sides of the Atlantic is found in the 1844 situation. The controversy arose when Joseph Belcher, the one-time secretary of the Baptist Union in England and newly arrived pastor of Granville Street Baptist Church in Halifax, began to ask questions about state aid for Acadia.[56] He had been involved in the refusal of English Baptists to take any state aid for education and had shared in their struggle to stop such aid going to others.[57]

The year 1843 had seen a key struggle over the Factory Act in Britain when the education clause had been withdrawn after the protest of the Nonconformists. This was because it would have provided money to the Anglican Church to educate the children who worked in factories. This whole struggle had been followed in the colonies, and *The Christian Messenger* in July of 1843 had commented: "It is not a little singular that the position of English Dissenters and Nova Scotia Baptists is not very dissimilar."[58] Belcher, however, felt the Nova Scotia Baptists were not being consistent by talking of the separation of church and state while taking government grants for their schools. He was assured that the funds were not used to teach theology but rather to teach the other subjects, but he was not to be swayed.[59] He wrote to his friends in England and when John Pryor arrived there seeking financial aid for Acadia he ran into a controversy. The response was much less than hoped and Belcher bore much of the blame among Nova Scotia Baptists.[60]

The 1846 Nova Scotia Association took steps to separate the chair of theology from the rest of the university and moved that the "work in theology at the College be committed to the Association."[61] Belcher, however, was forced out of Nova Scotia for he had come just after the Baptists had changed political allegiance to the Conservatives over the Acadia issue while he, as a typical English Baptist, supported the Liberals. Since the leaders of this conservative faction were also the leaders in his own church and they also owned the building, it is no wonder he left the church and later the city.[62]

The Nova Scotia Baptists had usually assumed that since one denomination received money that they were entitled to it as well. But their position began to change. In 1849 the Nova Scotia Association had to go to Britain for aid, with I. E. Bill and John Francis acting as agents. The British religious press again played up the question of government funds. Bill and Francis were forced to leave early because of the issue. The 1850 convention voted to have Acadia supported wholly by gifts and all government aid was to go to Horton Academy. In its vote of thanks to friends in Britain, the convention placed notes in all the periodicals that had been negative.[63] Bill seems to have been convinced of the voluntary principle for he commented about the improved situation at Acadia: "It brings out in bold relief the power of the voluntary principle."[64] When it was decided in 1865 to accept a government grant, Bill commented:

> We cannot but feel that the wiser course would be to keep perfectly clear of all government props in future. The whole-hearted support of a praying Christian community ought to be sufficient; without this, the paltry contributions of government treasuries are of little avail.[65]

When the issue of public schools came to the fore, Baptists in the Maritimes were in the midst of the fray. They followed the British model more closely by insisting that there should be no religious education at government expense and no government aid to church schools. The question of education had therefore caused Maritime Baptists to examine the issue of separation of church and state, and in the area of public education they were reasonably consistent. Part of that consistency came because of what had happened in England.[66]

The Baptists in Canada tended to follow more consistently the British model of complete separation of church and state in education. W. T. Whitley comments about clergy reserves and education in Canada that "the political contest was on very English lines, and the ends were gained."[67] This consistency may in part be explained by the fact that much of the articulate Baptist leadership in the struggle came from Britain. Scottish and English Baptists made their feelings known in opposition to clergy reserves and in favour of non-sectarian public education.[68]

Benjamin Davis and J. M. Cramp edited *The Canada Baptist*

Magazine and Missionary Register from 1837 to 1849. E. R. Fitch said that they dealt with the great issues "in a masterly way; and it is not too much to say that their work helped in no small measure towards the settlement of questions such as that of the Clergy Reserves, upon right principles."[69]

In 1854 William Winter founded *The Canadian Baptist* and, as an Englishman, stressed the separation of church and state. John Winterbotham, another English Baptist, became editor in 1856 and was a strong advocate of religious liberty.[70] He defined it this way: "Religious Liberty means no man shall be liable to pain or penalties, taxation or oppression, in being forced to support a system of religion in which he does not believe."[71]

The Canadian Baptist press thus had a distinct English flavour and played a definite role in involving Baptists in politics. S. D. Clark comments that educational institutions introduced a sense of responsibility to the community and forced them into politics.[72] Temperance, Sabbath observance, and slavery were other issues which drew Baptists into the political arena. All of these issues received widespread coverage in the denominational press.[73] An example of the English input in this area is the fact that over one half of the material of *The Christian Messenger* in Nova Scotia in the 1830s and 40s was from Britain.[74]

The periodicals were not the only English influence in the reading material of Canadian Baptists. In 1827, Dr. McCulloch of Pictou was thanked for bringing books back from British Baptists for use in Nova Scotia churches.[75] The 1841 Nova Scotia Association moved that "Brethren J. W. Nutting and J. Ferguson be appointed to open a correspondence with the London Colonial Missionary Society" and with the Baptist Book and Tract Society about the Sabbath Schools "in the hope that gratuitous supplies of books may be obtained for their use."[76] Numerous articles and books were circulated among the Sunday Schools. One was written in Halifax by S. Selden, an Englishman and active Baptist layman. It contained a catechism and hymns, one of which contained the following verse:

> The Sabbath-school, that blessed place
> Oh I would rather stay
> Within its walls, a child of grace,
> Than spend my hours at play.[77]

I. E. Bill gives a list of the books circulating in 1875 that included "Cramp's Baptist History, Carson on Baptism, Spurgeon's Sermons, Bunyan's Pilgrim, The Life of Judson, Theodosia Ernest, Mary Bunyan, Grace Trueman, Infidel's Daughter, and works like these have been placed in many hands."[78]

Because British materials were so widely read and because of the numbers of English Baptists coming to Canda in the nineteenth century there was a distinct English theological emphasis as a result. This was seen in particular in the communion question. The general trend in Britain had been from closed to open communion with Robert Hall as an early leader in the new direction. In the Maritimes the issue became a crucial one early in the century when the 1809 association meeting resolved to be a closed communion Baptist association.[79] The English preacher, David Nutter, who came a few years later, felt that it was the right decision and the real birthdate of Baptists in Nova Scotia.[80]

As the nineteenth century progressed, there were more and more open communion leaders coming from Britain to Canada. Philip Allwood suggests that part of Belcher's difficulties may be explained by his open communion position in closed communion Nova Scotia.[81] The issue played havoc with any efforts at the unification of Baptists, particularly in the Canadas. The Scottish open communion stance came into conflict with the regular and closed communion position of most of the Baptists in Upper Canada before 1820.[82] By 1840, however, the Scottish Baptists began to establish closed communion churches "as the newcomers from Britain came to accept the 'regular' norm in Canada."[83] John Gilmour, in a letter to a friend in 1840, lamented: "I sincerely wish our Brethren in the Upper Province tho' strict were not so strict — I do not see why close and open communion Baptists should not be able to co-operate in educational and missionary exertions."[84]

Gilmour reflected the frustration of the supporters of the Canadian Baptist College in Montreal. Neither students nor money had come from the closed communion western associations. When these associations withdrew from the original Baptist Union in Canada in 1848 to form the Regular Baptist Union of Canada on a closed communion base, the college was forced to close.[85] The high point of the controversy seems to have been reached in the decade following as the upholders of the closed communion position gained control of the associations in the west and took over *The Canadian Baptist* in 1859 from the open communion Winterbotham.[86] In 1859, Dr. Fyfe, as the new editor, used the paper to denounce C.H. Spurgeon for admitting unimmersed people to communion.[87] Fyfe's successor, Hayes Lloyd, was also a strong supporter of closed communion.[88] Even the Grande Ligne Mission was influenced by the debate and six of its missionaries signed a document that they would build "Regular Baptist Churches."[89]

By 1860 the issue began to lose some of its intensity as a concern about union took priority. Mary Hill comments that the widespread use of works by C. H. Spurgeon, Robert Hall and John Bunyan, as well as a growing number of open communion men coming from Britain, made the position more acceptable.[90] The impact of men of the stature of Edwards, Gilmour, Davis and Cramp was also considerable as all of them held to open communion.

As the century wore on, the educational institutions had an influence toward open communion as well.[91] R. J. Bean claims that the controversy "was primarily the result of a conflict between American and British traditions."[92] In the end it was the British open communion position that gained the day. The decline in theological tensions made union movements a possibility.

In Britain the nineteenth century saw Baptists moving toward union. In spite of tensions over the communion question, a General Union of Baptist Ministers and Churches was founded in 1813. Foreign and home missions were the chief reasons for this move.[93] While it was an age of fragmentation because of the large number of societies for various tasks, the general trend of the age was toward unity which culminated in the union of the Regular Baptists with the New Connexion Baptists in 1891 to form the Baptist Union.[94] British Baptists carried their concern about union and efficiency with them when they crossed the Atlantic and as a result were often in the forefront of efforts toward larger denominational structures.

Associations had played an important role very early in the history of Baptists in both the Maritimes and the Canadas.

Elder T. S. Rand is quoted in the 1800 by-laws of the Nova Scotia Association as saying: "That such a combination of churches is not only prudent, but useful; as has been proved by the experience of many years in England and America."[95]

In the Maritimes the British pastors took their place in the associations and gave support to the establishment of the Baptist Convention of Nova Scotia, New Brunswick and Prince Edward Island in 1846.[96]

The union movement in the Canadas had more direct British input than that in the east and the path was not as smooth. Associations developed very early, with close connections to the American Baptists. By 1836 the Baptist associations spanned Upper and Lower Canada and some voices were raised in support of a larger union. A single Baptist voice seemed to some to be a necessity in the face of the Anglican control of McGill College (Montreal) and King's College (Toronto), and in order to press for the secularizing of the clergy reserves.

In 1843 a convention was called at Paris, Ontario. An Englishman, the Rev. John Winterbotham of Brantford was named the first president of the Canada Baptist Union.[97] Two of the five western associations formed their own Western Baptist Missionary Society and published their own journal.[98] S. D. Clark and Mary Hill both make a strong point of the British influences in the formation of the Union. Clark suggests that the Baptist Canadian Missionary Society and its English missionaries in the east "led to the consolidation of English influence, and organization of the Canada Baptist Union in 1843."[99] He goes on to say that this was the first step of Baptists on the road from Sect to Denomination.[100]

The Canada Baptist Union floundered in 1848 on the rock of open communion as the western associations withdrew and in 1851 formed the Regular Baptist Missionary Convention of Canada West. Since this body excluded all open communion churches, the Canada Baptist Missionary Society East was founded several years later.[101] As the communion question waned in importance and the need for educational facilities, pensions for the clergy, a Baptist paper, and support for missions grew, the Baptists began to work more closely together.[102] By 1889 the Baptist Convention of Ontario and Quebec, made up of both open and closed communion churches, was incorporated by an Act of Parliament.[103]

Efforts to form an all-Canada union were made during this period. Cramp visited the Maritimes in 1844 and again in 1846 with a proposal of union.[104] H. H. Walsh commented that "isolation and poverty of mere provincial life constantly challenged Dr. Cramp and all those who sought to create a unified Baptist community in the Maritimes and in the Canadas to the extreme limits of their patience."[105] Distance and varied interests made an all-Canadian union impractical in the nineteenth century. Overseas missionary enterprises proved to be the only issue that could generate enough enthusiasm to have Baptists all across Canada work for a common objective.

British Baptists had a profound effect upon the Canadian Baptist concept of foreign missions. The funding of the Particular Baptist Missionary Society for Propagating the Gospel Among the Heathen in 1792 to send William Carey to India became a clarion cry to action that echoed throughout the English-speaking evangelical world.[106] Carey's career was followed closely in British North America. Saunders commented that "Every item of intelligence from Carey's mission, eagerly read by them, was fuel to the flame."[107] The year of 1814 was a memorable one when the association at Chester forwarded its first money for missions to the British and Foreign Bible Society.[108] In 1829 the missionary society at Saint John sent $70 to the English Foreign Missionary Society.[109] The first article of the *Baptist Missionary Magazine of Nova Scotia and New Brunswick* in January, 1827 was a memoir of the Rev. William Ward, one of the Serampore Missionaries.[110] In the years that followed, every edition of the paper carried exploits of English missionaries. There grew a conviction that Maritime Baptists should do something in foreign missions and in 1844 Richard Burpee sailed for Burma with half his expenses paid by Baptists of Nova Scotia and New Brunswick.[111]

The interest in foreign missions was not confined to the east. In October, 1867 the Rev. A. V. Timpany and his wife were chosen as missionaries to work with the American Baptist Missionary Union. Their support was to come from the Regular Baptist Foreign Missionary Society of Ontario and Quebec.[112] Eventually Canadians worked together to begin a Baptist work among the Telugu people of India.[113] The impact of Carey's vision continued throughout the century and Canadian Baptists celebrated the Carey Centennial in 1892 with a special missionary effort.[114] At the 1896 London Convention of Ontario and Quebec Baptists, the Rev. A. B. Reekie challenged Canadians to consider Bolivia as a second mission field. The proposal received a unanimous vote.[115] By 1910 there were fifty-three missionaries in Bolivia and India and a total yearly missions income among Canadian Baptists of $62,724.44.[116]

The impact of the missionary thrust upon Baptists in Canada was deep, and affected all levels of church life. E. M. Saunders commented that the emphasis upon missions was a natural outgrowth of the educational institutions and a response to the success of British and American overseas missions.[117] This missionary vision brought women's missionary organizations into existence, inspired home missions, and became a major incentive toward the growth of Baptist Conventions in Canada.

One significant area of British influence in Canada, difficult to evaluate, is the role of the man in the pew who had come to settle in this country. There must have been many who provided leadership in local congregations but it was only those who influenced the broader Baptist community who stand out. A few examples will have to suffice to illustrate a larger picture. One leading layman in Upper Canada was William Winter who emigrated to the Pickering area from England in 1832. While making a living buying and clearing land, he took time to found several churches and do some preaching. In 1854 he founded *The Canadian Baptist* while acting as a deacon in the Woodstock Baptist Church. After 1845 in Saint John there was a Baptist layman, Deacon Edmund Hillyer Duval, who provided leadership for his local church and preached in the local area. Duval was a key educator in the province and as such a man of wider influence.[119] The Baptist work on the west coast of Canada began with an Englishman, John Morton, who had gone to the gold fields in 1862.[120] Examples could be multiplied as laymen made their influence felt. Mary Hill comments that in Upper Canada the Scottish and English Baptists were numerous and influential in the larger towns and cities by 1850.[121]

It is much easier to identify British Baptist influence in the pulpit than it is in the pew. In the crucial area of pastoral leadership there were over one hundred men who came to British North America to fill pulpits or teaching positions. A few of these were employed as missionaries like the Rev. H. Wilkes, and the Rev. J. Edwards who served with the Baptist Colonial

Missionary Society in the 1830s and 40s.[122] Several others who filled key positions in education were sent from England by the same body. They include Benjamin Davis and J. M. Cramp for the college in Montreal, and Miss Bennett and Charles Spurden for the Fredericton Seminary. The impact of these and other leaders in the training institutions was immense upon pastoral students. Clark commented that most of these "overseas missionaries" were "men of cultural attainment."[123]

The list of distinguished Canadian Baptist leaders who had been trained in Britain is a long one. It would be much longer, however, if so many had not moved from Canada to the United States. *The Canadian Baptist Register* and the *Baptist Year Book for Ontario and Quebec* between 1868 and 1890 list thirty-five pastors who came from Britain, and by the latter date only eleven were still serving in Canadian churches.[124]

Some pastors came to Canada with the intention of going on to the United States while others came in response to direct requests for aid. Local congregations, like Germain Street Baptist Church in Saint John, often turned to Britain for pastoral leadership.[125] The Western Association of Nova Scotia wrote to the *London Baptist* and Dr. Stock to recruit pastors in 1874, and as a result five men came to the area.[126] Margaret Thompson tells of some who came to the Canadian West, several of whom were trained at Spurgeon's college.[127]

Most of those who came were pastors and not familiar with the revivalist emphasis of many of the Canadian-born leaders. Some like David Nutter, in the 1820s in the Maritimes, made a real contribution in a revivalist fashion.[128] An illustration of the different emphasis comes from Isaiah Wallace who describes the revivals at Acadia in 1855 with a comment about Dr. Cramp: "Having had but little experience in revivals, he gave the special services over to the students, assuring us always of his sympathies and prayers."[129] The British approach was more toward correct homiletical orations than the exhortations to repentance more common among frontier preachers.

Often the British-trained pastors moved into key positions of leadership in the city areas and provided a much needed intellectual thrust. The rural areas felt their presence to a lesser degree but even there the English training made them the people who produced papers for presentation to the local ministerial associations. An example of that type of thing was Stephen March who in 1889 and 90 presented papers on Annihilation of the Lost and Temperance to the Bridgewater Ministerial.[130] One notes the comments on these men, like Bill's assessment of the Rev. George Richardson who served many years in the Maritimes: "Having a strong clear voice, and a ready command of language, he was a forcible speaker."[131] In Fitch's evaluation, the Rev. John Gilmour was "a great leader of men and a thoroughly devout and consecrated Christian."[132] These and others like them had a profound effect upon the texture of Canadian Baptist life.

Some generalizations have been made about English Baptist influences in Canada by S. D. Clark and Mary Hill. They both follow the thesis that in the move of Baptists from a sect to a denomination, English leadership was the key ingredient.[133] This involved a move from the revivalist frontier-type of preacher to the educated professional pastor with many of the latter coming from Britain and those trained in Canada being taught by British Baptists.[134]

This whole struggle is then seen as a battle between American and English forces. This is partially supported by W. T. Whitley who comments that the first Baptist Union in Canada in the 1840s was English-orientated and therefore collapsed and had to be rebuilt upon American models. "For positive work, English traditions were insufficient, and it proved impossible to harness all in the English fashion."[135] As the century wore on, the structures that emerged were a cross between the American and British traditions.

Several conclusions naturally follow from this study that help to explain the direction of nineteenth century Canadian Baptist development. British Baptist influences were present to a significant degree after 1820 with the influx of Scottish Baptists and a few pastors coming to churches in Canada. Education was the major point of that influence as both finances and personnel arrived, resulting in an emphasis upon a trained professional clergy. In areas of leadership requiring skills in organization or in written and oral expression, British Baptists often came to the fore. Denominational papers, pamphlets, position papers and books had a large input from the British. Denominational structures had wide support from the British-reared pastoral leadership, particularly in Central Canada. When the large numbers of British periodicals, sermons and books are added, it is apparent that British Baptists helped to shape Canadian Baptist thinking in theology, missions, church-state relations and denominational development. Most of these influences were the result of British-trained pastors and laymen who came to Canada seeking to serve their Lord in the best way they knew and they naturally turned to the methods and skills they had learned in the mother country.

2 British Influence, R. S. Wilson

1. Stuart Ivison and Fred Rosser, *The Baptists in Upper and Lower Canada Before 1820* (Toronto: Univ. of Toronto Press, 1956), pp. 9ff and 82ff.

2. *Ibid.,* p. 9.

3. *Ibid.,* p. 9.

4. George Edward Levy, *With Pioneer Baptists in Nova Scotia: A Sketch of the Life of David Nutter* (Wolfville: Davidson Brothers, Publishers, 1929), pp. 12-13.

5. *Ibid.,* p. 10.

6. T. D. Denham, *The History of Germain Street Baptist Church, Saint John, N. B., for its First One Hundred Years: 1810-1910* (Saint John: Saint John Publishing Co., 1910), pp. 1ff.

7. I. E. Bill, *Fifty Years with the Baptist Ministers and Churches of the Maritime Provinces of Canada* (Saint John: Barnes and Company, 1880), p. 662. George E. Levy, "The United Baptist Convention of the Maritime Provinces," *Baptist Advance: The Achievements of the Baptists of North America for a Century and a Half,* ed. Davis C. Woolley (Nashville: Broadman Press, 1964), p. 141.

8. Bill, *Fifty Years,* p. 667.

9. *Ibid.,* p. 662.

10. Ivison and Rosser, *The Baptists,* p. 94.

11. *Ibid.,* pp. 94-95.

12. *Ibid.,* p. 94.

13. Stuart Ivison, "Baptist Beginnings in Canada", *Our Baptist Fellowship,* ed. J. Gordon Jones (Toronto: Baptist Convention, 1939), p. 21.

14. E. R. Fitch, *The Baptists of Canada* (Toronto: The Standard Publishing Company, 1911), pp. 106ff.

15. Mary Bulmer Reid Hill, "From Sect to Denomination in the Baptist Church in Canada" (unpublished Ph.D. thesis, State Univ. of New York, Buffalo, 1971), p. 80.

16. S. D. Clark, *Church and Sect in Canada* (Toronto: Univ. of Toronto Press, 1948), p. 227.

17. Fitch, *The Baptists of Canada,* p. 124.

18. Leslie K. Tarr, *This Dominion His Dominion* (Toronto: Fellowship of Evangelical Baptist Churches in Canada, 1968), p. 59.

19. Fitch, *The Baptists of Canada,* p. 124.

20. Clark, *Church and Sect,* pp. 226-227.

21. Fitch, *The Baptists of Canada,* pp. 118-119.

22. *The Baptist Missionary Magazine of Nova Scotia and New Brunswick* (Halifax, July 1835), pp. 148ff.

23. *Ibid.,* pp. 145ff.

24. Ernest A. Payne, *The Baptist Union: A Short History* (London: Carey Kingsgate Press, 1959), p. 63.

25. *Ibid.,* p. 69; Clark, *Church and Sect,* p. 230.

26. W. T. Whitley, *A History of British Baptists* (London: Charles Griffin and Company, 1923), p. 260.

27. *Ibid.,* pp. 257ff.

28. A. C. Underwood, *A History of the English Baptists* (London: Kingsgate Press, 1947), pp. 150ff.

29. Whitley, *A History,* p. 260.

30. Ivison, "Baptist Beginnings," p. 22; Clark, *Church and Sect,* p. 230; Gerald G. Harrop, "The Baptist Convention of Ontario and Quebec," *Baptist Advance,* p. 160.

31. *The Christian Messenger* (Halifax, June 2, 1837), p. 172; Fitch, *The Baptists of Canada,* p. 119.

32. *The Christian Messenger* (Halifax, January 13, 1837), p. 12.

33. *The Christian Messenger* (Halifax, June 2, 1837), pp. 172-173; Whitley, *A History,* p. 261. W. B. Gurney was the founder of the Sunday School Union in England in 1803.

34. *The Christian Messenger* (Halifax, June 2, 1837), p. 173.

35. *Ibid.,* p. 173.

36. Fitch, *The Baptists of Canada,* p. 119.

37. *Ibid.,* pp. 119-120.

38. *Ibid.,* pp. 113, 120.

39. *The Christian Messenger* (Halifax, July 28, 1837), pp. 236-237; Tarr, *This Dominion,* p. 60; Whitley, *A History,* p. 337.

40. Harrop, "The Baptist Convention," p. 163; Fitch *The Baptists of Canada,* p. 120.

41. Fitch, *The Baptists of Canada* p. 120.

42. H. H. Walsh, *The Christian Church in Canada* (Toronto: The Ryerson Press, 1956), p. 217; Whitley, *A History,* p. 333.

43. Hill, "From Sect to Denomination," p. 84.

44. *The Christian Messenger* (June 25, 1841), p. 163.

45. Harrop, "The Baptist Convention," p. 163.

46. Fitch, *The Baptists of Canada,* p. 121.

47. *The Christian Messenger* (Halifax, August 20, 1841).

48. Fitch, *The Baptists of Canada,* p. 121; Ivison, "Baptist Beginnings," p. 22.

49. *The Christian Messenger* (Halifax, January 11, 1839), p. 9.

50. George E. Levey, *The Baptists of the Maritime Provinces: 1753-1946* (Saint John: Barnes-Hopkins Limited, 1946), p. 115; Whitley, *A History,* p. 275; Walsh, *The Christian Church,* p. 160.

51. *The Christian Messenger* (Halifax, January 11, 1839), p. 9; Bill, *Fifty Years,* p. 585; Edward Manning Saunders, *History of the Baptist of the Maritime Provinces* (Halifax: Press of John Burgoyne, 1902) p. 235; Fitch, *The Baptists of Canada,* p. 80.

52. Bill, *Fifty Years,* pp. 333, 589; Saunders, *History of the Baptists,* p. 237.

53. Bill, *Fifty Years,* pp. 126-127; Saunders, *History of the Baptists,* p. 241.

54. Bill, *Fifty Years,* p. 122; Saunders, *History of the Baptists,* p. 357.

55. Bill, *Fifty Years,* p. 125.

56. Payne, *The Baptist Union,* p. 64.

57. Whitley, *A History,* pp. 262, 283-284.

58. *Ibid.,* p. 289; *The Christian Messenger* (Halifax, July 7, 1843), pp. 211-212; and (Halifax, July 28, 1843), pp. 234-235.

59. Saunders, *History of the Baptists,* p. 353.

60. *The Christian Messenger* (Halifax, June 2, 1837), p. 175; (November 1, 1844), p. 349; and (March 27, 1846) p. 102; Philip G. Allwood, "The Belcher Schism" (unpublished paper, Acadia Divinity College, 1978), pp. 2-3, 16.

61. Saunders, *History of the Baptists,* p. 353.

62. Bill, *Fifty Years,* pp. 114, 163ff.; Walsh, *The Christian Church,* p. 158; Allwood, "The Belcher Schism," pp. 5ff.

63. Bill, *Fifty Years,* pp. 109, 124-125, 356, 360-361; Walsh, *The Christian Church,* p. 159.

64. Bill, *Fifty Years,* p. 373.

65. *Ibid.,* pp. 126, 436.

66. *Ibid.,* pp. 115-116, 502, 523; Walsh, *The Christian Church, pp. 151, 232;* Charles E. Phillips, *The Development of Education in Canada (Toronto:* W. J. Gage, 1957), pp. 322-333.

67. Whitley, *A History,* p. 337.

68. Clark, *Church and Sect,* pp. 225-226; Walsh, *The Christian Church,* p. 172; Harold U. Trinier, *A Century of Service: The Canadian Baptist 1854-1954* (Toronto: The Board of Publication, Baptist Convention of Ontario and Quebec 1954), p. 7.

69. Fitch, *The Baptists of Canada,* p. 122; Hill, "From Sect to Denomination," p. 61.

70. Trinier, *A Century of Service,* p. 26.

71. *Ibid.,* p. 37.

72. Clark, *Church and Sect,* p. 253.

73. Almost every issue of *The Christian Messenger* in 1839 carried articles on temperance. Trinier, *A Century of Service,* p. 36; Clark, *Church and Sect,* pp. 254ff; Walsh, *The Christian Church,* p. 177.

74. *The Christian Messenger* in every issue carried British news. Its predecessor, *The Baptist Missionary Magazine of Nova Scotia and New Brunswick,* had done the same.

75. Bill, *Fifty Years,* p. 56.

76. Ibid., p. 101.

77. Stephen Selden, *A Scripture Catechism for Use in the Family, the Bible Class, and the Sabbath School* (Halifax: Christian Messenger office, 1868).

78. Bill, *Fifty Years,* p. 656. Underwood, *A History,* pp. 170-179; Whitley, *A History,* pp. 306ff;

79. Saunders, *History of the Baptists,* pp. 125-126.

80. Levy, *With Pioneer Baptists,* p. 22.

81. Allwood, "The Belcher Schism," pp. 13-14.

82. Ivison and Rosser, *The Baptists,* pp. 15ff.

83. Harrop, "The Baptist Convention," p. 169.

84. Clark, *Church and Sect,* p. 300.

85. *Ibid.,* pp. 301-302; Harrop, "The Baptist Convention," pp. 168-169; Walsh, *The Christian Church,* p. 217.

86. Trinier, *A Century of Service,* pp. 23, 48.

87. *Ibid.,* p. 48.

88. *Ibid.,* pp. 52ff.

89. Harrop, "The Baptist Convention," p. 169.

90. Hill, "From Sect to Denomination," p. 95.

91. *Ibid.,* p. 95.

92. Harrop, "The Baptist Convention," p. 168.

93. Underwood, *A History,* p. 184.

94. *Ibid.,* pp. 201-202; Payne, *The Baptist Union,* p. 54; Whitley, *A History,* pp. 309, 318-319.

95. S. T. Rand, *The Jubilee Historical Sketch of the Nova Scotia Baptist Association* (Charlottetown: James D. Haszard, Queen's Printer, 1849), p.8.

96. Levy, *The Baptists,* pp. 151ff.; Saunders, *History,* pp. 156, 170-171.

97. Ivison and Rosser, *The Baptists,* pp. 60-63, 82; Fitch, *The Baptists of Canada,* p. 115; Trinier, *A Century of Service,* p. 35.

98. Clark, *Church and Sect,* p. 300.

99. *Ibid.,* p. 204; Tarr, *This Dominion,* p. 160.

100. Clark, *Church and Sect,* p. 204.

101. Hill, "From Sect to Denomination," p. 61; R. R. McKay, "The Story of Our Convention," *Our Baptist Fellowship* (Toronto: Baptist Convention, 1939), pp. 32-33.

102. Walsh, *The Christian Church,* p. 217.

103. McKay, "The Story," p. 40.

104. Saunders, *History,* p. 286; Walsh, *The Christian Church,* p. 218.

105. Walsh, *The Christian Church,* p. 218.

106. Underwood, *A History,* p. 165.

107. Saunders, *History,* p. 208.

108. Bill, *Fifty Years,* p. 49.

109. Fitch, *The Baptists of Canada,* p. 78.

110. *The Baptist Missionary Magazine of Nova Scotia and New Brunswick* (Halifax, January, 1827), p. 5.

111. Levy, *The Baptists,* pp. 138-139.

112. McKay, "The Story," pp. 35-36

113. *Ibid.,* p. 35.

114. J. March, *A Brief History of the Foreign Missionary Enterprise among the Baptists of the Maritime Provinces of the Dominion of Canada* (Saint John: Paterson and Company, 1899), pp. 25-26.

115. McKay, "The Story," p. 36.

116. Fitch, *The Baptists of Canada,* pp. 137-138.

117. Saunders, *History,* p. 284.

118. Trinier, *A Century of Service, pp. 4-5, 24-25.*

119. Bill, Fifty Years, pp. 556-557.

120. Margaret E. Thompson, *The Baptist Story in Western Canada* (Calgary: The Baptist Union of W. Canada, 1975), p. 54.

121. Hill, "From Sect to Denomination," p. 60.

122. *Ibid.,* p. 52; *The Christian Messenger* (Halifax, March 29, 1839), pp. 100-101; (May 17, 1839), p. 157; (November 6, 1840), p. 358.

123. Clark, *Church and Sect,* p. 230; Saunders, *History,* pp. 364ff.

124. *The Baptist Year Books of Ontario and Quebec* (1862-1907); Walsh, *The Christian Church,* p. 282.

125. *The History of Germain Street,* p. 25; Bill, *Fifty Years,* p. 65.

126. Bill, *Fifty Years,* p. 652.

127. Thompson, *The Baptist Story,* pp. 43-44, 57.

128. Clark, *Church and Sect,* p. 228; Levy, *With Pioneer Baptists,* p. 6.

129. Bill, *Fifty Years,* p. 242; Isaiah Wallace, *Autobiographical Sketch with Reminiscences of Revival Work* (Halifax: Press of John Burgoyne, 1903), p. 16.

130. Stephen March, *Temperance:* A Paper Read before the Bridgewater Ministerial Association, February 10, 1890; and *Death the Penalty of Sin:* Revised and read before the Bridgewater Ministerial, May 1889.

131. Bill, *Fifty Years,* p. 343.

132. Fitch, *The Baptists of Canada,* p. 124.

133. Clark, *Church and Sect,* p. 224.

134. Clark, *Church and Sect,* p. 229, 252; Hill, "From Sect to Denomination," pp. 67, 101.

135. Whitley, *A History,* p. 337.

3

Witness in French Canada

W. Nelson Thomson

The aim of this chapter is to trace the development, *as an indigenous movement*, of the French-Canadian Baptist churches that have issued from the labours of successive generations of pastors, missionaries, teachers and colporteurs, beginning with the pioneer witness established in Grande Ligne, Quebec, in 1836, by Madame Henriette Feller, and by the Rev. Louis Roussy. These Swiss missionaries were themselves the fruit of an evangelical revival, sparked by the ministry in Switzerland of the Scottish evangelist Robert Haldane.

The story of the beginnings has been well documented, and it is not our intention to repeat it here.[1] But we will endeavour, by an examination of available written reports, to determine the degree to which the objectives of this work have been fulfilled, namely the establishment of French-Canadian local churches, composed of those who confess the Lordship of Jesus Christ in believer's baptism — while continuing to be identified with their original *milieu*. To what extent have the churches confronted their contemporaries with a viable alternative to the religious heritage of the majority?

Religious Background of French Canada

The Roman Catholic Church had not always enjoyed the prestigious influence which obtained when Madame Feller and Mr. Roussy arrived in Montreal in 1835. "Canada was long a bone of contention between Gallicans and Ultramontanes."[2]

Nevertheless the governor, Frontenac, determined that ecclesiastical control should be limited. "Thus under the French regime the state, far from being the handmaid of the church, gradually became its master."3

However, after the conquest by Great Britian in 1759, a number of factors combined to give to the Roman Catholic Church unparalleled influence and power. Eventually there were enshrined in the Quebec Act (1774) guarantees giving Roman Catholics the right to "have, hold and enjoy, the free exercise of the Religion of the Church of Rome" and to their clergy the right to "hold, receive, and enjoy, their accustomed dues and rights, with respect to such persons only as shall profess the said religion."4

In effect, the Church of Rome was given legal right to collect the tithe, or ecclesiastical tax, from Roman Catholic property-holders, a right which is still operative today. It remained only for the Constitutional Act of 1791, to give further *de facto* power to the clergy. Lower Canada was "to be retained by the French where, for the most part, the feudal customs and practices of the old regime would continue as they had prevailed under the Quebec Act of 1774."5

The clergy did not hesitate to use its influence on the political orientation of the people.6 In return for the entrenchment of its prerogatives, the Roman Catholic clergy responded accordingly. Bishop Brian urged support for the British during the American Revolution. He said to the people: "Your oaths, your religion impose on you an indispensable obligation to defend with all your power your country and your king."7 The French-Canadians in fact seemingly contented themselves with simple neutrality.

Similarly, "the War of 1812 yielded an opportunity to Bishop Plessis. His loyal and effective pastoral letters greatly assisted the British cause."8 He was duly rewarded with a stipend, recognition as Catholic bishop of Quebec (previously only the Anglican bishop was given official recognition in his episcopal role), and appointment to the legislative council.

It is in the light of the preceding facts that one can grasp the socio-religious situation prevailing in Canada when our pioneer missionaries arrived. Rebellion was in the air. The *patriotes*, led by Louis Joseph Papineau, were rousing the population to action in face of what was deemed political oppression on the part of the British. The clergy, understandably, supported the government. As a result, for the first time since the conquest, extreme tension existed between clergy and people. The intellectual elite in particular was by this time increasingly anti-clerical. In the effervescence of the period, the missionaries in Grande Ligne, along with several converts, were identified in popular thought with the British, and had to seek refuge for several months in New York State. One of the leaders of the rebellion, Dr. C. H. O. Côte of Napierville, who after his conversion in 1841 became a leader in missionary work during the early 1840s, perceived the situation thus (in 1837): "Seeing the conduct of the Romish clergy, and the support they gave to the government, he placed it on the same footing with the latter, and resolved in his heart to do his utmost to rescue his fellow countrymen from their ecclesiastical as well as political oppressors."9

It was after the failure of the rebellion that the Roman Church became a political and social force whose influence in French Canada is difficult to exaggerate. "She became the principal and all-encompassing institution, bringing security, stability unity and submission."10 Since the 1820s, education of Roman Catholics was entirely in the hands of the church. The parish structure (or *fabrique*) served as civil structure also, collecting taxes for such schools as existed. "The people. . .had only one privilege, that of being educated in the true religion, in the most certain doctrine. . .of natural law."11

Thus, having sketched the general framework, sociological and religious, within which the first Protestant French-speaking churches emerged, we can look more closely at their distinctive development. It is necessary for us to bear in mind as we do so that no sectarian spirit or personal animosity found any place in the hearts of the pioneers. Their frequent references to the Roman Church and its hierarchy are both lucid and historically accurate. Their love for the people among whom they worked is abundantly proved by their sacrificial living and their willingness to suffer for the Gospel's sake.

Missionary Labours up to 1868
1836-1851

By reading the earliest extant reports of the Mission, one gets a taste of the religious life of French Canada in this period, and can appreciate both the aims of, and the difficulties encountered by, early Baptist leaders there. Although originally from an evangelical wing of the Reformed Church, "Mme Feller and Mr. Roussy were baptized by Dr. Côte in 1847. It was then decided to seek affiliation with the Canadian Baptist Missionary Society."[12] This took place in 1849. The purpose of the missionaries was always the planting of a permanent testimony by the creation of believers' churches.

The first available printed report relates the events of 1848, a date we recognize as an important landmark in the nationalistic surge in Europe, specifically the beginning in Italy of the loss of the papal states, and the consequent refusal by Pius IX of modern secular movements. In the light of these facts, the missionaries observed an interesting repercussion. "Unhappily, here as in Europe, falsehood and superstition give place to infidelity."[13] What was to become a *leitmotif* in this history is further described in the same report: "It is thought best to preserve the appearance of living in the Romish religion, notwithstanding the want of faith in its practices and the entire contempt of its priests and their teachings."[14]

The method of the early missionaries was a combination of evangelism and education. Classes were held in Grande Ligne for both children and adults, where in addition to basic skills in reading and writing, Scripture was taught. Colportage and home meetings, distribution of Scriptures and personal testimony, all were used to bring people to a saving knowledge of Christ. By the year 1848 there were already nine preaching stations. There were four primary schools in addition to the school in Grande Ligne itself.

There were, of course, reasons enough to be discouraged, from a human point of view. Opposition to efforts to spread the Word of God was not long in coming. "One of the Oblate Fathers . . . who passes from parish to parish preaching temperance, is one of the most embittered enemies of the Divine Word."[15] Again, Christian readers of the report are reminded that "for want of means, schools have been closed, colporteurs dismissed, and missionaries generally hindered in their labours."[16]

1851-1868

Throughout this period the missionaries were confident of victory for the Gospel in French Canada. "The spirit of intolerance is more and more on the decline except on the part of the Priests. Protestants everywhere are met with politeness and respect."[17] A map was printed in 1852, showing no fewer than thirty-three places where evangelical meetings were being held, in halls or homes, and as labourers became available. This figure includes four towns in the state of New York, where many French-Canadians had emigrated.

In 1855 the society was incorporated as "The Evangelical Society of La Grande Ligne."[18] A motion was passed at the annual meeting:

> Resolved that Lower Canada presents a large and interesting field of evangelization and that we should be encouraged to continue and extend our missionary efforts among the French Canadians, in seeing the success with which these efforts have already been attended.[19]

It is worth noting that the work was directed from Grande Ligne. Leon Normandeau, secretary-treasurer for that year, received gifts and encouragement from English-speaking Baptists in the United States and Canada, but the society itself was genuinely indigenous at this time.

It was now possible to speak of "fifteen preaching stations, attended by 650 adult hearers and surrounded by thousands that willingly receive the visits of colporteurs and ministers. . . ."[20]

That the missionaries were attuned to the time in which they lived is evident. Continuing reaction to the hegemony of the Roman Church found expression in the general population. "Infidelity is spreading far and wide in our land even among the illiterate."[21]

The plan of action of the society was carefully elaborated: "Our mode of operation may be briefly stated in a natural division of four different departments, all intimately connected together . . . viz: the ministry; the work of evangelization by evangelists and colporteurs; the teaching in our Normal and Primary Schools; and finally the Press."[22] Concerning the last, literature was an effective tool. "Every week our French paper

'Le Semeur Canadien' pays a visit to its thousand sub-scribers."[23]

Educationally, there were two institutes, the one at Grande Ligne for young men, and the other at Longueuil (originally at St. Pie) for young ladies, the latter now named Feller Institute. These were in addition to eight primary schools serving 120 children. The report states: "There is a much larger number without school of any kind. . .We do not sacrifice evangelization to education, nor education to evangelization, for they are at bottom the same thing, and they must help one another."[24]

Indeed, one can only marvel at the fact that in just over twenty years of effort, beginning with no converts and no churches, the list of Christian workers in 1859 included fourteen French-Canadians out of a total of nineteen. Throughout this period indigenous French-Canadian Baptist work was a reality, and the whole was crowned by the birth of a fellowship of churches, which has held its annual meeting every summer from the year 1868 to the present.[25]

The Development of French Baptist Churches, 1868-1910

The First Annual Meeting

An event, the significance of which was evident at the time, confirms our conviction that the first generation of missionaries built well. Confederation was now one year old. Madame Feller having died a few months previously, the *Union des Eglises Baptistes de Langue Francaise* was officially formed on July 8, 1868. About Feller it was said: "We know that her joy would have been great indeed, and her gratitude profound, to see meet together the pastors and delegates of these young churches, for whose formation and development she so worked and prayed."[26]

Nine organized churches covenanted together to form a union. In the constitution the aim is stated as being "to cultivate the spirit of union and of peace by mutual relationships and by awareness of the state and needs of the churches; to progress in godliness and to cultivate, individually, the missionary spirit."[27]

1871-1891

a) Religious Climate
The period we are examining began with the completion of Pius IX's moves in the direction of doctrinal definitions and papal power. The Dogma of the Immaculate Conception (1854), the Syllabus of Errors (1864) and the Vatican Council Dogma of Infallibility (1870) were much in the news.

In response to the religious climate of the time, the 1873 report of the Evangelical Society of La Grande Ligne states:

> Three very different elements are at work to destroy the once imposing power, made up of political, religious and ecclesiastical interests. The first is the arrogant ultramontane faction, which to its ultimate woe, is pushing its intolerant assumptions to extremes, which no sensible government will tolerate. The second is a naked infidelity — the legitimate but monstrous offspring of Rome's superstitious teachings, and false miracles, which has reached the denial of the very existence of God. And the third is the Protestant evangelical element at work in all Catholic countries, by means of Protestant missions, the spread of the sacred Scriptures. . . .[28]

The 1876 report affirms, "We have never before met so many inquiring minds, and our meetings have never been so largely attended by Roman Catholics in almost all our stations, as during the past year."[29]

b) *The Growth of Factors Favouring Indigenization*
By 1884, the missionaries were heartened to note that the large Grande Ligne church built that year, was half paid for by the members themselves. It was by that time almost self-supporting.[30] The following year, marking the fiftieth anniversary of the arrival of Feller and Roussy, brought the knowledge that the ministry of the Gospel was effective.

> The leaven is constantly working. If we had no other means to know it, we would learn it from the pulpit of the Catholic Churches and from the Catholic press which are constantly admonishing their hearers and readers to beware of the French Protestants who are making converts.[31]

According to the constitution of the Evangelical Society of La

Grande Ligne, the object of the society was "the dissemination of the benefits of education and the propagation of a knowledge of the Gospel of Jesus Christ."[32] It was therefore urgent that Feller be not considered a terminus ad quem. Our early leaders envisioned French-language theological education: ". . . a preparatory school deserves that title and fulfills its end, only when affiliated to some higher institution, for which it becomes a natural feeder, which is not the case there . . ." (at Grande Ligne).[33]

In 1876 the Longueuil school was closed, and Feller Institute was united with the existing school in Grande Ligne. Committees were set up "to consider the establishment of a French department in the Newton Theological Seminary."[34] Finally, "in the fall of 1889 the French Department was opened with an attendance, the first year, of six students"[35] at the Newton Theological Institute of Massachusetts. From the absence of further reports, we conclude that this arrangement was short-lived. Otherwise some of our early pastors were trained in Geneva, Switzerland, and later on at McMaster University.

c) *Evaluation*

The period here under review enables us to compare stages of development in the process of indigenization. The report of the French churches for 1872 gives a list of sixteen French Baptist churches in Canada and the United States, of which nine were in Canada including one mission station in Nova Scotia, led by N. Normandin.[36] Ten pastors are listed, almost all French-Canadians, in addition to three working on fields without organized churches. A global report is offered in 1874, by way of inventory.

> It is estimated that over 4000 French Canadians have been led to embrace the truth of the Gospel through the direct instrumentality of this mission; fifteen churches were organized; over 2000 young people were educated in its institutions; and twenty-two young men were prepared for the work and sent into the field as ordained ministers, or as evangelists and colporters (*sic*).[37]

In 1888 there were in Canada:

> . . . eight organized French-Canadian churches and twenty out-stations. . . . The church membership in the French-Canadian

churches is comparatively small, for so many of the converts came
to the United States to escape annoyances and to better their circumstances.[38]

The exceedingly slow progress in the number of churches is
now easier to understand. One church reported in 1868 had
already ceased to exist by 1872 because of emigration. Let it be
said that periods of emigration to the United States have frequently affected the general population of the province of
Quebec, especially when members of large families left the
ancestral farms and were not always able to find work in the
cities. This factor was complicated for the Protestants by
religious persecution, which frequently included refusal of
work, even if available, to one who was a "heretic." "How
often have our converts been obliged to leave home on account
of family or social persecution. How often have they failed to
find employment or even a friendly helping hand, and so have
been forced to leave the country."[39]

1891-1910

The 1891 Mission report states: "We need young men, both
French and English, and women too, who will devote their lives
to this work."[40] This is the first specific reference we found to a
request for English-speaking workers, although there had been
a few English-speaking (bilingual) missionaries, and several
teachers. It was assumed, certainly, that they would learn
French. By far the majority of the team was French-Canadian.
Concerning Feller, the 1893 report says, "A very limited
number of English pupils is received."[41] The idea was excellent,
but as we shall see, the camel had his nose in the tent.

By 1894, it became evident that early hopes for evangelizing
the intellectual elite of French-Canada were not to be met with
immediate success. "Unable as we seem to be to reach the
educated and influential class of our French people, we are
creating an educated and influential community in our churches
and by our teaching institutions."[42] And the Mission could well
be proud of its leadership, even though the effort to permeate
the whole of society was not yet a reality. Nevertheless, indigenization was a reality already in terms of pastoral vocations.

At the present time thirteen of the missionaries working under the
Grande Ligne Mission board, and seven employed by our

American Home Mission Board, are men who found Christ while studying at the Institute, and it was there they first heard and heeded the Lord's command to preach the gospel.[43]

Persecution was unrelenting during these years. In 1893 colporteur Gendreau was put in prison in Sorel on the charge of disturbing the peace, for answering questions put to him in a public square. The next year windows were smashed in the *Salle de Réunions Evangéliques et de Lecture* in Quebec City. These facts only underline the effectiveness of the work. Of the provincial capital at that time it is reported: "Seldom have the meetings been held without 15 to 20 Catholics being present."[44]

These testimonies are confirmed independently, if we consult a French-Canadian political, literary and social periodical of the time. The language of the missionaries is non-polemical in comparison to that of *La Lanterne*:

> The clergy, which occupies the first place in our province, is ignorant, pretentious, coarse and often immoral. It is responsible for the lack of progress . . . and for the prejudices of our compatriots.[45]

In 1910, the Grande Ligne Mission Board decided on a change of policy, which was to involve a gradual dilution of the French orientation of the work. One should add that the official French-Canadian institutions (schools, the press, and society generally being organized on confessional lines) were scarcely hospitable to French-Canadian Protestants. It is understandable that Feller graduates would go to McGill or McMaster rather than to French universities. Nevertheless, anglicizing of the work was to be deleterious to the emergence of truly indigenous and mature French-Canadian churches.

Here then is the statement on bilingual work: "In Montreal [i.e., St. Paul's Church] the Board has decided to give the matter a full test, and there is now organized the first Bilingual Baptist Church in Canada, with a membership of 46 persons. So far the promise is bright, but it is an experiment."[46] Already English services were held as required in Marieville, Grande Ligne, Ottawa, Roxton Pond, St. Constant, Hull and Roussillon.

The Decline and Resurrection of the Indigenous Church, 1910-1979

"In all our congregations, many of the French are marrying into English families; and on the other hand, the English are marrying into French families."[47] Given the ease with which the newly-planted seedling could be transplanted into English soil, the end result was predictable: in the course of a generation these people were no longer French-Canadians, and the collective witness was to that degree weakened.

In 1914, St. Paul's Church reported: "The evening service is entirely in English, and it is in this connection that the stronger part of the work lies."[48] The attempt was also pursued in St. Constant, "one of the points where bilingual work brings complications and where patience and perseverance will be required before definite conclusions concerning the wisdom of continuing upon the present lines are reached."[49]

Again and again the contrast between the thoroughly French-Canadian emphasis of earlier days and that of the situation emerging prior to and after the first World War, became obvious. If one peruses the student newspaper of Feller Institute, *The Student*, one sees very little written in French, in the issues available for consultation (1915 to 1917). One significant article, written in French by the Rev. M. B. Parent, says: "Speak French. . .it is a means of helping the work of evangelism in our province."[50] The very fact that young people needed this kind of exhortation is an eloquent comment on the degree of anglicizing (in terms of staff, students, and course content) already in effect in the school itself — even though there was always a large proportion of francophone pupils (e.g., 119 out of 191 in 1921).

Some of the critics of the work were pointing to the closing of such fields as Sorel and Maskinongé, but in 1922, A. C. Brouillet replied that such ebb and flow was normal: "Let our detractors not forget to count the births (of new churches) as well as the demises."[51] Fair enough, for we have seen many of the factors which militated against the survival of the churches. Yet, with hindsight, one can regret that the progressive slide to anglicization was not recognized and remedied at that time.[52]

The 1932 association minutes include an exchange of views

concerning the fact that some bilingual churches send their letters to the annual conference in English. "The incident was
closed after applause from those present affirmed once again
our desire to remain exclusively French."[53] In the 1933 report
"l'Eglise de l'Est" states that this will be their last report as a
bilingual church.[54] Apparently the arrangement was less than
satisfactory. In spite of these healthy reactions, the reading of
the reports for the 1930s is painful for those concerned with indigenous French work. Several reports are in English, especially
those concerning youth meetings. Invited speakers frequently
were English-speaking; there is no record of their messages being interpreted.

Anglicization came to be an unquestioned fact of life. The
Mission report for 1927 refers to St. Constant, where the pastor
is an English brother; but "the people, though French, are
familiar with the English tongue, most of them having been
students at Feller Institute."[55]

In 1937, mention is made of the infamous Padlock Law which
gave the government wide powers with reference to any group
or meeting suspected of communism. "According to reports
from all our missionaries, Protestants are being described as
communists in public statements by the priest on many of our
fields."[56] Those familiar with the circumstances realize that
although communism was seen as an attractive option by many
people in the Western world during the depression years, there
was also, on the part of many in French-Canada, a specifically
religious disaffection. "Unfortunately very few know of any
other place to which to turn when they leave the church and the
tendency as a consequence is to drift into agnosticism or
atheism."[57] On the older fields, the tradition of a French Protestant church in town was by now an accepted fact of life, so
that people were inclined to be content with the *status quo*. Protestantism was seen not as a viable alternative, but as a matter of
family heritage. A Grande Ligne Mission survey committee gave
a report in 1946, but beyond some structural revamping,
nothing significant for the promotion of indigenous French-
Canadian work emerged.[58]

By the 1950s the alarm was being sounded. Said E. A.
Boisvert in 1951 to the annual conference of the French
churches: "We need more recruits for evangelism. . .if the executive of the association took an active part in our churches, it

would do good. Several young English Canadians are coming to work among us. That is good, but our churches are not giving us missionaries."[59] His reference to the need for the French-Canadian body, the association, to get involved with more than the organization of an annual meeting was a prophetic and strategic suggestion.

The next year Dr. Paul Chodat said: ". . .the penury of workers is such that we must call in English-speaking workers. If that continues the Grande Ligne Mission will not endure as a French mission."[60] That same year the association voted that one of the criteria for ordination would be the ability to speak French fluently. These statements indicate that the urgency of the indigenization was becoming apparent, and that changes were to be expected in the years to come. There were also other straws in the wind. L'Oratoire reported in 1956 the loss of ten members who had joined English churches.[61]

By 1958 the Rev. Charles Foster was telling the annual meeting of the association that the latter should be thinking of itself as a little convention of its own. Notice is taken of the new French Protestant school opened in Montreal.[62] During these years a French Baptist summer camp and a book service of French evangelical literature were organized by the present author. A resolution was passed in 1959 which, once again, expressed a search for greater involvement of the French churches and their pastors in the decision-making processes of the Mission:

> *Whereas* our Association, the Grande Ligne Mission, and the Conference of pastors are working for the same goal, the development of evangelical work among our churches, *it is resolved* that we encourage a closer cooperation and a more intimate unity by meetings of representatives of each of these organizations, at least twice a year, and any other method aiming at unifying and intensifying our missionary work.[63]

It is instructive to look at the list of pastors for 1960. They include one French-Canadian, two Swiss and six English-speaking Canadians who had learned French. (Other missionaries included two English-Canadians, one Swiss, and three French-Canadians.)[64]

The Mission itself was fully cognizant of and agreeable to the aspirations of the churches. The 1963 Mission report states: "It has been the policy of the Board to promote an attitude of self-reliance among our churches, to the end that they may steadily progress toward the goal of practical self-sufficiency."[65] Under the guidance of the Rev. Charles Foster, study sessions were conducted over a period of years, in which members of the French Baptist churches were invited to examine biblical principles and the history of missions, with the aim of educating the membership in the implications of indigenous work.

Notice of motion for a change in the constitution having been tabled in 1965, Dr. Albert Lefrancois proposed to the association in 1966 that henceforth we become a *union* of churches, and not simply an association within the Baptist Convention of Ontario and Quebec. "The Grande Ligne Mission . . . desires to transfer to our Union . . . the management of funds and the direction of our own work."[66] In 1969 the *Union d'Eglises baptistes francaises au Canada* was incorporated, and the first full-time general secretary, the Rev. Maurice Boillat, was inducted into office.

It is worth noting that both the Rev. H. C. Wilkinson (general secretary of the Grand Ligne Mission from 1948 to 1965) and the Rev. Emrys Jenkins (general secretary of the Grande Ligne Mission from 1965 to 1969) cooperated fully in the development of the French churches toward a more responsible role, as the work moved inexorably from the status of a mission, organized by English-speaking Baptists, to that of a union of French-Canadian churches. The Mission representatives met with those of the Convention of Ontario and Quebec, to consult on French-Canadian Baptist work, beginning November 26, 1966. The 1968 report of the Grande Ligne Mission explains the process that had taken place: "The people the Mission seeks to serve are French Canadians, therefore the need is for a French Canadian Baptist organization . . . The transformation of the 'French Association' into the 'Union of French Baptist Churches in Canada' was the answer to the need for a totally French Canadian structure."[67]

In 1968 Feller College (as it had been called for many years past) was sold. The efforts at meeting the needs of French-Canadians at Feller, latterly through the principalship of the Rev. E. A. Boisvert and the Rev. John Gilmour, especially following the Kitchen-Mallory study on Feller undertaken in

1959,[68] and evaluation of the decision to close, would occupy another chapter.

We shall not speak at great length about the history, during the 1970s, of the "French Union," except to say that at this writing, the Rev. M. Boillat has just resigned after ten years of outstanding leadership as general secretary. We are in the process of continual reevaluation, but it seems clear that the direction taken a decade ago was the right one. In 1970 the Union of French Baptist Churches in Canada was recognized by the Baptist Federation of Canada as a fourth constituent convention. That same year the Union reported: "The all-French Council of eleven members (seven laymen and four pastors) has proven to be a real working force." The report added, however, the important caution that the Union *per se* was not the basic unit. "Despite various means and methods used in promoting the Kingdom of God, the local church remains God's divinely appointed institution here on earth . . . the most effective tool of evangelism."[69]

Three years later, the report noted "a greater sense of stewardship and indigenous leadership . . . ."[70] In 1974 the following facts were underlined: ". . . several students preparing for future service . . . a keener desire on the part of local churches to establish new congregations."[71]

Membership, after a pruning of lists, is slowly but surely on the rise. The highest was 1008 in 1931, and the lowest 398 in 1972. It now stands at 650. Although theological courses were offered in French in Quebec City during the 1960s and in Montreal during the 1970s, we are at this time seeking to find a more adequate means of providing seminary-level training for our candidates. We believe that this, when accomplished, will signal a more fruitful and authentic way into the future for our now fully indigenous *Union d'Eglises baptistes francaises au Canada.*[72]

* * * * *

The indigenous concept of planting and fostering the development of local churches — self-supporting, self-directing, and self-propagating — has been the main focus of this paper. It is obvious that in an overview such as this one can only tentatively seek to draw provisional conclusions. In the early years of the work, prospects were good for a thoroughly French-Canadian church. This has now at last become a reality. Indigenous leadership is clearly on the rise in terms of missionary staff.[73] Our natural desire is for the growth of churches that will glorify God and witness to the saving power of Christ. It would be well to bear in mind that statistics do not tell the whole story. In 1902, the Rev. Theodore Lafleur, secretary of the Grande Ligne Mission, stated:

> If some friends of this cause think that, considering the space of time employed, the money spent, and the honest work done, we ought to be able to show greater results, we answer first, that these results, scattered as they are over all this northern continent, are very difficult to measure, and that our aim being chiefly a spiritual and moral reformation, visible results are not the adequate measure of the value of our work, and far less of its broad and varied influences.[74]

Undeniably, French-Canada today is no longer unanimously Roman Catholic. The ecumenical stance of the Roman Church since Vatican II and the new religious pluralism of the francophone population, present an entirely different picture than the monolithic situation which prevailed for so long. However, since the Great Commission has never been rescinded, our French churches will continue to witness to the Redeemer, and hopefully address themselves effectively to the new context — whatever it may be — both political and religious.

3 Witness in French Canada, W. N. Thomson

1. See J. M. Cramp, *A Memoir of Madame Feller* (London: Elliot Stock, n.d.), and Walter N. Wyeth, *Henrietta Feller and the Grande Ligne Mission: A Memorial* (Philadelphia: W. N. Wyeth 1898).

2. Mack Eastman, *Church and State in Early Canada* (Edinburgh: University Press, 1915), p. 31.

3. Walter A. Riddell, *The Rise of Ecclesiastical Control in Quebec* (New York: Columbia University, 1916), p. 129.

4. *Ibid.*, p. 157.

5. H. H. Walsh, *The Christian Church in Canada* (Toronto: Ryerson, 1956), p. 79.

6. This fact is extremely well documented in Charles Lindsay, *Rome in Canada* (Toronto: Lovell, 1887). See especially pp. 24, 27, 252, 397.

7. See the *Mandement* of May 22, 1775. ("Vos serments, votre religion, vous imposent une obligation indispensable de défendre de tout votre patrie et votre roi".) *Mandements des Evêques de Québec* (Québec: Imprimerie A. Côté et Cie, 1888), pp. 264-265.

8. Edmund H. Oliver, *The Winning of the Frontier* (Toronto: United Church Publishing House, 1930), p. 104.

9. N. Cyr, *Memoir of the Rev. C. H. O. Côte, M.D.* (Philadelphia: American Baptist Publishing Society, n.d.), p. 8.

10. "Elle devient l'institution principale et englobante, apportant sécurité, stabilité, unité et soumission". Jacques Grand'maison, *Nationalisme et Religion,* vol. 1 (Montreal: Beauchemin, 1970), p. 150.

11. "Le peuple . . . avait un seul privilège, celui d'être éduqué dans la vraie religion, dans la doctrine la plus sûre . . . du droit naturel." Jacques Grand'maison, *op. cit.*, vol. 2, p. 38.

12. E. R. Fitch, *The Baptists of Canada* (Toronto: The Standard Publishing Co., 1911), p. 203.

13. *Annual Report of the Swiss Mission (Canada East) for 1848* (Montreal, 1849), p. 1.

14. *Ibid.*, p. 2.

15. *Ibid.*, p. 3. This is doubtless an allusion to Father Charles Chiniquy, later to become a controversial Presbyterian minister.

16. *Ibid.*, p. 6.

17. *The Grande Ligne Mission Register*, January 1853, p. 1.

18. *Ibid.*, April 1852, p. 12.

19. *Report of the Evangelical Society of La Grande Ligne for 1855* (Montreal: French Bible Depository, 1856), p. 7.

20. *Ibid.*, p. 8.

21. *Ibid.*, p. 9.

22. *Report of the Evangelical Society of La Grande Ligne for 1856* (Montreal: French Bible Depository), pp. 3-4.

23. *Report of the Evangelical Society of La Grande Ligne for 1855*, p. 10.

24. *Ibid.*, p. 11.

25. With the apparent exception of 1869.

26. *Formation et Constitution de l'Union des Eglises baptistes françaises et Minutes des deux Premières Assemblées Anniversaires tenues à La Grande Ligne le 8 juillet 1868 et le 29 juin 1870* (Montréal: Imprimerie de l'Aurore, 1870), p. 3.

27. *Ibid.*, p. 21.

28. *Thirty-Sixth Annual Report of the Evangelical Society of La Grande Ligne* (Montreal, 1873), p. 3.

29. *Thirty-Ninth Annual Report of the Evangelical Society of La Grande Ligne* (Montreal, 1876), p. 3.

30. *Forty-Seventh Annual Report of the Evangelical Society of La Grande Ligne* (Montreal, 1884), p. 14.

31. *Forty-Ninth Annual Report of the Evangelical Society of La Grande Ligne* (Montreal, 1886), p. 15.

32. Appended to *Thirty-Seventh Annual Report of the Evangelical Society of La Grande Ligne, 1874, p. 30*.

33. *Ibid.*, pp. 7-8.

34. *Thirty-Eighth Annual Report of the Brooklyn Association in Aid of the Grande Ligne Mission for the Year Ending December 1887* (New York, 1888), p. 8.

35. Dr. H. L. Morehouse, "The French Canadian in Quebec and New England" in *The Baptist Home Mission Monthly*, December 1893 (New York, N.Y.: The American Baptist Home Mission Society). Reprinted as a pamphlet, n.d., p. 29.

36. *Rapport de la Quatrième Anniversaire de l'Association des Eglises baptistes de langue française au Canada*, tenue à Roxton Pond, le 3 juillet, 1872 (Montréal: Imprimerie de Mitchell et Wilson, 1872), p. 9. Cf. George Edward Levy, *The Baptists of the Maritime Provinces 1753-1946* (Saint John, N.B.: Barnes-Hopkins, 1946), pp. 164-165. Note the early change from a French *Union* to an Association.

37. *Forty-Fourth Annual Report of the Evangelical Society of La Grande Ligne (Montreal, 1881), p. 8*.

38. *Fortieth Annual Report of the Brooklyn Association in Aid of the Grande Ligne Mission for the Year Ending December 1888* (New York, 1889), p. 7.

39. *Sixty-First Annual Report of the Grande Ligne Mission* (Montreal, 1897), p. 26. Information on this factor is inserted here, although the phenomenon covers a longer period than the twenty years under consideration in this section.

40. *Fifty-Fifth Annual Report of the Grande Ligne Mission* (Montreal, 1891), p. 27.

41. *Fifty-Seventh Annual Report of the Grande Ligne Mission* (Montreal, 1893), p. 16. Beginning in this year the report concerns the current year, henceforth the year is October 1 to September 30.

42. *Fifty-Eighth Annual Report of the Grande Ligne Mission* (Montreal, 1894), p. 6.

43. *Forty-Sixth Annual Report of the Brooklyn Association in Aid of the Grande Ligne Mission for the year ending December 1894* (Brooklyn, N.Y., 1894), p. 9.

44. *Fifty-Eighth Annual Report of the Grande Ligne Mission*, 1894, p. 6.

45. *La Lanterne* (Revue Mensuelle), vol. 1, no. 1., Montreal, Nov. 5, 1903, p. 1.

46. *Seventy-Fourth annual Report of the Grande Ligne Mission*, 1910, p. 9.

47. *Seventy-Fifth Annual Report of the Grande Ligne Mission*, 1911, p. 7.

48. *Seventy-Eighth Annual Report of the Grande Ligne Mission*, 1914, p. 9.

49. *Ibid.*, p. 13.

50. *The Student*, Grande Ligne, Québec, vol. II, no. 5, April 1917, p. 2. The same observation could be made about *The Feller College* (from 1936) and the yearbook *L'Echo* (from 1949).

51. *Procès-Verbal de la Conférence Annuelle des Eglises baptistes françaises du Canada*, 1922, p. 13.

52. A. C. Brouillet did indeed analyze the reasons for the closing of Maskinongé in 1920 (mortality, emigration, mixed marriages, premature organization) in the 1931 Association report, p. 36, and of Sorel in 1902 (boycotting, persecution, illness, death) in the 1932 Association report, p. 30.

53. *Procès-Verbal de la Conférence Annuelle des Eglises baptistes françaises du Canada*, 1932, p. 5.

54. *Procès-Verbal de la Conférence Annuelle des Eglises baptistes françaises du Canada,* 1933, p. 12.

55. *Ninety-First annual Report of the Grande Ligne Mission,* 1927, p. 6.

56. *One Hundred and First Annual Report of the Grande Ligne Mission*, 1 October 1936 to 30 September 1937, p. 4.

57. *Ibid.*, p. 4.

58. *One Hundred and Ninth Annual Report of the Grande Ligne Mission, 1945-1946,* pp. 3-4.

59. Lettre circulaire, *Procès-Verbal de la Conférence Annuelle des Eglises baptistes françaises du Canada,* 1951, p. 3.

60. *Procès-Verbal de la Conférence Annuelle des Eglises baptistes françaises du Canada,* 1952, p. 5. Dr. Chodate did not realize that the new English-speaking workers were, to a man, committed to the indigenous concept.

61. *Procès-Verbal de la Conférence Annuelle des Eglises baptistes françaises du Canada,* 1956, p. 10.

62. *Procès-Verbal de la Conférence Annuelle des Eglises baptistes françaises du Canada,* 1958, p. 4.

63. *Procès-Verbal de la Conférence Annuelle des Eglises baptistes françaises du Canada,* 1959, p. 6.

64. *Procès-Verbal de la Conférence Annuelle des Eglises baptistes françaises du Canada,* 1960, pp. 14-15.

65. *One Hundred and Twenty-Sixth Annual Report of the Grande Ligne Mission 1962-1963,* p. 2.

66. *Procès-Verbal de la Conférence Annuelle des Eglises baptistes françaises du Canada,* 1966, p. 6.

67. *One Hundred and Thirty-First Annual Report of the Grande Ligne Mission 1967-1968,* p. 2.

68. See the *One Hundred and Twenty-Third Annual Report of the Grande Ligne Mission,* 1959-1960, p. 3. Also the *One Hundred and Twenty-Fourth Report of the Grande Ligne Mission* 1960-1961, p. 3.: "More emphasis on the bilingual character of Feller was laid this year than in years past." (Note that when bilingualism was first broached in the Mission, it was with reference to having some churches where English services could be held. By 1961 increased bilingualism at Feller had come to mean the reverse, namely more room for French.)

69. Union d'Eglises baptistes françaises au Canada, *Annual Report,* January 1 - December 31, 1970, p. 1.

70. Union d'Eglises baptistes françaises au Canada, *Annual Report,* 1973, p. 6.

71. Union d'Eglises baptistes françaises au Canada, *Annual Report,* 1974, p. 10.

72. "Fully indigenous" refers to leadership and responsibility which is now squarely with the French-Canadian churches. They are not yet completely autonomous from a financial perspective although they provide fully one-third of the total budget of our French work.

73. In 1979 there are eight active French-Canadian workers, four others whose mother tongue is French and eight whose mother tongue is

English. An interesting feature is that one of our workers, Mr. Emmanuel Pierre, is Haitian. In recent years Haitian immigration into Montreal has brought many of these brethren into our fellowship.

74. *Sixty-Sixth Annual Report of the Grande Ligne Mission* for the year ending October 1st, 1902, p. 8.

4

They Speak in Other Tongues: Witness among Immigrants

Jarold K. Zeman

What is Canada's greatest problem? . . . It is immigration. . . . If it be granted that in this question is wrapped up our greatest opportunity and our gravest peril, it clearly follows that our Canadian people should become thoroughly acquainted with the different nationalities that compose our immigration, their race characteristics, their number and distribution, their occupation and religion, and above all their accessibility to the gospel. But our people are not well informed on these subjects. We are safe in saying that not ten per cent of our church members have been seized with a sense of the magnitude nor of the peril of the immigrant tide that is rolling in upon Canada, nor have they been deeply impressed as to their responsibility in solving this problem.

Canada is God's last best country. No other country in the world has opened its doors and is inviting the industrious of all nations, tongues and races to homes given without money and without price.

With these words, C. J. Cameron, superintendent of the Baptist Home Mission Board of Ontario and Quebec, pleaded with fellow Baptists in his book *Foreigners or Canadians?* published in Toronto in 1913.[1] The timing of his appeal was ideal. In the same year Canada admitted a total of 400,870 immigrants, the highest number for any single year in Canadian history.

Cameron's claim that immigration constitutes the key factor in the development of this country could hardly be dismissed as a rhetorical exaggeration then, and even less so today. At the turn of the century, Canada's population totalled only 5.3 million. Today, it is estimated at 23.5 million. During these eighty years 23 million babies were born whereas deaths totaled less than 9 million. In the same period 9.2 million immigrants were admitted while 5 million persons are estimated to have left the country as emigrants, mostly to the United States. It would be difficult to determine what proportion of the emigrants originally arrived as immigrants and used Canada as a transit country. Any decrease in the number of native Canadians due to emigration would of necessity reinforce the cultural and economic impact of newly-arriving immigrants.[2]

Canada has no ethnic majority. The cities and countryside are populated by people who represent the races and cultures of the whole world. More than a hundred languages are spoken daily in Canadian homes and on the streets. Some of them can be heard on radio and television stations. Newspapers and books in many languages are printed in several centres. Multilingualism and multiculturalism is a fact of life in the central and western provinces of Canada.

For a century or more, Canadian Christians have faced the choice between negative and positive responses to "the whole world at their door."[3] Consciously or subconsciously, some perceived the sounds of their foreign-speaking neighbours as the curse of Babel where languages were confused so that people "may not understand one another's speech" (Genesis 11:7). Others recalled the wonder of Pentecost. The early Christians were enabled to speak in other tongues so that people gathered in Jerusalem from many lands could hear the Gospel "each in his own language" (Acts 2: 4-8).

The imposed limits of this essay do not allow for a comprehensive review of all major efforts of Baptist outreach among immigrants. The sources for such study are written in more than twenty languages and are scattered across Canada, most of them in the private collections of ethnic ministers and congregations.[4] The brief account presented here will be limited to New Canadian work sponsored by or undertaken in cooperation with the Baptist Convention of Ontario and Quebec.

The story of Baptist ministries to immigrants in Western Canada has been told in two recent publications.[5] Apart from port work, Baptists in the Atlantic provinces have had few opportunities for ethnic ministries.[6] Outreach among immigrants of German origin (North American Baptist Conference) is treated in a separate essay.[7] A review of the Swedish work (Baptist General Conference) which developed mostly in Western Canada, is available in print.[8] Difficulties encountered in the search for information led to the exclusion of data on missionary work in Ontario and Quebec sponsored by other Baptist groups, such as the Fellowship of Evangelical Baptist Churches.

Ethnic (Language) Churches and Missions

The development of Baptist ethnic ministries in Ontario and Quebec since Confederation (1867) appears to have passed through five distinct phases. In each period, the changing ethnic characteristics and methods of work were related to major waves of immigration determined by government policy. In its admission of immigrants, the Canadian government was influenced in varying degrees by economic needs of the country, by world events, and by humanitarian concerns.

During the second half of the nineteenth century, the large-scale immigration of people of German and Scandinavian origin led to the establishment of many congregations and missions in the German and Scandinavian languages, both in Ontario and in Western Canada. They constitute the oldest segment of Baptist ethnic work. Although some of the churches were revitalized by immigrants arriving in this century, most congregations are now English-speaking but maintain affiliation with their respective ethnic conferences.

During the brief period between the turn of the century and the outbreak of the First World War (1901-1914) nearly three million immigrants entered Canada. The focus of Baptist concern shifted to newcomers of Slavic origin. The arrival of the Rev. John Kolesnikoff in Toronto in 1908 prompted the opening of three "mission halls" in that city as well as missions in Hamilton, Welland, Oshawa, Fort William, Montreal and other centres. The channels for Slavic witness included mission halls, night schools, street meetings, lantern lectures, festivals, free dispensaries of medical aid, distribution of literature, training in domestic housekeeping, and employment information centres.

One cannot but admire the wholistic approach to the needs of immigrants.9

The twenty years between the two World Wars brought further diversification of ethnic missions. Slavic outreach was expanded to include Czech, Slovak, Polish and the languages spoken in modern Jugoslavia. Finnish, Hungarian and Romanian churches were established as well. The most significant growth occurred in Toronto and Windsor. However, since New Canadian churches were characterized by a burden for evangelistic witness among their fellow countrymen wherever they would be found, a network of mission stations in many languages covered most of Southern Ontario.

A typical New Canadian pastor would serve not only his congregation but also visit, on a regular basis, five to ten "preaching stations" or house churches in other cities and towns. Very few of these developed into organized churches. Nonetheless, hundreds of immigrants were brought to a personal commitment to Christ, and in most cases they and their Canadian-born children eventually joined English-speaking churches.

The names of two remarkable pastors-missionaries during the period deserve special mention. The Rev. John Cristea (1901-1950) came from Romania (Transylvania). After training at the Baptist seminaries in Bucharest and Louisville (Kentucky), he preached to Hungarian and Romanian immigrants in Windsor from 1931 until his premature death in 1950. In several printed pamphlets he ably interpreted for English-speaking Canadians the problems faced by immigrants, and the urgent task of winning them to Christ. During the difficult depression years, he also had to cope with communist propaganda among unemployed immigrants.

> While Winnipeg is the chief centre of Communism, and Toronto the second, there is no doubt in our minds but that Windsor is the third. . . . I have been ridiculed many times by the Communists who say that I am a capitalist of the first order and that I am not interested in the welfare of the poor people. Some have said, "If you go to hear Cristea preach, you will find out that he preaches justice mixed with capitalistic ideas." But despite all this criticism many Communists still come to hear my messages.10

The Rev. John Kaczowka (1893-1975), a former novice of the Redemptorist Fathers, came to Canada via the United States in 1913 as an immigrant from Poland. After conversion, he was trained at McMaster University and served as pastor of Polish Baptist churches in St. Catharines and Toronto (after 1944). His personal testimony and vast experience in immigrant ministries made him a much-appreciated spokesman for witness to nominal Roman Catholics.[11]

Baptist outreach to immigrants reached its climax in the years following World War II and up to the end of the 1960s. The influx of political refugees from Soviet-controlled territories strengthened many older congregations and led to the establishment of new ones such as the Latvian and Estonian churches in Toronto. The latter became known as the fastest-growing congregation in the Baptist Convention of Ontario and Quebec.

The mass immigration of Italians to Toronto and other cities also prompted an experimental approach in Italian work. Two missionaries from Italy, the Rev. Mario Acacia (in Toronto) and the Rev. Vincenzo Coacci (in Montreal) sought to link small Italian fellowship groups to existing English-speaking churches. By and large, the experiment failed.[12]

There was a marked change in the educational and social profile of many post-war immigrants, particularly those who left Europe for political rather than economic reasons. Many of them were professional people with advanced training and long experience. The "up-grading" was reflected in the calibre of several post-war New Canadian pastors who included former seminary professors (Rudolf Ekstein — Latvian, and John Keidann — Brazilian);[13] writers and poets (such as Peter Kolibaev — Russian)[14] and performing artists (such as Kaljo Raid — Estonian cellist). Two men completed academic doctorates while engaged in New Canadian work (Mario Acacia and Jarold K. Zeman).

Many ethnic pastors were involved in the writing and production of Christian periodicals and books in their respective languages as well as in the preparation of radio programs to be aired on Canadian stations and in shortwave transmissions to their homelands. Most of the ethnic congregations maintained a dual affiliation: with the Baptist Convention of Ontario and Quebec, and with their small ethnic conferences.[15]

The decade of the 1970s must be designated as a distinct phase in the development of Baptist New Canadian missions. There was a radical shift in the ethnic profile of newly-arriving immigrants. Whereas in 1956, 57.7 percent of all admitted immigrants came from the continent of Europe and 30.6 percent from the United Kingdom (for a total of 88.3 percent), in 1977 immigrants of European origin accounted for less than 20 percent, and those from the United Kingdom for less than 16 percent. In the same year, 27.3 percent of all immigrants came from Asia, the majority of them of Chinese origin, and 18.4 percent from the Caribbean, Central and South American regions. A visitor to Toronto and other cities in Ontario cannot but notice the presence of the new large black and oriental minorities.

Baptist response to the new trends in Canadian immigration has been threefold, thus far. While only one new mission in a European language was added (Portuguese), several large Chinese congregations were organized in Toronto, Montreal and elsewhere. These are the fastest-growing Baptist churches in Ontario at the present time.

With the exception of Haitian immigrants, black newcomers from the Caribbean region are mostly English-speaking. Their integration into existing English churches is underway with varying degrees of progress. A new sense of urgency prevails in many of these churches in the large cities as they seek to develop new strategies for survival and witness in their ever-changing neighbourhoods.[16]

The following table documents the impressive scope of Baptist attempts to reach newcomers in no fewer than twenty-eight languages, other than English and French. Other denominations, particularly the Roman Catholic, Eastern Orthodox, Lutheran and Anglican, have attracted much larger numbers of immigrants who naturally gravitate to the dominant church of their particular homelands. With the exception of Estonian and Chinese congregations, New Canadian Baptist churches have remained relatively small (less than one hundred adult members). But no other Christian body in Canada can match the record of Baptist witness in so many languages and over such a long period of time.

Baptist Missions to Immigrants
Listed by Language

Note: The places and dates of beginnings are listed where known but
do not necessarily indicate an organized church nor a continuing work. Some groups met only for a brief period of time and
no churches were established.

Indo-European

Germanic[17]
Danish
German—Bridgeport, 1851, and Neustadt, 1859[18]
Icelandic
Norwegian
Swedish—Waterville, Quebec, 1886; Kipling, 1902; Kenora, 1894

Slavic
Bulgarian—Toronto, 1908
Croatian (Jugoslavia)—Toronto and Windsor, 1920s
Czech—Toronto, 1942
Macedonian—Toronto, 1908
Polish—Toronto, 1920 (church, 1923)[19]
Russian—Toronto, 1908
Ruthenian—Toronto, 1908
Serbian (Jugoslavia)—Toronto and Windsor, 1920s
Slovak—Windsor, 1925 (church, 1927)
Slovenian (Jugoslavia)—Toronto and Windsor, 1920s
Ukrainian—Toronto, 1908 (church, 1952)[19]

Baltic
Latvian (Lettish)—Toronto, 1951

Romance
Italian—Toronto, 1961
Portuguese—Toronto, 1978
Romanian—Windsor, 1923

Hellenic
Greek—Toronto, 1913 and 1962

Armenian
Armenian—Montreal, 1961

Finno-Ugric
Estonian—Toronto, 1949 (church, 1951)
Finnish—Toronto, 1929
Hungarian—Toronto and Welland, 1924 (church, 1929)

Altaic
Turkish—Toronto, 1908

Oriental
Chinese—Toronto, 1967 (church, 1971)
Korean—Toronto, 1976

Canadian Christian Fellowship

The small ethnic congregations and their pastors-missionaries could not begin to meet the overwhelming needs, both spiritual and material, of the ever-increasing numbers of newcomers from other lands. English-speaking churches in the large cities and in many rural areas began to feel the impact of the changing ethnic composition of their communities. The challenge was taken up by women who were organized in local mission circles and raising substantial funds for their missionary projects at home and abroad.

Working in close cooperation with the denominational Home Mission Board, The Women's Baptist Home Missionary Society of Ontario West and its counterpart in Eastern Ontario and Quebec[21] had provided generous financial grants toward the salaries of ethnic pastors and missionaries among immigrants in Ontario and Western Canada since 1894. After the First World War the women initiated a new endeavour in Baptist outreach to immigrants. The appointment of Anna Phelps as the first "missionary to New Canadians" in 1919 marked the beginning of one of the most remarkable missionary projects on the Canadian scene.

Through five decades (1919-1969) the Baptist women's societies appointed and supported a total of fifty-five women home missionaries, most of whom served, for longer or shorter periods of time, among immigrants in the major metropolitan centres of Ontario and Quebec. Two of them, Charlotte Evans who served from 1929 to 1970, and Olive Hunter, 1927 to 1969, deserve special mention for their long and distinguished careers.[22]

The impressive achievements of the New Canadian outreach sponsored by the women must be attributed, first and foremost, to the ability of the women missionaries and the BWMS officers in the local mission circles, to mobilize large numbers of volunteer helpers, originally women, but in later years also men.

In the mid-1930s the programme became known as the Canadian Christian Fellowship (CCF) but its recorded beginnings can be traced to the concern of women in the Villa Nova Church and in other Baptist churches in Norfolk County, around Simcoe, a decade earlier (1925).[23]

A similar project called "American Friendliness" was developed by the Northern Baptist Convention in the United States after the First World War, and likely influenced some of the early organizational aspects of the Canadian programme.[24]

From its humble beginnings to its peak in the 1950s and 60s, the CCF programme included four main channels of ministries to immigrants:

- friendship through visitation, both in the homes of newcomers and through hospitality extended to them in Canadian homes, in order to provide moral and often also material support;
- teaching of English, undertaken by volunteers in the form of personal tutoring in homes or at teaching centres organized in Baptist church buildings;
- citizenship education as an aid to the immigrants' integration in Canadian society;
- evangelization of newcomers with a view to their personal commitment to Jesus Christ and membership in Baptist churches.

All aspects of the programme were undergirded by a network of prayer partners. Much energy was spent also on collection of food, used clothing and furniture for distribution to needy immigrants.

The relative emphasis on any of the four stated objectives varied from church to church and depended on circumstances and on the calibre of local leadership. The CCF programme was administered by the BWMS missionaries and by special committees organized at congregation, association, and convention levels. Annual reports from local centres were compiled and printed in *The Link and Visitor*. The following examples will indicate the scope of the work in major cities in Ontario and Quebec.

During the 1953-54 school year, 245 volunteer teachers taught English to 513 students in several Baptist churches in Toronto. Three years later, 1956-57, Baptist mission circles in the same city reported a total of 146 teachers who had taught over 6000 lessons to 572 pupils — of 21 different nationalities. The teachers were supported by 134 visitors to New Canadian homes and 54 prayer partners. For the same year, churches in Ottawa reported 35 teachers, 45 visitors and 40 prayer partners. In Montreal, 46 teachers gave 3600 English lessons while 21 visitors and 12 prayer partners carried on the other aspects of the programme. Teaching centres were in operation in several other cities, including Hamilton, Brantford, London, Sarnia and Windsor.

Through the 1960s, the government assumed increasing responsibility for instruction in English and citizenship in centres which were directed by paid professional teachers but also used volunteer tutors. Inevitably, the enrolment in the teaching centres operated by Baptist churches declined. During the 1964-65 school year, only 138 teachers, 66 visitors and 64 prayer partners were reported from the entire Convention. The fruit of the evangelistic efforts during the same year was perhaps more encouraging: 26 immigrants who had been reached through the CCF programme, joined Baptist churches by baptism; 48 did so by transfer of membership from another church, and two "by experience" (personal testimony); 25 others became adherents.[25]

In 1969 the concept and goals of the CCF were changed to "Christian Fellowship in Action" to meet the social needs of communites at large. A few volunteer tutors continued to teach in centres sponsored by the government but the Baptist teaching centres were phased out. Other aspects of the CCF programme appear to have been abandoned as well.

When one reviews the annual statistical reports filed by the BWMS missionaries, local teaching centres and the CCF secretaries, or reads the many moving accounts of particular personal incidents in New Canadian work recorded in words and pictures in the denominational or secular papers as well as in the preserved personal files, one cannot but be impressed by the dedication and perseverance of the Baptist church members involved in the CCF programme. What motivated these men and women of all ages and vocations to invest so much time and energy in mission to immigrants?

Writing during the depression years, the secretary of the CCF in Norfolk County, Mrs. E. Heath of Delhi, pleaded for greater involvement in New Canadian work and concluded her article with the following appeal:

> Let each of us be on the alert, watching for an opportunity to show some kindness to the stranger in our midst. Our only hope is to endeavour to make of these newcomers good Canadian citizens and to win them to Christ. If we do not do so and they turn to Communism in their hunger for friendship, and the agitator finds in them a receptive and responsive note, it will be entirely our own fault. The problems of these people are not imaginary, but are very, very real, and the time is not far distant, when the church may find she has lost her opportunity to reach the New Canadians.[26]

An official pamphlet published by the BWMS in the 1960s underscored the three basic goals of the programme as follows:

- *It is Canadian:* Through the ministry of the local Baptist church, Canadians extend a hand of friendship to strangers in our midst.
- *It is Christian:* It is a God-given opportunity to Canadian Baptists to share the knowledge of their faith with those of different nationalities who had not had the vital experience and relationship with our Lord Jesus Christ.
- *It is Fellowship:* It is the privilege of Canadian Christians to live out Christ, Who said, Love your neighbour as yourself.

The pamphlet also stressed the three main characteristics of the CCF work. It is *personal, practical,* and *prayerful.*[27]

No doubt, the predominant motive was determined by the theological outlook, type of personality, local circumstances and other variables. Humanitarian compassion was intertwined with patriotic concern for the future of Canada and with an evangelistic burden for the salvation of men.

One of the amazing aspects of the CCF outreach was its appeal to the entire cross-section of the Baptist constituency. Persons of high social rank from prestigious churches joined hands with members from small congregations in the blue-collar districts of the city. Christians with several university degrees taught English alongside those with only elementary education.

Another factor that explains, in part, why the CCF movement reached its peak in the 1950s and 60s was the excellent cooperation among leaders and workers in several sectors of Baptist life. Most of the BWMS missionaries in the major metropolitan areas gave energetic leadership and received wholehearted encouragement from the local mission circles and BWMS officers. The names of Charlotte Evans in Ottawa, Shirley Heatlie in Montreal and Stella Gaverluk in Toronto became synonymous with CCF concerns.

At the same time, several ethnic pastors (mentioned earlier) were men with unusual abilities to communicate the burden for immigrants to the Baptist constituency at large. Furthermore, the Home Mission Board (reorganized as the Department of Canadian Missions in 1964) provided a major impetus for New

Canadian work under its superintendents (secretaries) Dixon A. Burns (1951-1966) and Archibald R. Goldie (1964-   ), both immigrants from Scotland, and Jarold K. Zeman (1959-1968) from Czechoslovakia.

The New Approach to New Canadian Work

Concern for immigrants and support of ethnic pastors and missionaries had constituted one of the major responsiblities of the Home Mission Board since the turn of the century. However, only under the leadership of Dixon A. Burns, with his gifts in education and promotion, was the full potential of the missionary appeal of New Canadian work realized.

In his reports and presentations of home missions at the annual convention assemblies, he introduced personal testimonies by immigrants, and music by ethnic choirs and soloists. At mass rallies held in the large downtown churches in Toronto[28] choirs and instrumental ensembles from ethnic churches were combined with the pageantry of native costumes. Several busloads of choir members from the New Canadian churches in Toronto were brought to Kingston for the Home Missions program at the Baptist Federation Assembly in 1959.

Working in close cooperation with the CCF office in Toronto, the Home Mission Board printed and distributed colourful church bulletins, posters, placemats (for international church dinners) and Gospel literature as an incentive to local churches to observe annually a New Canadian Fellowship Week.[29] Conferences were held to provide better understanding of the immigrants and training for more effective methods of reaching them.

All of these measures reflected the so-called "New Approach to New Canadian Work" (1962). It was an attempt to transfer the main responsibility for New Canadian outreach at the local level from the women's mission circles to the whole congregation. It was proposed that "the Board of Deacons or Church Council should assume the general oversight of New Canadian work and delegate the responsibility for each particular phase to the different groups and organizations, e.g. the B.W.M.S., men's groups, the Baptist Young People's Union and Sunday School departments and classes."[30]

A concise manual for training volunteer workers was published in 1964 under the title, *The Whole World At Our Door.*[31] It included chapters on understanding the immigrant, his background and adjustment to Canada; the role of ethnic churches; integration as a two-way street; and practical steps in New Canadian outreach, among them "The New Canadian Sponsorship Plan."[32]

Without a comprehensive survey of local churches, their involvement in ministries to immigrants and the present ethnic profile of their membership, it is impossible to evaluate the response to and results of "The New Approach." If the pages of the denominational papers reflect the outlook and activities of local churches, one is inclined to conclude that the general interest and involvement in New Canadian work has declined rather than increased in the 1970s, and this in spite of continuing massive immigration. The younger generation of women appears to be concerned with other issues. The BWMS no longer assigns any of its missionaries specifically for New Canadian work. The women have relinquished their responsibility for immigrant work but the congregations, by and large, have not taken up the challenge. There is some evidence of revived concern in the churches of the Toronto Association as they face a large influx of new racial groups, particularly from the West Indies and Asia.[33]

Port Work

Up until the early 1960s, the majority of immigrants arrived by boat. The personal welcome and assistance to bewildered newcomers "at the gate" to Canada was an important aspect of the ministries to immigrants. Baptists cooperated with other denominations in providing part-time or volunteer port chaplains. Since no complete records are available only a few highlights of Baptist port work can be mentioned here.

Halifax, Quebec and Montreal served as the main ports of entry. A student from McMaster University, M. R. Hartley, served as Baptist port chaplain in Quebec, May 6 to September 22, 1912. During that short period of time, he welcomed 1900 Baptist immigrants.[34] Since the early 1920s, the Home Mission Board of the United Baptist Convention of the Maritime Provinces employed, on a part-time basis, an official Baptist representative to welcome immigrants arriving in the port of Halifax.[35] After World War II Mrs. Kenneth Miller, Mrs. David Davison, and Doris Wagner served as port chaplains in Halifax between 1948 and 1959. In one year alone (July 1, 1956 to June 30, 1957) Miss Wagner reported the arrival of nearly 58,000 im-

migrants in the port of Halifax, of whom 15,000 were Protestants. The total included 8,000 refugees from Hungary.[36] For
a limited time, there were also Baptist chaplains in Saint John,
New Brunswick (such as Rose Bullock in 1959) and in St.
John's, Newfoundland.

Under the auspices of the Home Mission Board, the ports of
Quebec and Montreal were served by part-time port chaplains,
among them Shirley Heatlie, the Rev. M. R. Simmonds, and A.
W. Fraser. There was a national coordinating Port Work Committee under the Baptist Federation of Canada.[37]

Refugees

Since the beginning of the Second World War, the Western
countries, including Canada, have faced the world-wide problem of refugees. Victims of wars and of political, racial or
religious persecution, millions of homeless and starving people
looked to North America as the main haven of safety and an opportunity to resume normal life.

The government of Canada repeatedly made special provi-
sions for the admission of refugees. The Canadian churches
played a significant role in their appeals to the government and
to the conscience of their members to respond to the refugee
problem. Major waves of refugees included the victims of Nazi
persecution in the late 1930s, the "Displaced Persons" (DPs) at
the end of World War II, refugees from communist countries,
especially from Hungary in 1956 and Czechoslovakia in 1948
and 1968, the Chilean refugees in 1973, and the Vietnamese and
Indo-Chinese "boat people" since 1975.

Canadian Baptists were involved in every phase of refugee aid
and resettlement. Working through international church agencies such as the Baptist World Alliance, the Mennonite Central
Committee and the World Council of Churches, local congregations sponsored refugee persons and families, not necessarily
Baptist, and assisted them in every way after their arrival in
Canada.[38] When emergencies arose, the Baptist Federation of
Canada raised and distributed substantial financial aid through
its Relief and Development Committee.[39]

Conclusion

In 1921 Mahatma Ghandi described the dream of global
multiculturalism: "I do not want my house to be walled in on all
sides and my windows to be stuffed. I want the cultures of all

lands to be blown about my house as freely as possible. But I
refuse to be blown off my feet by any."[40]

It was no mere coincidence that "the prophet of Canadian
multiculturalism,"[41] Watson Kirkconnell, was a Baptist and
one of the recognized leaders of the denomination.[42] In 1935,
Kirkconnell wrote:

> There is nothing so shallow and sterile as the man who denies his
> own ancestry. The "100%" American or Canadian is commonly
> one who has deliberately suppressed an alien origin in order to
> reap the material benefits of a well-advertised loyalty. There can
> be little hope of noble spiritual issues from such a prostituted
> patriotism. Unfortunately, it is abetted by the ignorant assump-
> tion of many an English-speaking citizen that alien origin is a
> natural mark of inferiority. He who thinks thus is a mental
> hooligan — whether he be a lawyer, a militia colonel, or a bishop
> of the church. What we sorely need, on the contrary, is enough
> common intelligence to recognize both the rich diversity of racial
> gifts on this earth and the strength that racial roots can contribute
> to the individual . . . .
>
> Prophetic hopes would envisage a future Canada in which every
> individual would be thus inspired to fuller citizenship by his
> realization of his origin, whatever that might be.[43]

Baptists constitute small and usually insignificant minorities
in countries from which most immigrants of non-British origin
have come to Canada. Yet the 1961 census of Canada revealed
the results of a century of continuous efforts by Canadian Baptists to present the Gospel to newcomers in many languages and
in a variety of ways. Baptists showed a higher proportion of
members and adherents who were of "other ethnic origin"
(other than British, French or Indian-Eskimo) than any other
"mainline" Protestant denomination indigenous to the Canadian scene. Baptists showed 23.7 percent as compared with 10.9
percent for Anglicans, 13 percent for Presbyterians, 17.8 percent for Roman Catholics, and 19 percent for the United
Church.[44]

The 1981 census will indicate whether or not Canadian Baptists have maintained the momentum of their missionary concern for newcomers during the past two decades. That may also
be an appropriate time to answer another intriguing question.
Why have Baptists in Canada been so heavily involved in
ministries to the total needs of immigrants, yet for most of the
time, strangely silent on their human rights, including the rights
expressed or denied by the immigration laws of this country?

4   They Speak in Other Tongues, J. K. Zeman

1. C. J. Cameron, *Foreigners or Canadians?* (Toronto: Standard Publishing Company, 1913), p. 5.

2. All immigration data in this chapter are quoted from the annual bulletins *Immigration Statistics* (Government of Canada: Manpower and Immigration) and from *Canada Year Book*. Cf. also the helpful interpretation "Canadian Population: Past Trends and Future Prospects," *Commercial Letter* 1979, No. 2 (Toronto: Canadian Imperial Bank of Commerce.).

3. Cf. J. K. Zeman, *The Whole World At Our Door* (Toronto: The Baptist Convention of Ontario and Quebec, 1964).

4. The records of ethnic churches deposited in the Canadian Baptist Archives (CBA) at McMaster Divinity College are so few and fragmentary that they are useless for any comprehensive treatment of Baptist ethnic ministries. Attempts to secure information from present leaders of New Canadian churches produced only limited response.

5. Margaret E. Thompson, *The Baptist Story in Western Canada* (Calgary: The Baptist Union of Western Canada, 1975, mimeographed, 528pp.) and Joseph Edwin Harris, *The Baptist Union of Western Canada: A Centennial History 1873-1973* (Calgary: The Baptist Union of W. Canada, 1976; based on the research by Thompson).

6. It is possible that the earliest mention of Baptists in Canada refers to immigrants of German origin who settled in the Lunenberg area of Nova Scotia in 1753. See George E. Levy, *The Baptists of the Maritime Provinces 1753-1946* (Saint John: Barnes-Hopkins Limited, 1946), pp. 1f. There are no ethnic Baptist churches in the Atlantic provinces at the present time.

7. See Chapter 5 by Edward B. Link. Cf. Thompson, *op. cit.*, pp. 304-322.

8. Cf. Adolf Olson, *A Centenary History as Related to the Baptist General Conference of America* (Chicago: Baptist Conference Press, 1952); David Guston, ed., *Fifteen Eventful Years: A Survey of the Baptist General Conference, 1945-1960* (Chicago: Harvest Publications, 1961) and Donald Anderson, ed., *The 1960's in the Ministry of the Baptist General Conference* (Evanston: Harvest Publications, 1971). See also Thompson, *op.cit.*, pp. 323-336.

9. On Kolesnikoff (d. 1917), see Cameron, *op.cit.*, pp. 42-58; C. H. Schutt, "Rev. John Kolesnikoff," *Canadian Baptist Home Missions Digest* (CBHMD) 2 (1955): 83-86; C. J. Cameron, "Sacrifice, the Supreme Law of Service," *Crusaders in Canadian Baptist Missions* (Toronto: B.Y.P.U., 1929-30), pp. 23-29; Ernestine R. Whiteside, "After Fifty Years," *Link and Visitor* (LV), November 1934, pp. 14-16.

10. John Cristea, *The Romance of Home Missions* (n.p., n.d., preface dated in Windsor, February 1939), p. 9. See also his booklets *Canada for Christ*; *The New Canadians*; *Personal Evangelism*, and his article "Non-

English Work," *LV*, June 1934, pp. 14-16. Cf. the obituary by C. H. Schutt in *The Canadian Baptist* (CB), 1 July 1950, p. 14.

11. Cf. "Our Polish Missionary - Rev. John Kaczowka," *CBHMD* 3 (1957): 106-112, and C. H. Schutt, "Tribute to a Worthy Pastor," *CB*, 15 September 1960, p. 6. See also the comprehensive report on New Canadian work across Canada during the late 1930s in *From Sea to Sea: A Study Book of Home Missions* (Toronto: The Women's Baptist Home Mission Board of Ontario West, 1940), pp. 184-235.

12. On Acacia, see the *Year-Book, Baptist Convention of Ontario and Quebec* (BCOQ) 1960-61, p. 140, and 1961-62, p. 167; *LV*, June 1961, p. 184. In December 1979, Acacia left Canada to become minister to Embassy Personnel in Washington, D.C. under the auspices of the Home Mission Board, Southern Baptist Convention.

13. On Ekstein (1899-1977), see *LV*, December 1951; *The Baptist World* (Washington, D.C.), February 1972, p. 8; and *CB*, April 1977, p. 34 (obituary). Dr. Joao Keidann was professor at the Baptist Seminary in Brazil and pastor of a large church prior to his arrival in Toronto in 1978 to work among the Portuguese immigrants. Cf. *LV*, November 1978, pp. 4-6.

14. *CBHMD* 5 (1961-62): 191-193.

15. See also the discussion of "the role of the ethnic church" in Zeman, *op. cit.*, pp. 11-15.

16. See the reports and expressions of concern in the monthly *Newsletter* of the Toronto Association of Baptist Churches during 1978-1979. A conference on "Ministering in our Multicultural Community" was held in Toronto in November 1979. Cf. also the comprehensive report *Canada's Ethniques* prepared by Mario Acacia for the Language Missions Department, Home Mission Board, Southern Baptist Convention (Atlanta, Georgia, 1979, 84 pp. mimeographed).

17. In Baptist missionary literature, the Danish, Norwegian and Swedish immigrant groups are often referred to as "Scandinavian." There is no Scandinavian language as such. From the available literature, it was difficult to determine whether there ever was Baptist work in the Danish, Icelandic and Norwegian languages in Ontario. It is recorded for Western Canada.

18. The 1978-79 *Year-Book*, BCOQ, p. 263, lists thirteen Baptist congregations in Ontario which are affiliated with the North American Baptist Conference.

19. In older Baptist literature, immigrants of Polish and Ukrainian origin were often called "Galicians" because of their roots in Galicia, a province in the old Austrian empire (up to 1918).

20. Outreach to French-speaking immigrants, including many from Haiti in recent years, has been the responsibility of the Grande Ligne Mission and now the Union of French Baptist Churches in Canada. See Chapter 3.

21. See the centennial history by Alfreda Hall, *Wheels Begin to Turn* (Toronto: The Baptist Women's Missionary Society of Ontario and Quebec, 1976), and the article on the earlier history of the Women's Baptist Home Missionary Society of Ontario West, 1884-1934, by Ernestine R. Whiteside, "After Fifty Years," *LV*, November 1934, pp. 3-26. The two regional home missionary societies merged with the corresponding two foreign missionary societies in 1953 to form the BWMS.

22. See the many reports by Evans and Hunter in the *LV*, and the Evans file of notes and clippings deposited in the CBA. For the list of all home missionaries, see Hall, *op.cit.*, pp. 92f.

23. Cf. Lee Bertran and Evelyn Slack, "Christian Fellowship in Norfolk County," *LV*, December 1941, pp. 415-418 (reprinted in part from the January 1934 issue). Cf. also several printed pamphlets on the Canadian Christian Fellowship work in the Evans and Gaverluk files, CBA.

24. The influence is acknowledged in the pamphlets mentioned in the preceding note, and in the manuscript "Glancing Through the Years of Home Missions in East Windsor" by Charlotte Evans (n.d., Evans file, CBA). In the early years of her service in Windsor (1928-1940), Miss Evans had contacts with Frances Priest, American Baptist missionary for the "American Friendliness" program in Detroit.

25. All statistics are quoted from the annual reports printed in the *LV* or deposited in the Evans and Gaverluk files, CBA. Research should also be directed to the minute books of the BWMS and its committees concerned with New Canadian work (all deposited in the CBA).

26. *LV*, April 1935, pp. 17-18.

27. *Canadian Christian Fellowship* (n.d., 1960s), 4 pp.

28. See the reports on the rallies in College Street Baptist Church, November 20, 1952, and in Walmer Road Baptist Church, November 3, 1954, in the *CB* and *LV*.

29. Collected samples of materials are deposited in the Gaverluk file, CBA.

30. J. K. Zeman, "The New Approach to New Canadian Work," *CB*, 1 May 1962, p. 8. The article was a summary of a fuller treatment in the *CBHMD* 5 (1961-62): 196-205, reprinted as a pamphlet in 1962. Cf. also the earlier plea by J. K. Zeman, "A Call to Reconsider Work among Immigrants," *LV*, May 1956, pp. 165-167.

31. See note 3.

32. The Sponsorship Plan was publicized also in the *LV*, October 1964, pp. 272f.

33. See the annual *Program Reports* and the monthly *Newsletter* of the Toronto Association of Baptist Churches from the late 1970s.

34. Cameron, *op.cit.*, pp. 18-22.

35. Adelaide M. Waghorne, "Meeting the New Canadians," *CBHMD* 1 (1953): 26-29.

36. Mimeographed report, June 30, 1957 (Gaverluk file, CBA). Cf. also her report "Welcoming Hungarian Refugees" in the *LV*, February 1957, p. 60, and the article by D. A. Burns, "Baptist Port Work in Halifax," *LV*, September 1954, p. 278. Mrs. David Davison, now in Wolfville, N.S., has kept a record of her port work in Halifax from July 1949 to May 1952 in two notebooks.

37. Cf. the reports in the printed minutes of the Council and Assembly of the Baptist Federation of Canada.

38. As an example of concern for refugees, see the report on the arrival of the Estonian refugee sail boat "Atlanta" in Saint John, N.B. in 1948, in *LV*, February 1949, pp. 46-49. No comprehensive review of Baptist assistance to refugees has been undertaken except in the book by William J. H. Sturhahn, *They Came from East and West . . . A History of Immigration to Canada* (Winnipeg: North American Baptist Immigration and Colonization Society, 1976).

39. See Chapter 10 by R. F. Bullen. For the wider context of this issue, see Gerald Dirks, *Canada's Refugee Policy: Indifference or Opportunism* (Montreal: McGill-Queen's University Press, 1977).

40. *Young India,* 1 June 1921. Reprinted in Krishna Kripalani, ed., *All Men Are Brothers: Life and Thoughts of Mahatma Ghandi as Told in His Own Words* (n.p.: World Without War Publications and UNESCO, 1972), p. 142.

41. The epithet was used by George F. G. Stanley in his address delivered at the dedication of the Watson Kirkconnell Room in the library of Acadia University on October 12, 1979.

42. Kirkconnell was chairman of the committee which prepared the plan for the first national Baptist body in Canada, the Baptist Federation of Canada (1944) and served as its fourth president (1953-1956). Cf. chapter 16, "Towards Baptist Unity," in his Memoirs, *A Slice of Canada* (Toronto: University of Toronto Press for Acadia University, 1967).

43. Preface to *Canadian Overtones* (Winnipeg: Columbia Press Ltd., 1935), quoted in Kirkconnell, *op.cit.*, p. 280. In a recent research report on racism in Toronto, based on a random sample of 617 white Torontonians, Frances Henry, anthropologist at York University, claims that "religious people are more racist than those who profess no religion. Within religious groupings, 'other protestants' (Baptists, Lutherans and Presbyterians) are the most racist." *The Dynamics of Racism in Toronto: Research Report* (February 1978; available from the Department of the Secretary of State of Canada, Ottawa), pp. 2 and 26.

44. The 1971 Census tables on "Religious Denominations by Ethnic Groups" (based on 33 1/3 per cent sample of population) indicated a less effective Baptist outreach among persons of "other ethnic origin". The following percentages were reported: 29.8 for Pentecostals, 21.8 for Roman Catholics, 20.2 for Baptists, 18.4 for the United Church, 13.5 for Presbyterians, and 12.7 for Anglicans. By contrast, 36.5 per cent of persons "with no religion" were of "other ethnic origin." Baptist involve-

ment with immigrants and refugees should always be interpreted in the total context of Canadian society. Note the following helpful studies: *The Canadian Family Tree* (Ottawa: Canadian Citizenship Branch, Department of the Secretary of State, 1967); Stewart Crysdale & Les Wheatcroft, eds., *Religion in Canadian Society* (Toronto: Macmillan of Canada, 1976); Leo Driedger, ed., *The Canadian Ethnic Mosaic: A Quest for Identity* (Toronto: McClelland and Stewart, 1978); Peter Slater, ed., *Religion and Culture in Canada/Religion et Culture au Canada* (n.p.: Canadian Society for the Study of Religion, 1977; available from Wilfrid Laurier University Press, Waterloo, Ontario); Dean D. Wood, *Multicultural Canada: A Teacher's Guide to Ethnic Studies* (Toronto: The Ontario Institute for Studies in Education, 1978); Jarold K. Zeman — Walter Klaassen, eds., *The Believers' Church in Canada* (Brantford, Ontario: The Baptist Federation of Canada — Winnipeg: Mennonite Central Committee, 1979).

5

North American (German) Baptists

Edward B. Link

Take a mix of German immigrants arriving in Canada during the last two centuries: the *Reichsdeutsche* from Germany; the *Volksdeutsche* from Russia and other European points; and the *Reichs-Volksdeutsche* coming via, and resettling from, the United States. Place them in Ontario and the Canadian West, but continually stir them up with migrations, and from time to time add extra-heavy doses of fresh immigration. Apply the preaching of a Bible-centered Gospel, the doctrines of the believers' church, and the polity of Pendleton's Handbook. Add the influences of German Baptists in the United States and Europe, and English Baptists in Canada. Stir in the pressures of integration, assimilation and materialism. Season with a pinch of coated racial guilt.

Let this ecclesiastical recipe ferment and cook for a century and a quarter.

The result is a group of some 14,000 members of the North American Baptists, residing in five provinces of Canada. Such an organization is well-qualified to join other Canadian bodies in a confusing denominational mosaic that defies classification, as church union-minded C. E. Silcox concluded in 1933.[1]

This brief essay is intended to shed some light on the German segment of the Canadian Baptist mosaic.

Unusual Beginnings in Ontario (Upper Canada), 1848-1875

Through five weeks of the humid summer of 1848, in the "Busch" of Waterloo County, Ontario, a born-again Lutheran pastor-colporteur representing the German department of the American Tract Society spoke with great zeal to large groups gathered in houses, halls and churches. A fifth-generation Lutheran pastor, highly trained in Germany, August Rauschenbusch had left his inherited church in Germany to come to the New World to serve in the vital role of Bible and tract distribution and evangelization. His Canadian listeners were part of the larger 40,000 German community made up of Lutherans and Mennonites who had moved to this area either directly from Germany, or via the United States as the Mennonites did as early as the period of the American revolution. According to Rauschenbusch these settlers were being neglected by their own denominational clergy and hungered for deeper spiritual experiences.[2]

When he left Waterloo County Rauschenbusch promised to send a permanent Tract Society colporteur to the area and by 1849 managed to get Heinrich Schneider, an earlier convert of his in Germany, to come and fill the position. Before Rauschenbusch found it possible to return to the area in 1851 he had followed the Lord in believer's baptism and became an enthusiastic Baptist. Consequently, he refused to baptize the Schneider's newborn baby. Instead, he convinced them and others to take the step of believer's baptism. On the tenth of September, 1851 these new Baptists were organized into the Bridgeport German Baptist Church.[3] Two months later Rauschenbusch represented these new Baptists at the first conference of the German Baptist Churches of North America held in Philadelphia.[4]

His presence symbolized two very important factors for the future of the Canadian churches. On one hand, it meant that the new German Baptist churches of Canada would belong to an international denomination, dominated by the United States segment. It did not matter that fourteen years later the first triennial conference of North American Baptists convened at Wilmot in Waterloo County. By 1875 the total Canadian membership added up to only 608, less that one percent of the overall denominational total.[5]

Secondly, the fact that Rauschenbusch represented Canada at the first conference pointed to his dominance of the Canadians in their formative years. Through lectures, articles, tracts and even debates he instructed the new constituency. In 1852 he preached Schneider's ordination sermon. In 1859 he strongly advised Ontario churches against the footwashing teaching of the Mennonites, and in 1871 he engaged the Lutheran pastor of Logan, Ontario, in a formal public debate on Baptist principles.

When Rauschenbusch began his long term as head of the German department of Rochester Baptist Seminary, his influence through his ministerial students proved to be enormous. Later his well-known son, Walter Rauschenbusch, emphazised the point that his father's teaching reached out to the whole denomination of German Baptists in both Canada and the United States.

A further influence upon the early settlers proved to be English Baptists. Evidence of this came to light in connection with Schneider's ordination in 1852. Although his examination took place in Rochester, New York, he was then recommended to the English-speaking pastors and churches in Canada for ordination.[6]

That same year the Bridgeport church decided to reduce long traveling distances to one central church by dividing into three churches named Berlin, Woolwich and Wilmot. In 1859 the Neustadt Baptists of Bruce County received recognition. Elmwood, Hanover, Tavistock, Logan, Zurich, and even Mulgrave in Quebec were organized before Confederation. The church at Killaloe gained the distinction of sharing its birthday with Canada, and was followed by Sebastopal, Lyndock and Arnprior.[7] These fourteen churches, founded within an eighteen year period, proved to be the only Ontario German Baptist churches formed for over eighty years.

Eastern Stabilization and Western Immigration, 1875-1900

The second quarter of the century began with an Ontario mini-revolution. The Canadians claimed that mission support was not always adequate, and when it did come the Canadian mission pastors suffered because of the lower value of the American dollar. Furthermore, Ontario churches were not represented on the central conference mission committee disbursing the mission funds. A July 1, 1876 letter to the Eastern Conference Mission Committee read: "Herewith we inform you that we in Canada have founded an independent mission society."[8]

However, seven years later, after the formation of the General Missionary Society of the German Baptists consisting partly of Canadians, the arrangement whereby actual mission grants would be determined by the committee proved to be acceptable. The Ontario German Baptists were restored to an equal partnership with the Americans. Throughout the whole twenty-five year period no new churches came into being but the total membership grew to 923. Immigration now tended to bypass Ontario and the new type of German-speaking immigrants coming into Canada streamed to the west, beginning in the early eighties.

In November, 1890 *Der Nordwesten* reported:

> Russia is taking active steps against the many German colonies in Wohlynian, Podolian and in the Kiev area. First the colonists were invited to settle, but now it's out with them or make them Russians.[9]

In 1891 the Rev. F. A. Mueller, a German pastor in Russia, received the sentence of banishment for baptizing a Russian. Before he left, some Baptists and Lutherans in the Wohlynian colony approached him and requested:

> When you get to America seek out an area for settlement where we can establish new homes and live in peace. Because of the intolerable religious and economic conditions we have decided to emigrate.[10]

Clearly, russification pressure was one of the more important reasons for the emigration of Russian-Germans.

Some of the earliest of these settled at a place they called New Toulcha near Regina in Saskatchewan. In 1890, an immigration official reported on their progress over a five-year period:

> How many old country farmers are $1,500 to the good at the end of three years, I should like to know? Let them come here, I say, and imitate the prosperous settlers of New Toulcha.[11]

When the Liberals came to power in 1896 the Sifton leadership produced an intensive immigration campaign. An 1897 Canadian Pacific Railroad propaganda map in the German language effectively described the lush western Canadian plains and their potential for farming. Letters written by already settled and satisfied immigrants, including some German Baptists, were included with the map.[12]

In 1886 *The Northwest Baptist* commented: "The Germans are coming in large numbers and the Baptists are the only body who has a ministry among them."[13] An energetic German-speaking businessman, J. B. Eshelman, who had moved to Winnipeg from Berlin, Ontario, and transferred his membership to the English Baptist Church of Winnipeg, prodded the Canadian Baptists into action. A founding member of the English-Baptist Red River Baptist Association mission board, he shared his concern that the thirty-member German Bible class he taught needed more nurture in German.

Also, he contacted the German Baptists of the United States. In response, in 1883, the first general missionary secretary, the Rev. J. C. Grimmel, himself baptized by Oncken in Germany and a pioneer of German Baptist beginnings in the States, made the first survey visit. He reported that the few German Baptists, "ein zerstreutes Hauflein," should be visited from time to time.[14] But the Rev. F. A. Petereit who made his first visit the next year returned to stay in 1886.

Trained in Rochester, Petereit foresaw the increasing number of Germans who "longed to hear the Word of God preached in their mother tongue."[15] Later he wrote:

> When in 1886 I assumed the position as German Baptist missionary I was the first German minister of all denominations in all of Winnipeg and the British North-West . . . .[16]

Almost from the beginning the support of Petereit was shared by the Canadian Baptists and the Germans of the United States. The first $200 came from the Women's Missionary Society of the Manitoba Convention. But the promised $400 by the Dominion Board of Eastern Canada never did arrive. Beyond a "predisposition to favour your special request," the Eastern leaders apparently found it difficult to get response for the needs of foreigners way out in the west.[17] However, in 1888 the

American German Baptists agreed to assume the $400 commit-
ment, and thus commenced the cost-sharing principle that,
although it was not systematized until 1902, bound the Canadian Baptists of the west in a common venture with the German
Baptists of the United States and Ontario.

By the end of the century this investment had produced eleven
churches with two organized mission stations, and a total
membership of 483. In 1886 the Rev. Petereit organized the first
western German Baptist church at New Toulcha, the settlement
described earlier. Employing the Bible, the *Glaubenstimme*
hymn book, and Pendleton's Handbook, he continued with further organizations at Ebenezer, Saskatchewan in 1888; at Winnipeg in 1899, and at Otaskwan, Alberta, in 1892. Other churches began in Gretna (1894) and Morden and Plum Coulee (1896)
in southern Manitoba; Leduc (1894), Wetaskiwin (1896) and
Josephsburg (1899) in Alberta, and Wolseley, Saskatchewan in
1894.[18]

By 1900 the combined membership of the German Baptists
north of the border numbered 1406 in churches begun through
the joint efforts of both the German Baptists of the United
States and the Canadian Baptists. To whom would they belong
in the future? In 1897 the Rev. G. B. Davies reported to the
English Mission Society:

> . . . they are coming . . . in a generation or two there will be no
> German language spoken in the West. The one system of National
> schools and the all devouring English tongue will make all Cana-
> dians speak the English language. Our German work is full of
> denominational promise.[19]

But in 1899 the German Baptist general missionary secretary
wrote: "the English are good at getting it out of the Germans."
He complained that some German Baptists drifted into English
churches, and enunciated the principle that those who are saved
in a German church owe their allegiance and missionary support
there.[20] Clearly, the contest between the "all devouring English
tongue" and "die Muttersprache" was on.

Organization and Alignment, 1900-1925

The interruption of the era of progress that initiated the first
quarter of the twentieth century by World War I, also meant

that the steady stream of immigrants to the west suddenly ceased. Furthermore, the German Canadians suddenly found themselves somewhat identified with the enemy. The question of alignment reached the critical point immediately after the war in 1919. After the Canadian churches opted for ties with German Baptists in the United States they found themselves not only without the mission aid of the Canadian Baptists, but also without the reinforcement of new immigration. Before these developments will be discussed it is essential that the general picture of organization be clarified.

By 1900 the 22,824 German Baptists in North America had set up a denominational structure consisting of smaller units of *Vereinigungen* or Associations. Each association concerned itself with matters of regional needs such as the planting of new churches. Associations formed seven larger units called *Konferenzen* or Conferences, also meeting yearly. The Ontario Association was part of the Eastern Conference, while the western Canadian German Baptists, having been handed over by the Ontario Association in 1894, were part of the Northwestern Conference which also included the Dakotas, Montana, Minnesota and Wisconsin. Every three years, a triennial session called the *Bundeskonferenz,* or the General Conference, brought representatives from all the German churches in North America together. As noted earlier the first such General Conference met at Wilmot, Ontario in 1867, and the first of the twentieth century met in Berlin, Ontario in 1901.

Three main interests of the General Conference included publications, ministerial education, and missions. The Publication Society began at the first conference and produced *Der Sendbote,* the important denominational paper. The seminary at Rochester, started in 1858 as the German department of Rochester Baptist Seminary under August Rauschenbusch, trained the bulk of the ministers. The General Missionary Society, organized in 1883 and responsible for both home and foreign missions, provided the necessary administration of inter-church affairs.

At the turn of the century Ontario's churches functioned within this framework, but the German churches of the far Canadian northwest needed to take significant organizational steps. The first came in 1900 when the first association met at Leduc, Alberta, with people from as far south as Josephsburg

(Irvine) joining the bulk of those in attendance from the Wetaskiwin, Rabbit Hill and Edmonton areas. Tears, midst great joy, streamed down faces at this first "re-union" of Russian-Germans since they had left Europe. The veteran English Baptist pioneer-pastor the Rev. A. McDonald delivered the main doctrinal address entitled, "How the New Testament Church Should be Organized." Fifteen papers by *ungeschulten* laymen were presented. The area representative to the territorial government at Regina, Mr. Rosenroll, who had promoted the $30 passage price for immigrants from Russia to the west, brought his well wishes from the government. Among other decisions, the Association urged the establishment of an organized church in Edmonton.[21]

The Alberta lead in the formation of an annual association fellowship was soon followed by Manitoba in 1905, and Saskatchewan in 1906. Ten years later the churches of the area between Medicine Hat and Maple Creek formed the fourth prairie association and called it Central, in spite of the fact that it was in the deep Canadian south.

Only two years after the first association, the entire Canadian West carved itself out of the Northwestern Conference, and at the suggestion of that mother conference called itself "Northern." General Missionary Secretary G. A. Schulte, who presided at the organizational meetings in Leduc, Alberta, wrote later:

> It not only awakened a greater interest on the part of the participants in the local Canadian work, but also influenced the churches to think more in terms of a denominational fellowship. Many churches were so isolated that they were barely conscious of the existence of other churches except possibly Winnipeg.[22]

Following the pattern of other conferences the new Northern unit elected a mission committee headed by a mission secretary to administer its regional affairs and report to the General Missionary Society.

However, an important participant at the founding conference was "Pioneer" McDonald who represented the Canadian Baptists. They definitely regarded this as "their" German work. In fact, the decision of the Northern Conference to give one half of its mission offerings to each of the Baptist bodies indicated a desire for a continuing dual relationship. In return for their share of the mission offerings the Canadian Baptists in turn provided one half of the mission needs of the Germans.[23]

At the 1909 Northern Conference the Canadian Baptists, through Dr. McDiarmid, president of the Baptist College at Brandon, invited the Germans to place a German professor on the Brandon faculty. The German response proved to be significantly negative:

> We do not consider the time opportune to appoint and support a German professor at Brandon. In the past our supply of pastors came from Rochester, and we find no reason to turn from that source of supply. Our German pastors must have their training in a German school; Baron von Uxkull has promised to organize a German 'Missionsschule' in Edmonton. For these reasons we do not deem it wise to undertake the support of two schools.[24]

The idea of the *Missionsschule* died in committee, but ten years later an enthusiastic student-pastor proposed to the Central Association the concept of Christian training institutes. They would serve the many Canadian young people who could not continue attendance at the public high schools, but had time on their hands through the long winter months. The proposal did not find acceptance, but within four years Pastor Wahl followed up his earlier idea by starting local church institutes or Bible schools of several weeks duration, the first being in Leduc in 1923.[25]

The rebuff of the Canadian Baptist efforts to tie in the Germans with their educational institution in Brandon proved to be an ominous signal that the Germans in the west would opt for a single alignment with the Germans in the United States. The German Baptists proposed that the Canadians send a lump sum to the German conference treasury in the United States from which the mission support would be disbursed. The Canadians countered with an offer asking the Northern Conference to sever organic connections with the American Germans. The reluctant choice of the Northern Conference was to maintain alignment with the German Baptists of North America, and end relationship with the Canadian Baptists.[26]

In his history of the churches in Canada, H. H. Walsh claimed that the German schism was one of several leading to the formation of several fundamentalist sects. He stated:

Differences arose between the German and English-speaking Baptists over the type of theological teaching at Brandon College. The Germans feared that the College was under the dominance of modernist teachers and withdrew from the Convention.[27]

However, Walsh did not document his hypothesis. There is no evidence anywhere to substantiate that interpretation. The break came on grounds of polity and language, not doctrine.

In Ontario, the crisis of alignment came during the middle of the war for the historic Berlin Baptist Church. In his history of Canadian Baptists, E. R. Fitch reveals how the prevalent concepts of Christianizing and nationalizing were interwoven under the theme of advancing Christian civilization. In his description of the German work in Ontario he noted that the churches were already in transition to English.[28] Indeed, as early as 1907 the Berlin church decided to conduct its evening services in the English language. This trend, undoubtedly, was accelerated by the anti-German feeling generated by the outbreak of the war. In 1917 the name of the city of Berlin, Ontario, was changed to Kitchener. That same year all services were conducted in English, and in 1919 the church conveyed its decision to the American German Baptists:

> For several years we have weighed the advisability of affiliating with the Ontario and Quebec Convention of Canada. It was difficult to make this decision, but after careful prayer it was unanimously voted that we take this step on January 1, 1920.[29]

O. E. Krueger attributed this loss to the pro-German sentiment expressed by the American churches while their country was neutral but Canada was already at war.[30]

Although not all of the Ontario churches joined the Canadian Convention immediately, a trend was started that contrasts with the desire of the western German Baptists to remain German. Obviously, for the more recent immigrants who kept arriving in the west until the outbreak of hostilities, *Der Sendbote* in their own language, and the German-trained pastors from Rochester were both understandable and influential. *Die Muttersprache* had won over the "all devouring English tongue," and in the process the population of German Baptists in the west had more than doubled. The membership of 3,061 indicated a baptism ratio of 1:14 as compared to 1:10 in 1900.

With the loss of Kitchener, the Ontario Germans showed a loss of about 200 and ended up with only 732 members. Nevertheless, the combined east-west total of nearly 3,800 grew to over 11 percent of the total North American German Baptist group.[31]

The Time of Testing, 1925-1950

With the basic organizational structure determined and the alignment with the American German Baptists solidified, the German Baptists of Canada faced the testing of the directions they had chosen. One obvious test would be the pressure of assimilation involving the question of transition to English as children educated in English schools grew into positions of leadership. However, one standing at the portals of the second quarter of the twentieth century could not have envisioned that this test would be complicated by the arrival of a new surge of immigrants, a major drought and depression, as well as another world war involving the country of the *Muttersprache* as the prime enemy.

Even before this era started, denominational leaders showed concern about the long-range future of the ethnic group. In his 1924 history of the North American German Baptists, Professor Ramaker of Rochester Baptist Seminary suggested that the ethnic mission was perhaps a temporary one, and that the anglified German Baptists would, in the long run, enrich the larger national Baptist bodies.[32] In a parable published in *Der Sendbote* as early as 1922, the Rev. F. A. Bladeow portrayed the predicament rather well. He compared the older German Baptist generation with a mother hen who valiantly tried to raise a brood of ducklings. All was well until they ventured near a slough. The ducklings plunged in and swam, but the mother hen could not swim along. The younger generation, wrote Bladeow, likened to the ducklings was plunging into a world that the older generation could not and would not enter, especially when it came to the things of the church.[33]

However, just as the leaders tried to come to grips with this problem a new surge of immigrants descended upon the Canadian west. With a cackle of relief the "mother hen" greeted their arrival for it forced the churches back into usage of the *Muttersprache,* and into the fellowship of brethren fresh from the German culture. Due to fresh immigration from 1926 to

1932 the German Baptist population of the west grew dramatically from 3000 to 5000 in that short period.[34] Some of this growth could be identified by new immigrant churches such as Minitonas and St. Rose, Manitoba, organized in 1928, and also, by the general enrichment of the existing churches. In his description of this period the Rev. F. Benke correctly identified another important factor in immigration. When uprooted immigrants come to a non-German land they are open to evangelization.[35] It must be concluded that many new converts amongst the recent immigrants strengthened the population of the churches. Dr. M. L. Leuschner wrote: "While the people of the world around them were cavorting in the revelry of the 'roaring twenties' these Baptists were deeply concerned about the needs of their fellow Baptists who were arriving at their shores as refugees, immigrants and strangers."[36] The *German Baptist Immigration and Colonization Society* founded in 1928 under the leadership of Herman Streuber had both sought out the immigrants in Europe and rallied the Canadian German Baptists to receive them.[37]

The test of the "great depression" together with severe drought in some areas challenged the predominantly rural German Baptists who without adequate returns for their crops, or without crops, had to struggle to survive, or migrate to more productive areas. The Rev. H. Schatz reported about the struggles of his Rosenfeld church in the heart of the arid area around Medicine Hat. Although a number of families moved away, those who stayed aided each other and the poorly paid pastor as best they could. A strengthened bond of fellowship was forged through this adversity, and revival broke out as people stripped of material possessions called upon God in faith.[38] Those who migrated often showed up in churches in the better areas, such as the Olds, Alberta, church which was started in 1929.

The final decade of this era began with World War II and Canada at war with Germany again. During the first two years pressures were put upon the German Baptists so that for a time churches such as Olds conducted all services in English.[39] In 1941 the Northern Conference did not convene because of the suspicions about Germans gathering in large groups. However, as the war progressed more favourably for the Allies, and as German Baptists gave evidence of genuine patriotic participation in the war effort, the pressures lessened; German services resumed, and Northern conferences and associations were freely held. However, German names of local churches were changed to English, and the whole denomination became known as the *North American Baptist General Conference.* Migrations to British Columbia produced five churches that opted to join the Pacific Conference. The six-year period of the war showed a growth of 600 members contributing to a total number of 3,500 new members in the west.

This was in marked contrast to the situation in the east where the number of churches in Ontario dwindled to six with a membership of 661. These contrasting pictures indicated that the continuing American alignment produced different results for east and west. Without the immigration it would appear that this era of testing meant stagnation. With immigration there was impressive growth, and the fact that most of the surge of immigration came to Canada meant that Canadian North American Baptists were growing faster than their American brothers. The all-Canadian membership of 6,700 now stood at 16 percent of the total denominational fellowship. However, the baptismal ratio now showed only 1:22.[40]

Two other factors for the preservation of the emerging generations also were most important. The *Baptist Herald,* started as a youth paper in 1923 was fast becoming a rival to *Der Sendbote* as the denominational paper. The predominantly-English Bible schools held in local churches, and leading to the beginning of the Christian Training Institute in 1940 made significant contributions to bilingual churches. This became evident not only in the training of lay leadership but also in the challenge to youth to enter the ministry or mission fields. It is noteworthy that over one half of the students at the seminary in Rochester were Canadians.

The New Era of Opportunity, 1950-1975

This last quarter century is similar to the previous one in that it began with another surge in immigration, now also a factor in Ontario. It differs in that there is neither a war with Germany nor a severe economic recession.

The Rev. W. Sturhahn, appointed in 1950 to be coordinator of the Baptist immigration program in Canada, described the arrival of the mass of immigrants, mostly refugees called "Displaced Persons."[41] As a result, in the east new immigrant churches began in Toronto, Hamilton, Windsor, and in Kitchener for the first time since the 1920 withdrawal. In the west, new churches were planted in places such as Prince Rupert, Terrace and Lethbridge; and in the cities such as Edmonton, Calgary, Vancouver and Winnipeg, the existing churches surged in growth before new mission churches or splits spawned new churches. In all, the total growth over the main 1950-1956 immigration period added up to 3,300 in the west. The immigration factor in the east took effect from 1954 to 1960 resulting in a near doubling of the membership from 660 to 1250.

Meanwhile, another important factor for growth emerged when the programme of church extension was initiated by decision of the General Conference at Philadelphia in 1952. Committed to bringing the Gospel to communities regardless of their ethnic composition, church extension recognized that assimilation was not the end of an ethnically-rooted denomination.[42] In his study of 1952, the Rev. K. Korella concluded that German Baptists constituted a psychologically-normal group in that the historic-cultural background of German Baptists, and specific problems arising from it, had no extremely adverse influence upon the personality development of the group. He found that his subjects were closer to normal Albertans than to the MMP standardization group, thus indicating the socio-cultural impact of the total community.[43] Thus declared "capable of integration" the Canadians launched church extension efforts. In both west and east new church units supported jointly by mother churches, the association, and the whole denomination, proved that North American Baptists could enter the cosmopolitan community and effectively begin churches. Enriched by the factor of migrations, especially to British Columbia and Alberta, by 1975 the number of churches in the west grew from fifty-three to eighty-seven, with an all-time high membership of 12,493. In the east churches grew from the low of six to fourteen, with a new record membership of 1,719.[44]

The combined Canadian total membership of 14,212 has moved Canadians to over 25 percent of the whole denomination revealing not only the growth value of immigration but also indicating the rapidly growing role of Canada in the North American Baptist continental picture. In 1958 the Triennial Conference at Edmonton shattered all attendance records and voted to begin a B.Th. theological programme at the Bible college. After twenty years over 60 percent of the pastors in Canada are products of that programme.[45]

This year a Master of Divinity programme is being introduced at the North American Baptist College in Edmonton which also continues to offer programmes in areas of lay leadership, music, religious education, and a Bachelor of Arts in religion.

In conclusion, it must be noted that there is need for cautious optimism for the last quarter of the century. Without a new surge of immigration a baptismal ratio of 1:23 is not good enough. How can a greater growth rate be achieved?

Dr. S. J. Mikolaski has rightly discerned that the ethnic barrier to growth is a myth. But is his call to double the membership within ten years realistic? In three years (1976-1978) only 139 new members have been added.[46] The low number indicates that people in communities permeated by materialism are not as easy to win as hungry immigrants. Is it possible that today's North American Baptists, who actually are "fattened up" immigrants and their children, are not hungry enough in their desire to win great victories for the Lord?

5 North American (German) Baptists, E. B. Link

An expanded version of this paper will appear in a forthcoming book to be available from the History Department at North American Baptist College, 23 Ave. & 115 St., Edmonton, Alberta T6H 4N7.

1. C. E. Silcox, *Church Union in Canada* (New York: Institute of Social and Religious Research, 1933), p. 416.

2. W. Rauschenbusch, *Leben and Wirken von August Rauschenbusch* (Kassel, Germany: J. Oncken Nachfolger, 1901), pp. 167-71.

3. Eastern Conference Archives (NAB College, Edmonton), 1852, pp. 16-20.

4. *Ibid.*, p. 15.

5. Table One (EBL Reference of compiled statistics, hereafter referred to as EBL-CS).

6. General Conference Minutes (NAB College, Edmonton), 1852, p. 8.

7. Eastern Conference Minutes, 1875.

8. Eastern Conference Minutes, 1876, p. 10.

9. *Der Nordwesten,* 28 Nov., 1890, p. 2.

10. F. A. Mueller, *Goldenes Jubiläum: Leduc, 1894-1944,* p. 3.

11. Canadian Sessional Papers, p. 158.

12. Karte von Manitoba und der Canadian Nordwest Territorien (NABC Archives).

13. *The Northwest Baptist,* 1 May, 1886.

14. Northwestern Conference Minutes, 1884.

15. *Der Nordwesten,* 28 Nov., 1890, p. 1.

16. 75 Anniversary Brochure, McDermot Ave. Baptist Church, 1964, p. 6.

17. *Northwest Baptist,* 1888.

18. Northwestern Conference Minutes, 1900.

19. *Baptist Year Book,* 1896-97, p. 167.

20. *Der Sendbote,* January, 1900, p. 56.

21. *Ibid.,* July, p. 229.

22. G. A. Schulte, *Erruennerungen* (Cleveland: Roger Williams Press, 1911), p. 157.

23. C. C. McLaurin, *Pioneering in Western Canada* (Calgary: The Author, 1939), p. 352.

24. Northern Conference Minutes, p. 10.

25. Dr. E. P. Wahl, personal interview with author, Feb. 11, 1964.

26. Northern Conference Minutes, 1919, pp. 84-5.

27. H. H. Walsh, *The Christian Church in Canada* (Toronto: The Ryerson Press, 1956), p. 62.

28. E. R. Fitch, *The Baptists of Canada* (Toronto: The Standard Publishing Company, 1911), p. 84.

29. Eastern Conference Minutes, 1919, p. 205.

30. O. E. Krueger, *In God's Hand* (Cleveland: Roger Williams, 1958), p. 62.

31. Table One (EBL-CA).

32. A. J. Ramaker, *A History of German Baptists* (Cleveland: Roger Williams, 1924), p. 112.

33. *Der Sendbote,* 1922, 3 May, p. 7.

34. Table Two (EBL-CS).

35. F. Benke, "German Baptists and Missions in Canada" (unpublished paper, 1938), p. 42.

36. Martin L. Leuschner, "North American Baptist General Conference," *Baptist Advance,* ed. Davis C. Woolley (Nashville: Broadman Press, 1964), pp. 227-250.

37. William J. H. Sturhahn, *They Came from East and West* (Winnipeg: North American Baptist Immigration and Colonization Society, 1976), p. 21.

38. Rev. H. Schatz, Interview with author, August 2, 1963.

39. E. B. Link, Personal Remembrances.

40. Table One and Three (EBL-SC).

41. W. Sturhahn, *op.cit.*, p. 16.

42. General Conference Minutes, 1952.

43. K. Korella, *Personality Adjustment of German Baptists of Alberta* (Edmonton: University of Alta., 1952), no. 55.

44. Table One (EBL-SC).

45. Table Four (EBL-SC).

46. S. J. Mikolaski, "The Present Crisis in The North American Baptist Conference" (unpublished paper, 15 May 1979), p. 8, 10.

Editor's Note

The influences and relationships between Baptists in Canada and the United States were examined in symposium papers presented by Robert T. Handy, Winthrop S. Hudson, Gordon H. Poussett and A. Ronald Tonks. For information about the publication of their essays, see Appendix II.

Part Two

Public Life

and

Social Responsibility

6

Baptists and Human Rights, 1837-1867

Paul R. Dekar

We live in the most dangerous period of history. At a time when we have discovered the means of exterminating humanity, we are witnessing throughout the world a near total breakdown of all standards of public morality. Governments systematically utilize torture, genocide, arbitrary arrest, detention, forced exile and the denial of liberty of conscience. Such repugnant practices generally are adopted in the name of economic development, maintaining national security, defending Christian civilization or advancing human rights. Ironically, liberation groups which oppose oppressive governments almost inevitably behave no better.

This general breakdown in public morality constitutes one of the fundamental religious issues of our time, and religious bodies have a responsibility to speak out regarding the nature of our crisis and the need to establish human rights as the cornerstone of moral obligation and social order. One would expect this to be true especially for people called Baptist because of their historic advocacy of liberty of conscience. Canadian Baptists inherited the legacy of seventeenth-century English nonconformists who pressed classic Protestant teaching regarding the freedom of Christian men and women to its most radical conclusion. One of these nonconformists, Thomas Rainborowe, articulated during the Cromwellian upheavals the standard by which we may judge modern Canadian Baptists on human rights questions. "The poorest he that is in England hath a life to live as doth the greatest he."[1] This standard, which I believe to be Christ's rule, would require that we must enable the poorest he and the poorest she to live as do the richest he and the richest she. We can do no other.

To what extent have Canadian Baptists lived accordingly? Because of the potentially vast scope of the question, this paper is restricted chronologically, geographically and thematically. Specifically, it explores, for the period 1837-1867 in what became Ontario and Quebec, Baptist attitudes to the rebellions of 1837-1838, fugitive slaves and women. There are at least three reasons for restricting the study in this manner. First, the period was a formative one in Canadian history. During the three decades before Confederation, Baptists were among the loudest and most consistent proponents of separation of church and state, and their voice on such questions as temperance, university charters and public education prompted the historian John Moir to call them, "the most dynamic religious force in the Maritimes."[2] On a more limited scale, the generalization is valid also for the Canadas.

Second, although scholars have studied Baptist involvement in social issues for the period, they have focused largely on issues such as the Clergy Reserves and nonsectarian education which most directly impinged on Baptist prerogatives. Baptist concern for these issues stemmed from what might appropriately be called enlightened self-interest. Numerically weak and theologically divided, Baptists confronted the very real possibility that the Church of England would be established as Canada's official religion. In the struggle of Baptists to ensure their right to practise Christianity freely and without prejudice, the question of consistency naturally arises. That is, how consistent were Baptists in applying to others the standard of human rights they advocated for themselves? The record is more mixed than one might expect or hope.

Finally, the issues considered below all have relevance for today because of widespread concern for political prisoners, racial minorities, and women's rights. Canadians tend to think of their country as a peaceable kingdom, an ethnic mosaic and a bastion of democratic protection of human rights. One need only recall the treatment of Japanese-Canadians during World War II, the sorry conditions in which many native Canadians live, and the suspension of constitutional rights during the crisis of 1970 to question how accurate these images may be. Again, the record is more mixed than one might expect or hope. To the extent that Baptists share in national myth-making, they need to be alert to the danger of idolatry and to the need for vigilance in the protection of human rights.

The Rebellions of 1837-1838

In a country forged without a revolution, there was at least one rebellion. More accurately, in Lower Canada and Upper Canada, Canadians fought one another in two rebellions. The main outcomes of their suppression, apart from the imprisonment and temporary exile of some of the participants, were the bridling of Canada's radical tradition and the speeding up of the country's evolution toward responsible government. A series of economic, political and social crises preceded the troubles of 1837-1838, and grievances were real enough.

"I confess," wrote Louis-Hippolyte La Fontaine, lieutenant of Papineau, "that penury is great and misery complete in Canada."[3]

These grievances proved catalytic during a time of incipient French and English-Canadian nationalisms, frontier expansion and love-hate identification with powerful social forces in the United States. In short, the troubles of that time helped to forge the unique Canadian nationality that crystalized in a way of compromise between the old and the new worlds.

During the years before Confederation, religion was a serious matter in the Canadas.[4] Unlike our tendency today to distinguish sharply between things sacred and things secular, religion was evident in the ebb and flow of everyday life. At least in Protestant circles, people read their Bibles daily and organized to build churches, to combat "demon rum" and to ensure that Bible and prayers formed part of school curricula. People met frequently to renew church covenants. Baptists, for example, met regularly to admonish and discipline church members on such matters as non-attendance at church, drinking, brawling, dancing, sexual misconduct, hypocrisy, slander or behaving at camp meetings in an unseemly manner. Camp meetings and revivals, adapted to the Canadian frontier from Wesleyan revivalism and such American traditions as circuit-riding and long communions, were prominent in free church circles, especially Methodist and Baptist.

The revivals tended to be emotional and to emphasize individual self-examination, but they met other needs as well. People experienced welcome respite from harsh frontier conditions. "God was in the camp," they could affirm in the warm atmosphere of Christian community. "The sound of the trumpet was heard."[5] They may even have had simply a good time, for as one contemporary critic put it, "More persons go for a frolic than to obtain any spiritual benefit."[6]

This close identification of things sacred with things secular created a popular impression which equated religious and political reforms. Thus, Baptists, who opposed Church of England Bishop John Strachan on the Clergy Reserves issue, were perceived to be decidedly radical in politics *and* religion. According to one article in a Church of England publication, "(Their) religious opinions have in every age been republican and their political views revolutionary."[7] Similarly, Sir Francis Hincks recalled the crucial 1836 election in Upper Canada as follows:

> Bearing in mind that there are exceptions to all general rules, I think that I am not wrong in my belief that the members of the Church of England and the Presbyterians generally voted for the Tory candidates, while the Roman Catholics and the Baptists, Congregationalists, &c., voted as uniformly for the Reformers.[8]

It is not surprising, then, that people implicated Baptists in the troubles of 1837-1838. The Church of England again published letters accusing Baptists of disloyalty. For example, referring to the London District, the Rev. Thomas Green wrote that, "not a few . . . of the Quakers of Norwich township have been suspected, and very many professed Baptists have been found arrayed in the ranks against our Sovereign Lady, the Queen."[9]

Fifty years later, the Rev. E. R. Stimson reported, "Taken singly, the Baptists were reputed to be the least reliable in the article of loyalty," although he went on to conclude that, "it cannot be said they were unpatriotic or selfish."[10]

Several reasons lay behind this distrust of Baptists. For one thing, they had close ties with the United States. Even though an influx of English, Scottish and Welsh immigrants had brought about a shift in the background, especially, of Baptist leadership, many congregations retained connections with Baptists in Vermont and upstate New York where pro-rebellion sympathies ran strong. Baptist revivalism and voluntarism also fed suspicion in Tory circles, as did Baptist resistance to laws which favoured the Church of England. For example, Baptist preachers had gone to jail on charges of using seditious language and for defending their right to solemnize marriages. Finally, ignorance of Baptist distinctives resulted in misconceptions. Thus, the 1841 census grouped Baptists with Anabaptists, which prompted Benjamin Davies, editor of the Montreal Baptist *Register,* to deride those who framed the questions as incompetents and bungling bigots.

> The bigotry . . . is betrayed in using the name Anabaptists for a body of people who have always protested against it, as being false and malicious when applied to them. If there are any Anabaptists in Canada (which we do not suppose), they ought not to be coupled with Baptists, who never administer the rite but *once,* and therefore cannot be said to *re-baptize.* [11]

Baptists probably did support reform, and somewhat later Alexander Mackenzie, a Clear Grit Liberal and a Baptist, became Canada's second prime minister. But with a few exceptions Baptists did not support the radicals who rebelled in Upper or Lower Canada. Captain Peter Matthews, executed for high treason on April 21, 1838, was a Baptist, as were perhaps a dozen men who rallied to Charles Duncombe's forces in December, 1837. [12] Other possible sympathizers were either disciplined or repudiated. At a covenant meeting held at Yarmouth Church on April 7, 1838, Brother Andrew McClure repented of having caused his brothers and sisters grief by going away under arms. "If it was to do again, he would not do so, as he now thinks it is wrong for Christians to take up arms at any time." Dundas Church went so far as disapproving the conduct of Brother Hooper for joining government forces during the disturbances, because militia duty prevented him from "filling up his place in the house of prayer and preaching to the people." [13] By contrast, Port Burwell Church resolved that:

> those who are called out on militia duty are not to be censured by the Church nor any person pertaining to them. And if any

member of this Church is knowing to any conspiracy against the Government and not make it known (he) is liable to be excluded from the Church.[14]

On April 10, 1838 the Delhi church decided to "receive Sister Elisa Reed's confession for her imprudent conversation on Poloticks (sic)"[15] while, in a strong editorial, the Montreal *Register* called the insurgency "strange and unnatural" and expressed strong criticism of Baptists in the United States who favoured the rebellion.[16]

Baptists found their loyalty challenged, and they were quick to respond. Thus, the editor of the *Register* argued:

Nor are we backward in enjoining upon our hearers the duty of obedience "to the powers that be," and that "not only for wrath but also for conscience sake;" believing that government is an ordinance of God for the general benefit of mankind. There is nothing in the single tenet by which we are distinguished from other Christians that is calculated to destroy the peace of society, or loosen the bonds of moral obligation. Baptism on a profession of faith has surely no very peculiar tendency to make men rebels.

He went on to apologize,

If there be any persons, in the London District, calling themselves Baptists, who have ranged themselves under the standard of rebellion, we are sorry to hear of it. We know nothing of them — who are their teachers; or what they have been taught. We renounce them altogether: they are as widely recreant from our principles as from those of our Episcopal Brethren.[17]

Elsewhere, in a letter to the Canada Baptist Missionary Society, an itinerant preacher named Tapscott, wrote that, although Blenheim Church had been greatly injured as a result of the rebellion, "I could not learn that anyone of the members of that or any other Church had been actually implicated."[18] Another Baptist minister, George Ryerse of Woodhouse Township, gave further testimony of Baptist loyalty. A man of influence in the district, Ryerse was asked by the lieutenant-governor's private secretary, John Harris, to act as an intermediary with Scottish Baptists in London who refused to pay tithes in connection with setting up rectories. Before setting out, he reported on the Baptists as he had known them previously:

I found them to be subject to strong prejudices, much influenced in politics by the poisonous writings of their countryman, W. L. Mackenzie, and are notorious for their hatred of national churches, and although I endeavoured to expose Mackenzie as far as consistent, yet I found them kind-hearted and loyally disposed at that time.[19]

In his subsequent report, Ryerse reported that, while pacifist views forbade them to engage in carnal warfare, they were absolutely loyal, "being determined not to do anything that might be thought to endanger the peace of the country in these excited times." Regarding the general state of Baptist opinion, Ryerse wrote:

I know of at least 16 Regular Baptist Ministers this side of Toronto who are strictly loyal, there are 8 or 10 others whose political principles I am not acquainted with but have never heard anything to be relied upon against any of them.

One reason Baptists protested their innocence to all treason charges was their innate social conservativism. According to the sociologist of religion, Samuel Delbert Clark, sectarian groups in Canada early favoured liberal or reform politics but subsequently moved in a more conservative direction and consistently constituted "a distinctive conservative influence in the community." In their defense of the existing social order, Baptist leaders resembled Catholic clergy who according to Charles Lindsey, "did more than even the British troops to crush the insurrection in Lower Canada."[20]

Baptists expected co-religionists to be sober citizens, and they tended to suspect any direct involvement in political affairs. Imperial feeling generally was on the rise, and Canadian Baptists shared a growing conviction that British constitutional rule resulted in special blessings of civil and religious liberty. Grievances there were but, as the Rev. John W. Maxwell, editor of the *Toronto Baptist Missionary Magazine,* put it, "the errors of Government present nothing which should rationally engage much of our time, or create within our bosoms any thing like envy or discontent." For Maxwell, the rebellion in Upper Canada reflected a "deep stain of ingratitude to God" and "selfishness, pride and arrogance." He went on to argue:

> There is a wondrous alliance between Rebellion and Infidelity . . .
> The land where the name of God is known, and this authority
> recognized — where thousands are enlisted under the banner of
> the Prince of Peace — the land of peculiar revivals, where God
> has long delighted to pour out his Spirit — the land where the
> kindly and benevolent affections are constantly in opera-
> tion — the land of Missionary enterprise — surely its sons and
> daughters would never sanction the proceedings of men raising a
> Rebellion without a cause.[21]

A more practical reason lay behind Baptist opposition to the
rebellions. The disturbances interfered with worship and
evangelism. Louis Roussy and Henrietta Feller were forced to
flee Lower Canada, while the Canada Education and Home
Missionary Society regretted that, "owing in part to the unsettled
state of the country, we have not been furnished with returns
from our missionaries." The report, dated Demember 24, 1837,
added that, "even in the awful transactions of the last three
weeks, during which a civil war was raged around us, we are
constrained to acknowledge the 'hand of the Lord.' " The
church in St. Catharines recorded that no covenant meeting was
held in January, 1838, "in consequence of the commotion that
still prevails in the land about," while Norwich, Springford and
Blenheim churches were all "greatly injured by the rebellion."
The editor of the *Register* lamented that the crisis diverted
people's attention "from spiritual objects and pursuits" and
displaced "the sentiments and habits of more quiet times." The
editorial went on to urge that heads of Christian homes take
special care for the claims of their own souls and of those who
were placed under their care.[22]

After suppression of the uprisings, the question on
everybody's mind was the fate of the prisoners. Popular opinion
held that Mackenzie and Papineau had simply deluded their
sympathizers into believing theirs was the cause of justice and
liberty, but few Canadians were inclined toward clemency. As
late as 1849, public outcry against the Rebellion Losses Bill
reveals a dual attitude of alarm and vindictiveness.[23]

Baptists mirrored the general mood. The editor of the
Register stressed the need for subjection to the powers that be,
while an editorial in the *Christian Messenger* argued that the
rebels' crime was so heinous as to warrant severe punishment.
Baptists had been known to defend the death penalty, so it is

not surprising that they were not prominent among those who organized the petitions, signed by anywhere from 8,000 to 30,000 on behalf of Samuel Lount and Peter Matthews. "The execution of Lount and Matthews is no more than everyone must have expected," wrote one Baptist. The editor of the *Baptist Missionary Magazine* went further. He argued that government leniency was a matter of regret for:

> although a full opportunity was granted to those men to leave for ever this country, where they say they have suffered so much, they still hover around our shores, gathering the weapons of war, exciting the passions of our kind and peaceable neighbours to help them "to burn our city — rob the Banks and inhabitants opposed to them — murder the Officers of the Government, and overthrow the laws and constitution of the Provinces."[24]

There is little evidence that Baptists even took note of the plight of the prisoners. This resulted in part from the fact that Baptist strength centred away from the prisons and courts where some two thousand cases were processed. Nonetheless, conditions were horrible, and influential religious leaders throughout the province complained about the severity of treatment.[25] Methodist, Presbyterian, Congregational and Roman Catholic clergy ministered among the prisoners, while the only notable Baptist effort was that of Grande Ligne missionaires, themselves exiled briefly in the United States, among some refugees there. This work resulted in the celebrated conversion of Dr. Cyrille-Hector-Octave Côte and his wife Margaret. One of the most radical, anti-clerical leaders of the revolt in Lower Canada, Côte served the evangelical cause from 1841 until his death in 1851. However, more typical of exiled prisoners' attitudes to Baptists was that of Elijah Woodman, a universalist who criticized Methodist and Baptist evangelistic practices as a menace to true religion.[26]

We may conclude this section by observing that Baptist records indicate no sensitivity to the social forces which precipitated the revolts of 1837-1838, nor to the human needs of participants and innocent victims. Baptists regarded the events as dangerous and a nuisance; as a result, they ignored the most potent human rights issue of the day, namely, the question of the prisoners and their rights.

Canadian Baptists and the Fugitive Slave

For nearly three hundred years blacks have been the most invisible racial or ethnic component of the so-called Canadian mosaic. Although slavery was barred from Upper Canada in 1793 and throughout the British empire by imperial act implemented between 1833 and 1838, actions not followed by legal segregation, blacks nonetheless have been subjected to discrimination, prejudice and human rights violations. During the war of 1812-1814 and the troubles of 1837-1838, blacks responded to their relatively favoured status in Canada with a mixture of gratitude and fear of return to bondage. They supported the loyalist cause and encouraged brothers and sisters fleeing from the United States to seek refuge in Canada. During the 1840s and 50s, as numbers increased and conditions deteriorated, the status of blacks in Upper Canada became a pressing social concern. As Ida Graves observed in a pioneering monograph, *The Negro in Canada:*

> Their welcome vanished with the cause in which it originated; the people who had regarded the abolition of slavery as an urgent moral task had no interest in the future of the Negro as such, and the race found in Canada as elsewhere that there are more subtle and pernicious forces of hostility than legal slavery.[27]

Initially few in numbers, blacks tended to settle in predominantly black neighbourhoods of growing towns — St. Catharines, Hamilton, Toronto, Chatham, Sandwich and Amherstburg — where they worked in menial jobs or, less frequently, in commerce and the professions. Most were farmers, and three rural utopian communities — Wilberforce, Dawn and Elgin — attracted much attention, favourable and unfavourable, after 1829.

There were, of course, black churches. Not all blacks in Canada were Baptist, but Baptists dominated, in part because many of the fugitives already were Baptist, in part because of evangelistic efforts by Canadian Baptists among the fugitives, and in part because of the stand Canadian Baptists took against slavery. In this Canadian Baptists inherited from English Baptists, a strong anti-slavery tradition. Two English Baptist missionaries, William Knibb of Jamaica and Joseph Clark of West Africa, were prominent abolitionists, and their activities, which included the rehabilitation of freed slaves, received favourable comment in early Canadian Baptist newspapers.[28]

In Upper Canada, or Canada West, Baptists opposed slavery in the United States and relatively early sought to minister among fugitives in the province. In 1838 a correspondent to the *Canada Baptist Magazine* strongly condemned slavery and prayed, "that the time may speedily come when slavery shall no longer exist." In February 1841, St. Helen Street Church, Montreal, resolved "to withhold communion at the Lord's Table or admittance into their pulpit, from every person known to be the holder of a slave, or the abettor of such as persist in maintaining a system so cruel, iniquitous, and unchristian." The Canada Baptist Missionary Society and Johnstown Baptist Association passed similar resolutions, while the Ottawa Association passed a resolution "rejoicing" in the formation of the American Baptist Anti-Slavery Convention. The Haldimand and Long Point (Western) Associations took similar action, as did the Free Will Baptists who fellowshipped only with strongly anti-slavery Baptists in the United States.[29]

Many congregations as well as the Grande Ligne Mission had connections with American Baptists. Generally, northern Baptists joined the abolitionist cause and in some instances, Canadian Baptists fueled anti-slavery feeling in the United States. For example, in 1852, the Rev. Robert Alexander Fyfe, then pastor in Warren, Rhode Island, advocated civil disobedience against the Fugitive Slave Act, while the Rev. Robert Dick of Toronto gave leadership through his interdenominational *Gospel Tribune for Alliance and Intercommunion throughout Evangelical Christendom*. During the Civil War Newton Wolverton, future principal of Woodstock College, joined his brother in fighting with northern troops. Later as principal of Bishop College in Marshall, Texas between 1891 and 1898, Wolverton incurred the wrath of white southerners by developing an institution "superior to any school in that part of the South, either for negroes or whites."[30]

Initially, most Baptist congregations admitted people of colour, and the first predominantly black congregations began on an interracial basis. However, separation of the races became the rule, although some congregations (for example, Dundas, Jerseyville and North Cayuga) resisted the trend toward segregation. To an extent, the initiative for segregation came from blacks. Leaders such as Henry Bibb, publisher of the *Voice of the Fugitive* and driving force behind the Refugee

Home Society, and the Rev. Josiah Henson of Dawn Institute openly favoured the formation of self-segregated churches as the most certain route to attaining independence, pride and respect. But growing white racism was much more significant as a factor in the developing pattern of Canadian segregation.[31]

William Lyon Mackenzie first noted this development in his *Sketches of Canada and the United States* (1833). In one article he described the capture of a black girl by "two hired scoundrels, who hauled and pulled her through the village . . . . To the everlasting disgrace of the inhabitants of Queenston, they stood by, many of them, and allowed the poor African lass to be placed by main force on board the ferry-boat which was to carry her back to slavery . . ." A leader of the Black Baptist movement, Elder Isaac Rice of Amherstburg, observed that, "the plan of founding settlements (coloured) in this part of Canada, is not from prejudice of the colored against white people, but because of an unwillingness on the part of the white population to associate with the colored." Rice himself was charged with undermining the position of blacks by Mary A. Shadd (Cary), editor of the *Provincial Freeman* and a leading critic of the Canadian churches. But allegedly well-meaning white missionaries such as David Hotchkiss of the American Missionary Association at Amherstburg and a notorious racist, received the main brunt of her attack:

> The testimony of reliable persons here is, that years ago, before Rice, and his co-adjutors, came hereabouts, the children were in the same schools and the fathers worshipped at the same altasr [sic]; but the Missionaries recommended schools, churches, and donations for fugitives, and hence the separations prejudice, distrust, &c. [32]

In additon to exposing racism as it existed in Canada West during the 1850s this statement reveals a serious rift in the black community. Leading black abolitionists, including Mary Shadd and Samuel Ringgold Ward, concluded that white Canadian abolitionists were too mild in their vision and too patronizing of the fugitives, but they directed their strongest attacks against other leaders of the black community, such as Bibb, Henson and Rice, for playing into the hands of white racists. By accepting funds for the development of segregated churches, settlements and organizations, Bibb, Henson and Rice were accused of increasing rather than diminishing prejudice against blacks. As Dr. Samuel Gridley Howe concluded after his investigations on behalf of the Freedman's Inquiry Commission:

> when they congregate in large numbers in one locality, and establish separate churches and schools, they not only excite prejudices of race in others, but develop a spirit of caste among themselves, and make less progress than where they form a small part of the local population. [33]

Whatever the merits may have been of separate institutions, racism existed, and blacks keenly felt the full force of exclusion. Even despite the existence of a white voice on behalf of the fugitives, including Baptist pastors Fyfe and Dick and leading laymen such as Alexander Mackenzie, for the most part white Christians played no role in aiding the blacks. If anything, the opposite was the case. As Robin Winks observed, "Most Negroes were Baptists and Methodists, and so too were the whites who wished to exclude them."[34] Not surprisingly then, the main impetus for anti-slavery, pro-fugitive activity among Canadian Baptists came from two black groups, the Amherstburg Association and the Canadian Anti-Slavery Baptist Association.

The Amherstburg Association began in 1841 with three member churches and forty-seven communicants and grew by 1861 to nineteen member churches and 1060 communicants. These statistics included churches in Michigan. In a sense, the primary focus was not racial but religious. The pioneer black Baptists saw God as Lord over all of life. Like white Baptists, the blacks organized temperance societies, Sabbath schools and other moral agencies. They promoted the advance of the Gospel. They disciplined church members who failed to maintain high standards of Christian living and fellowship. But the Amherstburg Association made its main contribution by opposing slavery in the United States; by caring for fugitive slaves in Canada; and by prodding white churches on the matter of race. When they first met to organize as an association, the delegates resolved, "that we ought to form ourselves into an Association *because we cannot enjoy the Privileges we wish as Christians with the White Churches in Canada.*" Henry Nettles of Amherstburg preached a sermon based on Exodus 7:16, a text liberation theologians still cite, "Thou shalt say unto him, the Lord God of the Hebrews hath sent me unto thee, saying Let my people go, that they may serve me in the wilderness."[35]

From these modest beginnings the Amherstburg Association emerged as a powerful Christian witness for justice and human dignity. Year after year association churches assisted fugitives, hosted myriad abolitionist meetings and spoke out strongly against white racism. In 1851, for example, Elders Horace Hawkins and Isaac Rice noted in a circular letter, "Almost constantly is our mission house at Amherstburg an asylum for the sick, and also for arriving families and persons who escape the oppressor." Somewhat earlier, in 1846, Hawkins expressed on behalf of all coloured people indignation over a resolution passed earlier by the white Baptist Long Point Association:

> The time has come when it becomes us as an Association composed as we are denominated, 'the people of *color'*, to stand like men of war, in defence of the truth, and our peculiar privileges, and to expose the base and ignominious misrepresentations of the 'Long Point or West Baptist Association' in Canada West. Since we have come out from them, and have formed ourselves into an independent Association and cast off the yoke of Antichristian bondage and no longer to be set at naught in their Ecclesiastical councils, to be looked upon with contempt, to be insulted whenever and wherever we meet with them as we suppose to worship the true and living God. They have raised the cry that we are not recognized as being in fellowship with them. We desire no fellowship with Antichristians . . . War is declared, the battle has commenced and we intend to push the victory to the gate and shout the triumph on the high battlement walks of our persecutors. O Lord God of host speed on the victory of thy son, and we will follow the wheels of his triumphal chariot and shout as we go, Hosanna to the son of David, blessed is he that cometh in the name of the Lord. The half have never been told you. But be you sure your sins will find you out.

Circumstances which provoked this breach in fellowship between white and black Baptists included the fear of whites that blacks were encroaching upon their territory. Much more serious, however, was the simple fact of white racism. As a leading white abolitionist, the Rev. Thomas Henning, put it, Presbyterians, Methodists and Baptists were dilly-dallying over the question of fellowship. A correspondent to the *Voice of the*

Fugitive went so far as to describe the situation in terms of an outbreak of a "contagious disease" called "colour-phobia":

> more destructive to the mind than to the body . . . . Its symptoms are various. It makes them sing out "darkey," "nigger," sometimes "long-heel" . . . . It excites them awfully when colored passengers enter the rail cars, or stage coaches, but not when they come in the capacity of waiters or servants.[36]

The response of the Amherstburg Association to the situation was clear. In 1853, as in earlier years, it resolved that:

> baptism performed by slave-holding ministers however sincere the candidate be not considered lawful bible baptism in the churches of this association nor shall such ministers be considered as the children of God so as to be permitted to approach our communion, believing that he who will sell his brother or sister for gold or silver today, is unfit to baptize tomorrow.

The second agency of Canadian Baptist anti-slavery, pro-fugitive work, the Canadian Anti-Slavery Baptist Association, was born out of a schism in the Amherstburg Association. Its brief history illustrates the tendency of Canadian blacks to become their own worst enemies. As we have already seen, blacks divided, often bitterly, on the question of whether relief funds should be channeled through integrated or separate institutions. In 1850 the issue arose specifically with reference to moves by the American Baptist Free Mission Society to control Josiah Henson's Dawn Institute. Initially the Amherstburg Association welcomed new support from American Baptist sources, but it backed away when serious difficulties arose. Seven churches continued to defend Henson, Dawn and the Free Mission Society against opposition from the Amhertsburg Association and individuals such as Mary Shadd and Samuel Ward. For six years these churches constituted the Canadian Anti-Slavery Baptist Association. While details of the schism need not concern us, it should be stressed that at issue was the whole matter of black self-respect, freedom and sense of security in Canada. In their 1851 circular letter mentioned above, Elders Hawkins and Rice expressed feelings of the Amherstburg Association blacks as follows:

> Strange accusations and incriminations have no doubt reached

your ears. Listening to bitter words, and witnessing the very brethren, once in happy junction and sweet union, sundered in professed Christian actions, and the work of a world's redemption — perhaps forever — is painful, like thorns in the flesh. You, who have fled the lash and died a thousand deaths, to reach a spot of quiet and peace, are now made merchandise of by those, who professedly, and in all probability do, seek your good — your elevation in this land . . . . We regret to learn that a few have consented to bow under racial prejudice again, and suffer a foreign body to manage, through paid agents, and by proxy, your church matters; to set up minorities in place of majorities; and say, under the garb of religion, of benevolence, of love to you, the minority shall henceforth be constituted and is the majority, the church. And whosoever shall not consent to break Baptist usage and declare that the minority shall rule, shall henceforth be branded as a slaveholder . . . .[37]

In contrast to this view, Canadian Anti-Slavery Baptist Association blacks believed that seeking white support did not constitute begging. They considered their principal function to upgrade feeble churches and to emphasize evangelism, temperance and other religious purposes.

The outcome of this controversy proved happy. In 1856-1857 the two associations reunited, resulting, almost at once, in spiritual renewal and numerical expansion. But this dénouément should provide twentieth-century Canadian Baptists no reason to rejoice. As long as blacks were few in number in Canada West, white Baptists welcomed, assisted and evangelized them. As black numbers increased and conditions worsened, especially with the threat of return to slavery after 1850 when the United States Congress passed the Fugitive Slave Act, the main burden of Baptist support for the fugitive fell upon blacks whose resources and capacity to respond were severely limited. With some notable exceptions, white Canadian Baptists limited their concern for the black opposition to slavery in the United States. The refugee in their midst received scant notice.

Canadian Baptists and Women's Rights

One of the persistent discrepancies between the ideal and practice of Christianity concerns women. According to the ideal, the church has recognized all persons as equal before God and in every aspect of life. In practice, the church has subordinated women in almost every respect. This has been most ob-

vious in terms of ministerial leadership. For example, in principle Federation Baptists have for some time endorsed the ordination of women. However, in practice Baptist women seeking ordination elicit a response similar to that Hannah Maria Norris
confronted when she made her first appeal for funds to enable
her to go to Burma as a missionary. She went to the office of a
friend and, as she recalled:

> On my way [another] friend . . . overtook me in his sleigh . . .
> When I told him what my errand was, I remember distinctly how
> his laugh rang out, loud and clear on the frosty air as he said,
> "Well if you are foolish enough to propose such a thing, it is a
> comfort to think he is too wise to do it."[38]

Norris persevered, as did many other determined Canadian
Baptist women, despite real opposition to women entering
church vocations. Until recently, the story of efforts by early
Canadian Baptist women to obtain equal opportunity, status
and sense of self-worth with men has been sadly neglected. This
has been a great loss, for the Spirit of God was manifest in the
desire of women to advance God's kingdom, even as the Spirit
of God is manifest today in the lives of women eager to share
their gifts for ministry.[39]

As a part of a larger story, this section will explore early
Canadian Baptist attitudes toward women. The experience of
the first English separatist congregations must be kept in mind.
In 1589 Henry Barrowe and John Greenwood sent from prison
a simple creed, *A True Description out of the Word of God of
the Visible Church*, which provided, among the officers of the
church, for widows who had to "be sixty years of age . . . [and]
well reported of for good works." Similarly, in 1607 John
Smyth wrote, as pastor at Gainsborough, that deaconesses and
widows, whom he classified together, had to be sixty years of
age. Their work was to relieve cheerfully the bodily infirmities
of the saints.[40] The Helwys group also provided for the appointment of deaconesses, and the *Propositions and Conclusions
Concerning True Christian Religion*, perhaps penned by Smyth
in 1612, allowed the appointment of "Deacons, men and
women: whose ministry is, to serve tables and wash the saints'
feet."[41]

The last statement reflected Anabaptist influence on the first
English Baptists, since women unquestionably played a signifi-

cant role in Anabaptist life. They did in Baptist circles as well. In the early 1600s congregations appointed deaconesses to do such work as was required of them. A generation later the Calvinist Particular Baptists accepted that women should be allowed to speak in church on designated occasions, while one source denounced a certain Mrs. Attaway as, "the mistress of all the she-preachers in Coleman St.," the main General Baptist Church in London.[42] *The Brownists' Conventicle* of 1641 included the following instructions:

> And in this our thanksgiving let us remember all the blessed pastors and professors, whether at Amsterdam or elsewhere; as also for our she-fellow labourers, our holy and good blessed women, who are not only able to talk on any text, but search into the deep sense of the Scripture, and preach both in their families and elsewhere.

Another source stated, "many more of their women do venture to preach among the Baptists than among the Brownists in England," and the widespread practice of women preaching among sectarian groups was vigorously attacked through the 1640s and 50s.[43]

John Bunyan provides striking evidence of the prominence of women in early Baptist life. According to *Grace Abounding* Bunyan's first wife gave him books which greatly influenced him, while the testimony of "three or four poor women" whom Bunyan happened to overhear set in motion his conversion. "They were to me as if they had found a new world . . . [and] my own heart began to shake."[44] Later, Bunyan's second wife courageously presented petitions on behalf of Bunyan, and during his long period of imprisonment various women called on him and sustained the Bedford congregation. While women are notoriously absent from the first part of *Pilgrim's Progress*, they dominate the second part and are the subject of the following observations of an innkeeper named Gaius:

> 'Twas a Woman that washed [Christ's] Feet with Tears, and a Woman that anointed his Body to the Burial. They were Women that wept when he was going to the Cross; and Women that followed him from the Cross, and that sat by his Sepulchre when he was buried. They were Women that was first with him at his Resurrection morn, and Women that brought Tidings first to his

Disciples that he was risen from the Dead. Women therefore are highly favored, and shew by these things that they are sharers with us in the Grace of Life.[45]

Despite these positive efforts to enhance the status of women in the church, Baptists went on to follow a pattern characteristic of sectarian movements. After occupying positions of leadership, women subsequently found themselves excluded. Claiming reasons such as inadequate biblical authority and the tendency of organizations originating in caring functions to institutionalize, and hence to constrict caring ministries, Baptists denied women opportunities to preach or serve as deaconesses. By the mid-nineteenth century, there were only isolated examples of Canadian Baptist women holding church offices. And on the matter of church vocations, the overwhelming attitude favoured the exclusion of women. Thus, although early Baptist church rolls included roughly equal numbers of men and women, only rarely did women hold a church office. In 1859 a Sister Barnes served as treasurer of North Cayuga church, while in 1834 the York Mills church voted to thank Sister Bond, "for her kind attention to their pastor in assisting Brother Finch in his deacons office in his absence." One hesitates to read too much into this minute, for some years later, when the York Mills church had virtually no male members, other Toronto churches appointed a full roster of external male officers.[46]

Concerning ordination in the United States, Free Will Baptists commissioned single women as foreign missionaries as early as 1846. Some Free Will Baptist congregations ordained women, but apparently not in Canada. The first woman I can presently document to have pastored a Baptist congregation in Ontario was the Rev. Jennie Johnson, a black woman from Chatham born in 1867. The Free Baptist Convention ordained her at Gablesville, Michigan, in 1909. The next year she returned to Chatham to pastor the Prince Albert Baptist Church. There she encountered opposition. As she explained:

When I returned from my Ordination, I found a certain amount of prejudice against ordination of women, and this . . . made it impossible for me to carry on there in the church that had largely been built by my own efforts. No crime had I committed against the laws of God, rather had I encountered the coldness of man-made rules and regulations.[47]

As a result of attitudes that prevailed throughout much of the Canadian Baptist churches, Jennie Johnson ministered during a long and remarkable career largely in Michigan parishes.

Despite exclusion from church offices and vocations, women explored other outlets to exercise their gifts of ministry. As early as 1800 Baptist women began to organize missionary and mite societies, and to give leadership during the monthly covenant renewal meetings. Others began to find ways to manifest their discontent with their constricted role in the church through moral reform agencies; for example, by promoting the abolition of slavery, sabbath observance and temperance, or by teaching in Sunday, female and public schools. Yet others became social critics and ultimately pioneered the women's rights movement. Even though Canadian Baptist women tended to restrict themselves too narrowly to evangelistic activities, they nonetheless contributed significantly to the elevation of the status of women both in the church and in society. They developed a positive sense of their abilities and challenged the emerging "cult of domesticity" which prescribed subservience to males and dedication to home and family.[48]

Easily the most prominent Canadian Baptist woman of the period was the Swiss-born Henrietta Oden Feller. In 1834 the widowed Madame Feller accepted a missionary call to francophone Canada despite family opposition and the formidable challenge of evangelizing Roman Catholics. Although she came to the Grande Ligne Mission in the more conventional role of teaching young girls, circumstances and personality catapulted her into a place of leadership in the mission until her death in 1868. Because she towered above other women missionaries such as Margaret Côte, Madame Roux, Madame Prospère Ledoux and Sophie Jonte, Feller effectively lessened their legacy. Nonetheless, her principal biographer emphatically insisted that she never overstepped apostolic limits or usurped authority.[49] Her example prompted women to seek additional opportunities for service and enabled advocates for women missionary service to counter prevailing attitudes.[50]

When the French Union first met at Grange Ligne on July 8, 1868, shortly after her death, the memorial minute compared her with Moses, who led the people of God through the wilderness but was denied the privilege of entering into the promised land.[51] While the French-Canadian Baptists had in mind the enormous task of evangelizing Canada, they also anticipated the extent to which Feller inspired a younger generation of women to service in the church.

The Grande Ligne Mission, and Baptists generally, pioneered female education in the Canadas. Feller campaigned tirelessly on behalf of female education and insisted, "if Christian women realized more what their sex owes to the Gospel, there would be no lack of means to carry it where women are still treated as slaves."[52] With other advocates, male *and* female, she served to raise the consciousness of women to their fundamental human rights. Thus, Susan Moulton McMaster became a leader in Christian education and benefactrice of a major institution of higher learning for women, Moulton College; Alexander Robert Fyfe, Mrs. Revell and other early faculty at the Canadian Literary Institute insisted on providing for the "intellectual and moral training of their [Canadian Baptist] daughters. The Institute presents advantages to both sexes which are seldom surpassed."[53] Before their times, the pioneer Baptists of Upper and Lower Canada recognized their obligation for the "moral and intellectual training . . . of both sexes . . . superior than that which was available through the common school system."[54]

The feminization of teaching and school attendance developed rapidly after 1840 in the Canadas. The Baptist contribution to changing female education patterns was real, but Baptists did not support greater opportunity for women on the basis of any strong conviction of women's rights or needs. Rather, they restricted offerings to courses designed to ensure the place of women in the home. Only unintentionally did Baptists elevate the status of women in society or the church.

Conclusion

In Canada, Baptist advocacy of religious liberty has not resulted in corresponding concern for human rights. Prominent Baptists have championed human rights, but they have done so as individuals without denominational backing. To an extent Baptist polity precludes such support, but Baptist polity has not prevented Baptists from taking strong stands on moral concerns such as temperance or political issues such as the Clergy Reserves and non-sectarian education. Baptist involvement has derived from perception, however enlightened, of their own interests or from an evangelistic style which centres on personal salvation rather than the kingdom of God. While this paper has explored only three issues, Baptist insensitivity to the human rights of political prisoners, fugitive slaves and women was part of a larger pattern of inaction and irresponsibility relative to much of the Gospel. Lacking a theological framework which would permit, indeed demand Baptists to work on behalf of oppressed peoples, Baptists have been paralyzed to respond to such difficult human rights concerns as conscientious objection during wartime; the plight of the Jews during the 1930s, and mistreatment of Japanese Canadians during World War II. Baptists must reflect upon the fact that it was one of their own co-religionists, Frederick Charles Blair, who as director of immigration during the 1930s formulated the policy which virtually excluded Jews from Canada and ordered, on May 15, 1939, the return of 907 desperate Jews aboard the St. Louis to certain death in Germany.[55] By severely limiting their understanding of the Gospel, Canadian Baptists have failed to measure up to the requisite standard of consistency, vision and faithfulness.

6 Baptists and Human Rights, P. R. Dekar

1. Richard John Neuhaus, "What We Mean by Human Rights, and Why," *Christian Century* 95 (December 6, 1978): 1180.

2. John S. Moir, *The Church in the British Era: From the British Conquest to Confederation* (Toronto: McGraw-Hill Ryerson Limited, 1972), p. 150.

3. Joseph Schull, *Rebellion: The Rising in French Canada 1837* (Toronto: Macmillan of Canada, 1971), p. 32. For this section I have consulted numerous studies, including Gerald M. Craig, *Upper Canada: The Formative Years 1784 - 1841* (Toronto: McClelland and Stewart Limited, 1963): Aileen Dunham, *Political Unrest in Upper Canada 1815-1836,* intr. A. L. Burt (1927; Toronto: McClelland and Stewart Limited, 1963); Edwin C. Guillet, *The Lives and Times of the Patriots: An Account of the Rebellion in Upper Canada, 1837-1838 and of the Patriot Agitation in the United States, 1837-1842* (Toronto: University of Toronto Press, 1968); William Kilbourn, *The Firebrand: William Lyon Mackenzie and the Rebellion in Upper Canada* (Toronto: Clarke, Irwin & Company Limited, 1956); Fred Landon, *Western Ontario and the American Frontier* (Toronto: Ryerson Press, 1941); Stanley B. Ryerson, *1837: The Birth of Canadian Democracy* (Toronto: Francis White Publishers Limited, 1937); see also Geoffrey Bilson, "Cholera in Upper Canada, 1832," *Ontario History* 67 (1975): 15-30; Chester W. New, "The Rebellion of 1837 in Its Larger Setting. Presidential Address," *Canadian Historical Association Report* (1937): 5-17; W. H. Parker, "A New Look at Unrest in Lower Canada in the 1830's," *Canadian Historical Review* 40 (1959): 209-18.

4. John S. Moir, "The Canadianization of the Protestant Churches," *Canadian Historical Association Report* (1966): 56-59 and "The Upper Canadian Religious Tradition," in *Profiles of a Province: Studies in the History of Ontario,* ed. Edith G. Firth (Toronto: Ontario Historical Society, 1967). Also, see M. A. Garland, "Some Phases of Pioneer Religious Life in Upper Canada before 1850," *Ontario Historical Society Papers and Records* 25 (1929): 231-47, and David J. Green, "An Investigation into the Role of the Baptist Church as a Moral Court on the Niagara Frontier," (term paper, McMaster University, n.d.), Canadian Baptist Archives, McMaster Divinity College, Hamilton, Ontario (hereafter CBA).

5. Arthur E. Kewley, "The Beginning of the Camp Meeting Movement in Upper Canada," *Canadian Journal of Theology* 10 (1964): 202.

6. Susanna Moodie, *Life in the Clearings versus the Bush,* intr. Robert L. McDougall (London, 1853; Toronto: Macmillan Company of Canada Limited, 1959), p. 110.

7. *Register* 1:22 (November 23, 1842): 2, commenting on an article in the *Church* for October 21, 1842.

8. Francis Hincks, *Reminiscences of His Public Life* (Montreal: William Drysdale & Co., 1884), p. 17.

9. *Canadian Baptist Magazine and Missionary Register* 2:3 (August 1838): 58, commenting on an article in the April 18 London *Times* and reprinted in the *Church*. Published monthly in Montreal from June 1837, the *Canadian Baptist Magazine and Missionary Register* became the bimonthly *Register* from January 5, 1842 through 1849.

10. E. R. Stimson, *History of the Separation of Church and State in Canada* (Toronto, n.p. 1887), p. 25.

11. *Register* 1:6 (March 23, 1842) :3.

12. Guillet, p. 270, publishes a brief biography of Peter Matthews written by William Lyon Mackenzie who characterized Matthews as, "a baptist, unfriendly to high church ascendancy, a true patriot, and indignant at the treacherous, fraudulent conduct of the detestable junto who, in 1837, governed Canada." George Rudé, *Protest and Punishment: The Story of the Social and Political Protesters transported to Australia 1788-1868* (Oxford: Clarendon Press, 1978), p. 51, mentions Baptist participants from the United States who aided the patriots. Additional sources for this section include Murray Meldrum, "Baptists, Politics and the Rebellion of 1837," (term paper, York University, 1972), CBA; W. G. Pitman, "The Baptists and Public Affairs in the Province of Canada, 1840-1876," (M. A. dissertation, University of Toronto, 1956), CBA; Colin Read, "The Duncombe Rising. Its Aftermath, Anti-Americanism, and Sectarianism," *Social History* 9 (1976-1977): 47-69.

13. Yarmouth Church Minutes, April 7, 1838; Dundas Church Minutes, December 31, 1837, CBA.

14. Port Burwell Church Minutes, January 30, 1838, CBA. According to an entry for April 28, 1838, Brother John Denton was, "excluded from this Church for signing the political union with those opposed to the British Government and other misconduct."

15. Delhi Church Minutes, April 10, 1838, CBA.

16. *Canada Baptist Magazine* 1:8 (January 1838): 192.

17. *Canada Baptist Magazine* 2:3 (August 1838): 59. The editorial referred to the slander cited in note 9 above. Responding to the same slander, a correspondent who signed as "Scotchman" insisted in the *Canada Baptist Magazine* for October 1838, pp. 106-8, that "a rebel has not been known amongst [the Baptists of Glengary and Ottawa regions]."

18. *Canada Baptist Magazine* 2:5 (October 1838): 114.

19. Pitman, pp. 41-43, and Read, p. 57, n. 35, cite two letters dated November 18, 1838 and December 15, 1838. The only indication I have found of possible Baptist support for Mackenzie was an appeal by him published in the Halifax *Christian Messenger* 1:47 (December 1, 1837): 411. However, the *Christian Messenger* opposed the rebellion in strongest terms.

20. S. D. Clark, *The Developing Canadian Community* (2nd ed., Toronto: University of Toronto Press, 1962), p. 136; id., *Church and Sect in*

Canada (Toronto: University of Toronto Press, 1948), pp. 224-59; Charles Lindsey, *The Life and Times of Wm. Lyon Mackenzie,* 2 vols. (Toronto: P. R. Randall, 1862), 2:49; Fernand Ouellet, "Les insurrections de 1837-38: un phénomène social," *Social History* 1 (November 1968): 54-82.

21. "Rebellion in Upper Canada," *Baptist Missionary Magazine* 2:4 (January 1838): 73-77. A similar attitude is found in the Halifax Baptist *Christian Messenger* 2:1 (January 5, 1838): 2. On the confluence of religion and nationalism, see Carl Berger, *The Sense of Power Studies in the Ideas of Canadian Imperialism 1867-1914* (Toronto: University of Toronto Press, 1970) and S. F. Wise, "God's Peculiar Peoples," in *The Shield of Achilles: Aspects of Canada in the Victorian Age,* ed. W. L. Morton (Toronto: McClelland and Stewart Limited, 1968).

22. *Canada Baptist Magazine* 1:7 (December 1837): 161-64; 1:8 (January 1838): 186-88; 1:9 (February 1838): 215; 2:5 (October 1838): 114; 2:9 (February 1838): 206-8; minute books for St. Catharines, January 6, 1838; Springford, November 4, 1837; Norwich and Blenheim, CBA.

23. In addition to sources cited above, see J. Bellomo, "Upper Canadian Attitudes towards Crime and Punishment (1832-1851)," *Ontario History* 64 (1972): 11-26; James A. Gibson, "Political Prisoners, Transportation for Life, and Responsible Government in Canada." *Ontario History* 67 (1975): 185-98; Douglas Hemmeon, "The Canadian Exiles of 1838," *Dalhousie Review* 7 (1927): 13-16; George F. G. Stanley, "Invasion 1838," *Ontario History* 54 (1962): 237-52; R. C. Watt, "The Political Prisoners in Upper Canada 1837-8," *English Historical Review* 41 (1926): 526-55.

24. *Christian Messenger* 2:19 (May 11, 1838): 147; *Canada Baptist Magazine* 2:5 (October 1838): 108; *Baptist Missionary Magazine* 2:4 (January 1838): 74. For a Baptist view on the death penalty, see an article entitled "The Murderers Lately Executed at Sydney, Cape Breton," *Baptist Missionary Magazine of Nova Scotia and New Brunswick* 1:2, n.s. (March 1834): 48-5.

25. R. S. Longley, "Emigration and the Crisis of 1837 in Upper Canada" *Canadian Historical Review* 17 (1936): 29-40; C. B. Sissons, *Egerton Ryerson, His Life and Letters,* 2 vols. (Toronto: Clarke, Irwin & Company Limited, 1937), 1:454. The only related expression of Baptist concern that I have found were protests against arts of self-defense and dueling in the *Canada Baptist Magazine* 2:4 (September 1838): 84-86 and 2:6 (November 1838): 134-36.

26. On Côte, see Narcisse Cyr, *Memoir of the Rev. C. H. O. Côte, M.D.: with a Memoir of Mrs. M. Y. Côte and a History of the Grande Ligne Mission, Canada East* (Philadelphia: American Baptist Publication Society, 1851); Franklin W. Morgan, "Sketch of Cyrille Hector Octave Côte," *Canadian Baptist* (April 15, 1967): 8, 12; Aegidius Fauteux, *Patriotes de 1837-1838* (Montréal: Les Editions des Dix, 1950), pp. 183-84; on Woodman, see Fred Landon, *An Exile from Canada to van Dieman's Land. Being the Story of Elijah Woodman, Transported*

Overseas for Participation in the Upper Canada Troubles of 1837-38 (Toronto: Longmans, Green and Company, 1960), p. 60.

27. Ida G. Graves, *The Negro in Canada,* McGill University Economic Studies, no. 16 (Orillia: Packet-Times Press, 1930), p. 43.

28. For example, *Canada Baptist Magazine* 4:3 (September 1840): 70-80; 4:4 (October 1840): 81-84; 5:2 (August 1841): 48, *Register* (June 22, 1842): 1-3; *Baptist Missionary Magazine of Nova Scotia and New Brunswick,* n.s., 1:1 (January 1834): 36-38; *Christian Messenger* 1:17 (April 28, 1837): 132-33; 1:19 (May 12, 1837): 147.

29. *Canada Baptist Magazine* 1:9 (February 1838): 205-6; 4:10 (April 1841): 239, 243; *Register* 1:1 (January 5, 1842): 4; 1:2 (January 19, 1842): 3; Long Point (Western) Association Minutes, 1842, CBA; Robin W. Winks, *The Blacks in Canada: A History* (New Haven: Yale University Press, 1971), pp. 219-220; Marilla Marks, ed., *Memoirs of the Life of David Marks, Minister of the Gospel* (Dover, N. H.: Free-Will Baptist Printing Establishment, 1846), pp. 311-12, 377, 399-400 et passim; "Canadian Colonization," *Free-Will Baptist Quarterly* 1 (1853): 403-16.

30. J. E. Wells, *Life and Labors of Robert Alex. Fyfe, D. D., Founder and for Many Years Principal of the Canada Literary Institute* (Toronto: W. J. Gage & Company, n.d.), pp. 241-49; *Gospel Tribune for Alliance and Intercommunion throughout Evangelical Christendom* 2:1 (May 1855): 18, 27 and many subsequent articles; *Globe,* May 2, 1857; A. N. Wolverton, *Dr. Newton Wolverton. An Intimate Anecdotal Biography of One of the Most Colorful Characters in Canadian History* (n.p., n.p., ca. 1932), p. 83.

31. On the formation of black Baptist congregations, the best secondary source is James K. Lewis, "Religious Life of Fugitive Slaves and Rise of Coloured Baptist Churches 1820-1865, in What's Now Known as Ontario," (B.D. thesis, McMaster Divinity College, 1965). Mr. Lewis is presently preparing the manuscript for publication. Also, Dundas Church Minutes, November 22, 1845; Jerseyville Church Minutes, November 14, 1824; North Cayuga Church Minutes, August 1848, June 1899, CBA; numerous editorials in the *Voice of the Fugitive,* published from 1851 to 1852. On Bibb, see his *Narrative of the Life and Adventures of Henry Bibb, an American Slave* (1849; New York: Harper and Row, Publishers, 1969). On Henson, perhaps the original Uncle Tom, see especially Winks, *Blacks in Canada,* pp. 178-232, and William H. Pease and Jane H. Pease, *Black Utopia: Negro Communal Experiments in America* (Madison: State Historical Society of Wisconsin, 1963).

32. Margaret Fairley, ed., *The Selected Writings of William Lyon Mackenzie 1824-1837* (Toronto: Oxford University Press, 1960), p. 33; Pease and Pease, p. 17; *Provincial Freeman and Weekly Advertiser* 2: 33 (December 22, 1855): p. 130.

33. S. G. Howe, *The Refugees from Slavery in Canada West* (Boston: Wright & Potter, 1864), p. 102, cited by James K. Lewis, "Negro Migration to Upper Canada (1800-1865) and the Wilberforce Community,"

(term paper, University of Western Ontario, 1971), p. 50, CBA. On Ward, see his *Autobiography of a Fugitive Negro* (1855; New York: Arno Press and New York Times, 1968); *Dictionary of Canadian Biography,* s.v., "Ward, Samuel Ringgold," by Robin Winks, 9, 820-21; and many letters in the *Voice of the Fugitive* and *Provincial Freeman and Weekly Advertiser,* established by Ward to oppose whatever influence Bibb may have had after his death in 1852.

34. Robin W. Winks, "Negro School Segregation in Ontario and Nova Scotia," *Canadian Historical Review* 50 (1969): 178.

35. Amherstburg Association Minutes, October 8, 1841, p. 1, CBA (my emphasis). In addition to the sources cited above, the following draws from James K. Lewis, "Religious Nature of the Early Negro Migration to Canada and the Amherstburg Baptist Association," *Ontario History* 57 (1966): 117-32, and Dorothy Shadd Shreve, *Pathfinders of Liberty and Truth. A Century with the Amherstburg Regular Missionary Baptist Association, Compiled from the Minutes and Historical Essays Written by Its Members* (Amherstburg: Amherstburg Regular Missionary Baptist Association, 1940).

36. Thomas Henning, *Slavery in the Churches, Religious Societies, etc. A Review with Prefatory Remarks by J. J. E. Linton* (Toronto, 1856); *Voice of the Fugitive* 1:11 (May 21, 1851): 2. Henning was a Presbyterian minister and brother-in-law of the leading white defender of blacks in Canada, George Brown of the Toronto *Globe.*

37. Amherstburg Association Minutes, 1851, pp. 121 ff; details of the schism are in Lewis, "Religious Life of Fugitive Slaves," pp. 76-85, and Lewis, "Religious Nature of Early Negro Migration," pp. 125-30.

38. E. C. Merrick, *These Impossible Women. 100 Years. The Story of the United Baptist Women's Missionary Union of the Maritime Provinces* (Fredericton: Brunswick Press, 1970), p. 81.

39. G. G. Harrop, "A New Duty for a New Occasion," *Canadian Baptist* (May, 1979): 8-9.

40. A. Maude Royden, *The Church and Woman* (London: James Clarke & Co., n.d. [1924]), pp. 94-95; Charles W. Deweese, "Deaconesses in Baptist History: A Preliminary Study," *Baptist History and Heritage* 12 (1977): 53.

41. William L. Lumpkin, *Baptist Confessions of Faith* (rev. ed., Valley Forge: Judson Press, 1969), pp. 121-22, 138.

42. Royden, p. 97; for the Particular Baptists, see B. R. White, ed., *Association Records of the Particular Baptists of England, Wales and Ireland to 1660,* 3 vols. (London, Baptist Historical Society, 1974), 1:28-29, 3:184-85.

43. Royden, pp. 95-97; E. M. White, *Woman in World History: Her Place in The Great Religions* (London: Herbert Jenkins Limited, 1924), p. 368.

44. John Bunyan, *Grace Abounding to the Chief of Sinners,* ed. Roger Sharrock (Oxford: Clarendon Press, 1962), pp. 8, 14-51.

134 Paul R. Dekar

45. John Bunyan, *The Pilgrim's Progress from this World to That which is to Come,* ed. James Blanton Wharey, rev. Roger Sharrock (Oxford: Clarendon Press, 1960), p. 261.

46. York Mills Church Minutes, April 6, 1834, CBA.

47. Jennie Johnson, *My Life* (pamphlet, ca. 1950, CBA).

48. Nancy F. Cott, *The Bonds of Womanhood: "Woman's Sphere" in New England 1780-1835* (New Haven: Yale University Press, 1977); Ann Douglas, *The Feminization of American Culture* (New York: Knopf, 1977).

49. J. M. Cramp, *A Memoir of Madame Feller. With an Account of the Origin and Progress of the Grande Ligne Mission* (London: Eliot Stock, ca. 1876), p. 244. For biographical data on other Grande Ligne women missionaries, see Ida B. Therrien, *La femme et la mission de la Grande Ligne,* 1940, ms, CBA; Eugene A. Therrien et al, *Baptist Work in French Canada* (Toronto: American Baptist Publication Society, n.d.); E. R. Fitch, *The Baptists of Canada: A History of Their Progress and Achievements* (Toronto: Standard Publishing Company, Limited, 1911), p. 226.

50. Nathan S. S. Beman, *A Plea for the Swiss Mission in Canada: A Discourse, Delivered in the First Presbyterian Church, Troy, October 15, 1843* (2nd ed., Troy, New York: Young & Hartt, 1845); R. Pierce Beaver, *All Loves Excelling. American Protestant Women in World Mission* (Grand Rapids: William B. Eerdmans Publishing Company, 1968); Wendy Mitchinson, "Canadian Women and Church Missionary Societies in the Nineteenth Century: A Step towards Independence," *Atlantis* 2/2, pt. 2 (Spring 1977): 57-75.

51. *Formation et Constitution de l'Union des Eglises Baptistes de langue française, et minutes des deux premières assemblées anniversaires tenues à la Grande-Ligne le 8 juillet 1868 et le 29 juin 1870* (Montréal: L'Aurore, 1870), p. 1.

52. 35th *Annual Report of the Evangelical Society of la Grande Ligne,* 1872, p. 8.

53. *Canadian Baptist Register,* 1863, p. 40.

54. *Canadian Baptist Register,* 1858, pp. 28-29.

55. Arbella, Irving and Harold Traper, "The Line Must Be Drawn Somewhere: Canada and Jewish Refugees, 1933-9," *Canadian Historical Review* 60 (1979): 179-209. On Baptists and conscientious objection during wartime, the attitude of future Prime Minister John Diefenbaker, who opposed such status for the Doukhobors and other pacifist groups, is illustrative. See George Woodcock and Ivan Avakumovic, *The Doukhobors* (Toronto: McClelland and Stewart Limited, 1977), pp. 309-10. For background, see Paul R. Dekar, "Baptists and Peace," in *The Believers' Church in Canada,* ed. Jarold K. Zeman and Walter Klaassen (Brantford and Winnipeg: Baptist Federation of Canada and

Mennonite Central Committee Canada, 1979) pp. 325-332. On Baptists and the Jews, preliminary comments may be found in Reuben Slonim, *Family Quarrel: The United Church and the Jews* (Toronto: Clarke, Irwin & Company Limited, 1977), p. 50 et passim; on Baptists and Japanese Canadians, Ken Adachi, *The Enemy That Never Was: A History of the Japanese Canadians* (Toronto: McClelland and Stewart Limited, 1976) and Tamatso Morikawa, "The Japanese in Canada," (B.D. thesis, McMaster Divinity College, 1958).

7

A View of Some Canadian Headlines, 1860-1912

W. Gordon Carder

To our pioneer forefathers the latter half of the nineteenth century was an era of abounding optimism coupled with unlimited possibilities for human progress. This spirit was affirmed to them again and again by new and amazing technological applications and inventions of the period. Most people in the western world saw these wonderful developments as the basis of unfailing progress on the road to a great new golden age for mankind.

The Canadian Baptist (hereafter cited as *CB*)[1] joyfully reported on many of these mighty, forward leaps. One such event was the opening of the Suez Canal in 1869. That same year Canadian missionary, John McLaurin, Sr., traveled to India via the Suez. Only two years before, his brother-in-law, pioneer Timpany had to travel the much longer and more difficult route around the Cape. Later the *CB* paid tribute to Suez engineer de Lesseps in the spirit of the century: "Bonaparte broached the plan of cutting through Suez. Half a century later engineer de Lesseps did it. He actually changed geography. He broke a continent in two for the world's commerce."[2]

"S. S. The Great Eastern" and Trans-Atlantic Cable
For some years the *CB* reported news items related to "The

Great Eastern." This iron wonder of 22,500 tons was then the largest vessel afloat. Launched in 1858, she was the pride of Britain and one of the wonders of her time. She had been built at the then fabulous cost of $5 million. She had five funnels, two sets of engines with a single screw and two gigantic side paddle wheels.

"The Great Eastern" did passenger service between London and New York from 1860 to 1863. Whenever the ship was in port at New York, crowds traveled from near and far to see her. Canadians took trains from Montreal, Toronto and Hamilton to join the throngs. But the "Eastern's" seaworthiness was questioned, and the passenger service did not make a profit. The good ship, however, proved herself in the laying of five trans-Atlantic cables. During July, 1866 the weekly issues of the *CB* gave detailed reports of the cable project that had Valentia, Newfoundland, for one terminus. This record included a day-by-day diary of the project. The cable was put into the sea at the rate of about one hundred miles per day. The *CB* rejoiced in the success of the venture and observed that now news would cross the great ocean with the speed of lightning. The *CB* printed a prayer for the venture:

> May sea monsters, and all other denizens of the briny deep keep clear of the slender path over which the thoughts of the old and the new continents are to be interchanged. May a kind and gracious God . . . accord His providential protection and blessing so this may be a means of cementing international goodwill and hastening the era of universal peace.[3]

Sunday Streetcars, Toronto

One Toronto item of progress, Sunday streetcars, was strongly opposed by Baptist leaders, in cooperation with the Methodists and Presbyterians. An editorial in the *CB* in 1886 expressed the feelings of many concerned Christians of the time:

> Persistent attempts are made to have the quiet of our city Sunday broken in upon by the running of streetcars . . . Some plausibility is given to the demand by representing it in the interests of church-goers to have the cars run at certain hours or part of Sunday . . . He would be a sorry Christian worshipper who would not ten times rather walk the length of the whole city or leave the church of his choice for one nearer home, than to be the means of taking away from some of his fellow citizens their Sunday privileges.[4]

A Public Hanging in Brantford, Ontario

Headline news in Upper Canada, June 7, 1859, was the hanging of two black men in the public square of Brantford, Canada West (now Ontario). The men were condemned for the murder of a mail carrier. From dawn of the day of the hanging people began to arrive in Brantford to witness the event. By nine o'clock about eight thousand people thronged the city square, considerably more than the total population of the city at that time. The mob included not only men and boys but also numbers of women and girls. The condemned men died at 9:13 A.M. The convicts were attended on the scaffold by a Baptist and a Methodist minister. They bowed together in prayer, then began to sing a hymn. The Baptist paper described the final drama:

> . . . The ropes were adjusted, the caps were drawn down over their faces . . . The Prisoners commenced to sing that solemn stanza "Hark from the tomb" and as the word tomb escaped from their lips, the bolt was drawn and in an instant they were ushered into the presence of their God.[5]

The Baptist editor, who generally left social concerns to others, was stirred by this event to advocate social change. The paper noted that curiosity rather than horror clothed the faces of the majority in the crowd and that the effect on people was a hardening and brutalizing of persons. The editor wrote:

> . . . its tendency was vicious. Not a word do we say against capital punishment — in fact we believe in it — but our voice is raised against public executions. Had these criminals been executed inside the walls, in the presence of a few respectable witnesses, the law would have been administered. Curiosity might not have been gratified, but the community would know that justice was meted out to the guilty . . . . We have witnessed a public execution in Brantford. God grant that another such opportunity may never be afforded the inhabitants of this rising town.[6]

Ontario Oil Fever

By May, 1862 the *CB* began reporting on oil drillings in Southern Ontario. A commercial oil well was begun at the Black Creek settlement, in the Sarnia area, in 1857. By 1861 rock drilling had proven successful in this district. The *CB* reported in May, 1862 that there were ten flowing wells in the Black Creek region and that to all appearances the number would increase indefinitely, if a market could be found for the product. In 1863 the *CB* noted that the first iron tankship, "The Ramsey," was beginning service between Liverpool and New York. By 1865 the market for oil began to be more apparent and the fever for "black-gold" spread widely in Ontario.[7]

At Hamilton the Barton Oil Company was set up with one hundred shares of twenty dollars each. This was typical of many companies formed to drill for oil all over southern Ontario. The Johnston Oil Company financed operations around St. Thomas. The organizers of this joint stock company promised to work night and day until their efforts were rewarded with flowing wells. By 1866 *The Baptist* reported that Oakville, near Toronto, had oil fever, and oil well boring was proceeding there with every expectation of success.

The Baptist reported many other drillings at Port Stanley, Oneida, Dunnville, Drumbo, Scarboro and Markham. Baptists tended to strongly support this type of private enterprise along with the get-rich-quick dream. This hope was more constructive for our nation than the present gamble of "Loto" Canada.

Slave Trade

Dramatic stories on the horrors of the American slave trade were common items in the *CB* in the early 1860s. An article in the Baptist paper put the issue in Canadian context as follows:

> To know that ministers, deacons and members of Baptist churches do hold thousands of slaves and actually engage in the buying and selling of human beings is enough to arouse sorrowful indignation which words fail to express . . . . The slavery we have to deplore in Canada is of a different class . . . . It is the slavery of the soul induced through ignorance and wilful neglect of the Bible . . . and the slavery of the soul resulting from papal influence in this province.[8]

About 1860 the paper noted that while Britain was spending a million pounds a year trying to wipe out the slavery traffic on the high seas, the business was thriving around Cuba, backed by wealth from New York and Boston. As many as fifty ships were said to be carrying slaves through the port of Havana.

The American slave war had various effects on Canada.

American influence on the Canadian economy is about as old as our nation. *The Baptist* observed that the immense number of horses destroyed in this war would raise the price of horse-flesh in Canada for years to come. In 1862 the *CB* noted that around Kingston, American agents had purchased several thousand horses at high prices for use in their northern armies. In the fall of 1863 the paper reported that one thousand horses had been shipped from Windsor for use in the war. I searched in vain for any Baptist comment on cruelty to animals in this context.

The assassination of American President Abraham Lincoln in 1865 was extensively reported in the *CB*. The paper noted: "The news of his death paralyzed our people for a time. Flags have been hung at half-mast in token of the event . . . . Southern sympathy has received a decisive blow in Canada by this act of barbarity."[9] Apparently the editor and Canadian Baptists of the day had a great admiration for the life and example of President Lincoln. The *CB* noted that this Christian man, out of an annual salary of $25,000 had saved $50,000 and invested it in government bonds for his country. *The Baptist* observed that Lincoln's living in the White House was unpretentious and frugal; that he carried on in Washington the simple, inexpensive habits of his former lifestyle in a small town. The *CB* implied that these virtues were to be commended to all. "Lincoln did nothing for show or effect," reported *The Baptist*.[10]

A Baptist Response to the Death of Queen Victoria

The death of Queen Victoria on January 22, 1901 was an occasion for extensive comment in the *CB*. The paper noted that no sovereign had ever had a higher place in the reverence and love of her subjects than Queen Victoria. The editor wrote:

> Her place has been unique and supreme . . . . What has won her this homage? It has been the simplicity of her character, of her Christian faith, of her life, maintained on the dizzy heights of one of the greatest thrones of the world and of the ages . . . . She has been true to the purest instincts of womanhood, and has manifested all the sweet devotion to husband, children and home which we look for in the best life.[11]

The editor assumed that all Baptists were enthusiastic supporters of the British monarchy.

On the Titanic Tragedy

The dramatic "Titanic" disaster became the occasion of much soul-searching and the basis of many solemn utterances from clergy and churchmen across Canada. *The Baptist* recorded that sermons and observations from the various denominations had been printed in many local papers all across the nation. The tragedy happened about one hundred miles south of the Grand Banks of Newfoundland on Sunday night of April 14, 1912. The *CB* editor wrote:

> No calamity of recent years has so stirred the sympathies of the people of two continents as the loss of the Titanic . . . . The interest in the great steamship was world wide, owing to the fact that she was the last word in ship-building as to size and equipment and that she was making her maiden voyage . . . . The heart of America and Europe has throbbed with deep sympathy. In public and in private this theme has largely displaced other topics of discussion. [12]

The *CB* noted that a very impressive memorial service was held in Massey Hall, Toronto, on the Sunday following the disaster.

Many people wondered, perhaps with a deep sense of guilt, if pride in human achievement, a boasting about human accomplishments represented in the construction of this great "unsinkable" ship was not somehow the cause of her doom. The *CB* editor saw the craze for speed, a new record for Atlantic crossings, as the basic reason for the disaster. He wrote:

> . . . But grief is not lessened when there are manifest reasons for concluding that these unfortunate victims have been sacrificed as a result of craze for speed . . . . In the light of the terrible loss it is not difficult to say that the price of speed is too high! [13]

Out of the darkness and grief of this sad calamity, *The Baptist* recorded a positive and constructive theology:

> We do not propose to cast the blame for this catastrophe upon the Lord of power and grace . . . . We do believe that the Lord is gracious . . . . His heart of love was toward the 1600 men and women who perished; and His tender mercy is with those seven hundred and more who found deliverance from the perils of the sea. God is good, even though transgression of His inexorable laws of nature has brought death and suffering and sorrow in its

train. Provision and protection, guidance and blessing, are every day convincing evidence of His providential care, notwithstanding the sad and dark experiences of life . . . even perils of the sea, staggering, terrible, incomprehensible do not rob us of our faith in Him.[14]

*   *   *   *   *

The Baptist responses to current events noted in this paper show identity with and sensitivity to the Canadian culture of the time. The expressed feelings and ideas were in harmony with the Canadian Protestant sentiments. The Baptist voice in Ontario was apparently more influential in the nineteenth century and up to the First World War than in later times when attention was focused on internal controversies and schisms.

7 A View of Some Headlines, W. G. Carder

1. *The Canadian Baptist* was pioneered in October 1854 as a weekly, printed and published in Brantford, Ontario. It was moved to Toronto in July 1859. The paper was first called *The Christian Messenger*. The name was changed to *The Canadian Baptist* in January 1860.

2. *CB,* November 19, 1891, p. 5.

3. *CB,* August 2, 1866, p. 3.

4. *CB,* August 1, 1889, p. 4. The Baptist, Methodist and Presbyterian Ministerial Associations all passed resolutions condemning the proposal to run street cars in Toronto on Sunday. *CB,* December 10, 1891, p. 8.

5. *The Christian Messenger,* June 9, 1859, p. 2. The names of the condemned men were reported as Robert Over and John Moor.

6. *Loc. cit.*

7. The early discovery of oil in Ontario was made near Sarnia, in the Enniskillen Township of Lambton County. This was known as the Black Creek settlement. A brook in this very flat countryside had been named Black Creek. The Black Creek settlement was incorporated as the village of Oil Springs in 1865. In this area, Oil Springs, Petrolia and Bothwell became the main centres of the crude oil flow. About 1,000 oil wells were drilled around Oil Springs and 2,000 around Petrolia. Flowing wells around Oil Springs rapidly declined after 1865 and so did the population from about three thousand persons to about 300 in the village. In 1863 the *CB* reported that crude oil was selling at 65¢ to 75¢ a barrel. By 1865 the price rose to $2.50 per barrel.

8. *The Christian Messenger,* February 14, 1856, p. 2.

9. *CB,* April 29, 1865, p. 3.

10. *CB,* June 22, 1865, p. 3.

11. *CB,* January 22, 1901, p. 8. Queen Victoria came to the British throne as a young girl in 1837 and reigned for 63 years. Her eldest son Edward VII reigned for nine years and four months. He died of pneumonia at Buckingham palace on May 6, 1910. At the time of his death the *CB* reported: "King Edward lived in the hearts of his people as perhaps no other British Sovereign has done, except Queen Victoria. He had a feeling for all classes and conditions in the Empire. May the mantle of Edward fall upon His Majesty King George V." (May 12, 1910, p. 11).

12. *CB,* May 2, 1912, p. 1. The editor of the paper at this time was Rev. W. J. McKay, B.D., L.L.D.

13. *CB,* April 25, 1912, p. 8. The S.S. Titanic (46,000 tons) was then the most luxurious and largest liner afloat. She had a double-bottomed hull with sixteen water tight compartments. Even if one quarter of these were flooded the ship was still buoyant. Therefore she was popularly dubbed an unsinkable ship. But the crash with the iceberg made a 300 foot gash

in her side that flooded five of the sealed compartments. Some 1,513 persons perished in the icy waters.

14. *Loc. cit.*

8

The Canadian Baptist *and the Social Gospel Movement, 1879-1914*

John S. Moir

Despite the acknowledgment by Canadian historians that the movement called the Social Gospel was and is one of the most important formative influences in our national development, to date only one scholarly monograph and a few articles have been devoted to its study. Furthermore, for reasons peculiar to Canadian historiography, those few studies have been usually concerned with Methodist involvement in the movement.[1] Nevertheless, it is widely suspected and now at least partially proven that reactions to the Social Gospel varied widely, not merely from denomination to denomination, but within individual denominations as well. Historians have also begun to look at the Presbyterian and Anglican responses to the Social Gospel.[2] Although several papers and Professor C. M. Johnston's recent history of McMaster University touch tangentially on the topic of Baptists and the Social Gospel,[3] as a research theme it remains virtually unexplored despite its obvious importance.

The purpose of this paper is to examine briefly the attitude of the editors of *The Canadian Baptist* toward the Social Gospel over a period of some thirty years. Clearly the constraints of time and space must reduce this to a mere overview, but perhaps even such a preliminary examination will serve to arouse interest and by suggesting certain tendencies may point the way for further research.

There was of course nothing new in the ideas of the Social Gospel — the parable of the Good Samaritan is but one of many biblical affirmative answers to Cain's eternal question, "Am I my brother's keeper?" What made the development of the Social Gospel distinctive in the late Victorian era was its sharp contrast in emphasis from the highly individualistic evangelism that had preceded it. Basically this contrast was a shift in emphasis rather than a difference in Gospel message or repudiation of evangelism. But the fact that the Social Gospel was enunciated in response to the problems of modern urbanization, industrialization and materialism attracted to the so-called Social Gospel so much public attention that at times it seemed that its teachings constituted some newly-revealed panacea for the ills of this world.

Historians do not agree as to where or when this broad concept of religiously-motivated social improvement came into being. C. H. Hopkins, the benchmark historian of the movement, has traced its amorphous lineage to the close of the American Civil War.[4] Certainly the writings of Walter Rauschenbusch at the turn of the century constitute not the proclamation of but the popularization of ideas already accepted by many Christian leaders in Europe and America. Thus, although *The Canadian Baptist* did not become the official organ of the convention until 1882 or, in strict legal terms, until 1887 when it was gifted by the will of William McMaster,[5] it is not surprising to find evidences of the Social Gospel ideas in its pages even while it was still a private publication.

It is vain of course to look so early for any full-blown statement of a Social Gospel philosophy. Indeed it can easily be argued that the Social Gospel never was a systematized philosophy — that at best it can be described as an umbrella concept covering a wide range of ideas and plans for social and moral improvement with which none of its advocates would be in total agreement, but from which all would draw such emphases as would suit their own purposes at any given time and under any given circumstances.

While *The Canadian Baptist* was still the property of William Muir, its editorial column frequently expressed Social Gospel ideas. On one occasion Muir called on Baptists to bear witness to "practical Christianity" in everyday life, because the secular and religious worlds in fact are inseparable. On other occasions he commented on the need for purity in politics, on the church's responsibility to meet the temptations besetting youth in an urban environment, on the need for systematic care of the deserving poor, and on the urgency of combatting pornography and prostitution.[6] For Muir the simple cure for fraud, dishonesty, avarice, strikes, lockouts and even wars, was to love your neighbour as yourself.[7] Such a sampling from the editorial pages of *The Canadian Baptist* does show that a tradition of social concern and activism already existed before the newspaper was acquired by William McMaster and the Standard Publishing Company in 1882, and before the Rev. E. W. Dadson was appointed editor in August of that year.

Dadson soon showed a more forceful and topical style in his editorial writings although the themes were those already bruited by Muir. Dadson continued the call for purity in politics, but he was more vocal on the subjects of prohibition and sabbatarianism, in part no doubt because each passing year made them more urgently Canadian problems. By 1884 Dadson was prepared to take a very positive position on specific social problems. Regarding poverty he called for investigation and remedial action, and pointed to everyman's right to work to avoid the humility of direct charity.[8] An annual income of only $350 constituted a bare subsistence for a worker's family, and occasional relief collections were not enough. Basic cures were needed for the economic ills of Canada. In Dadson's opinion, the law of supply and demand was "unchristian"[9] — the church must offer leadership "for the solution of all these great social problems."[10] With a modernity that would not be universally acceptable even today Dadson suggested that gambling was a disease. Similarly his steady support for prohibition — "annihilate," not "regulate" the liquor traffic — was typical of most Social Gospellers.[11]

On at least one occasion Dadson did pronounce the ultimate solution presumed by the Social Gospel — improving the social environment, he wrote, would "prevent the manufacture of criminals."[12] Nor was remedial social action to be left to private individuals. It was the politician's job to remove the "iniquitous causes" that promoted socialism.[13] Too often capitalism divorced morality from business practice — the truly Christian industrialist would ensure that his workers got "such a share in the profits as justly belonged to him."

With the outbreak of troubles in the Canadian Northwest, Dadson found yet another Christian cause to espouse, namely native rights. Injustice had driven the Métis and Indians to rebellion,[14] so God-loving Canadians owed it to the natives to educate them so that they could share in the good life of a Europeanized, Christianized (and presumably Protestantized) Canada.[15] This theme of justice for native Canadians became a recurrent editorial topic in the columns of *The Canadian Baptist* for several years thereafter.[16]

In 1886 the growth of trade unionism also attracted Dadson's interest and sympathy. "Is it not wonderful that the toiling millions, whose lives are one long, weary struggle to keep the wolf from the door, should conclude that there is something wrong in a system which, for every one it makes rich condemns hundreds to hopeless poverty."[17] Trade unionism would redress this imbalance, Dadson believed, and he called for Christian cooperation between capital and labour.

A case in point arose almost immediately when the Toronto Street Railway Company fired all union members who had gone on strike. "There is no excuse for the Company's action in its effort to interfere with personal liberty. That was a bit of petty persecution, the intolerance of commercial bigotry."[18] The company had demanded that the workers subscribe to an "unrighteous test act," and the blame for the resulting violence lay entirely at the company's door. When the workers won their contest against the company *The Canadian Baptist* was jubilant. The combination of political democracy and trade unionism would bring future improvements in working conditions of the labouring class, for whom Dadson was convinced real freedom of contract did not exist. "Justice requires that the poor man as well as the rich should have a voice in the legislation by which both alike are governed."[19] Profit-sharing was again advocated by *The Canadian Baptist* as a partial solution to industrial unrest.

Later that same year, moves to reduce working hours and to force early closing of shops were hailed by *The Canadian Baptist* as "late but sweet fruits of the goodly tree whose roots are fed and watered by the principles of the Sermon on the Mount."[20] The fact that ministers of many denominations had supported these reforms was "grand proof of the practical character of Toronto Christianity."

But Dadson used this episode as a springboard to advocate other needed social changes. The long, toiling hours of housewives deserved similar consideration, and what were Christians going to do about gambling, lotteries, professionalization of sports, child abuse, vivisection and similar debasing practices?[21] Laws restricting child labour and ensuring equal rights for working women were sadly needed in Canada.[22] Equal educational opportunities for the poor was another long-term solution to social injustice that had Dadson's blessing.[23]

By the time Dadson resigned as editor of *The Canadian Baptist* in September, 1889 he had unquestionably made the newspaper into an avowed vehicle for Social Gospel ideas, although his preferred description of such reformism was "practical Christianity." At the same time he had made it clear that *The Canadian Baptist* was totally the organ of the convention. No one, at least no one in the convention, disagreed with these policies — the proof lies in the appointment of Dr. J. E. Wells, an experienced lay journalist, as Dadson's successor.

It would be easy to dismiss the decade in which Wells occupied the editorial chair by saying that Wells' policies were simply a continuation of Dadson's. True, most of the same issues — prison reform, sabbatarianism, prohibition, justice to native Canadians, the need for inner city missions, purity in politics, sweat shop industries, profit sharing, protection for children, women's rights, poverty in the midst of plenty, etc., — continued to attract editorial attention, but two conjoined tendencies noted in Dadson's days became more evident under Wells. In the first place Wells' approach to Social Gospel ideas assumed no doctrinaire position. *The Canadian Baptist* responded to specific social issues — it did not theorize about remaking society with any panacea to produce instant and total reform. The key expression, "practical Christianity" was still employed frequently. The second and related emphasis can be described as increased specificity. Like Dadson, Wells wrote not about problems in the abstract but about specific issues as they arose, yet if anything, he was more forthright and more detailed, both in describing and denouncing social problems.

Well's approach to the labour question shows clearly this change of degree of editorial concern. He steadily defended the right to strike and accused the churches of alienating the working class by always supporting the capitalists' cause.[24] Unions were needed to protect the white slaves in the sweat shops of the garment industry.[25] When a strike against Carnegie Steel in the United States led to loss of life, Wells expressed sympathy for the workers and contempt for Carnegie's "considerable pretensions to philanthropy." The barons of industry were reducing the pay of "already poorly paid workmen, in order to increase their own lordly incomes . . . ."[26] The issue, said *The Canadian Baptist,* was the conflict between legal and moral rights.[27]

In 1894, when the "Industrial Army" of unemployed marched on Washington demanding work, *The Baptist* commented at length on the "cruel inequality" in the distribution of wealth. "Is there no legitimate and rightful way in which some portion of this immense national capital, itself the product of labor though now in the possession of the few, can be made available to save multitudes of laborers from destitution, by supplying them with work instead of charity?"[28]

Two months later, when violence in the Pullman strike had caused some public sympathy for the workers, Wells pointed out that the power of the capitalists put the workers at the mercy of their employers. Since company unions were too weak a defence, was compulsory arbitration the answer to this "ruthless law of supply and demand"?[29] In a similar vein *The Canadian Baptist* attacked the unfair practices of Rockefeller and the Standard Oil Company. Many men had succeeded in business without resorting to "heartless" and "principleless" practices that victimize the weak in society.[30]

Wells also became increasingly vocal about the plight of the poor. He had high praise for the relief policies of the Salvation Army which provided the poor with opportunities to earn the necessities of life.[31] Baptist churches had already supported a "city missionary" to Toronto's poor and unchurched for a decade, but Wells believed the churches could and should do much more.[32] It was dishonest to say that the poor man could become rich by working hard — let churchgoers put themselves in the shoes of the poor and see how a life of poverty and oppression really felt.[33] Wells called for the creation of county houses of refuge to assist "the destitute poor, who are guilty of no crime but poverty. . . ."[34]

"The reporting of Wells," comments H. U. Trinier in his history of *The Canadian Baptist,* "was not only accurate and reliable; it was often blunt and to the point."[35] As a Christian social critic Wells had probably carried the newspaper even further in the direction of the Social Gospel than Dadson had. But Wells' sudden death in "harness" in September, 1899, at the age of sixty, produced a crisis and eventually a change in the affairs of the newspaper.

An editorial committee of Professor Calvin Goodspeed, Archibald Blue and George R. Roberts was appointed. A year later the Rev. W. H. Cline replaced Roberts until Roberts was elected editor by the convention in November, 1901. During those three years *The Baptist* was virtually devoid of specific social comment.

Roberts began his work in 1902 with the support of a fourteen-man editorial writing committee. Soon *The Canadian Baptist* had occasion to voice its opinion on certain social questions.[36] Two strikes — one by Toronto's streetcar workers, the other by American coal miners — each drew critical comments because of the inconvenience caused to the public and because of the strikers' use of violence.[37] The main issue of the day, however, was that old war-horse, prohibition, which *The Baptist* asserted would bring an end to child abuse.[38] The provincial referendum on prohibition held in December, 1903, was hailed as a mighty victory for the "drys" — in fact prohibition failed to carry by a mere 13,000 votes out of more than 300,000 cast. More significant to the historian is the fact that rural Ontarians favoured prohibition overwhelmingly, but the urban wets outnumbered the urban prohibitionists eight to seven.[39]

In April, 1903, the anonymous editor was stressing the need to evangelize New Canadians to protect Canadian values, yet by the end of the year the paper was repeatedly speaking of evangelism in exclusively individualistic terms. This apparent ambivalence continued into early 1904 with a series of articles on socialism. Christian socialism was apparently acceptable because its aim was to "right the wrongs of society by the education of the working classes and by co-operative associations."[40] This was to be achieved by reforming the individual — non-Christian socialism that wanted to reform society was "largely the outcome of German rationalism."[41] In conclusion the editorial writer declared, "The price of labour, like any other commodity, is regulated by supply and demand," and unionism in attempting to alter this natural law was merely protecting incompetence.

If Roberts wrote this piece, it was virtually his last editorial word for in May, 1904, he was replaced by W. J. McKay, an acknowledged success as a scholar and pastor. In his journalistic valedictory Roberts expressed surprise at his firing, and stated that his editorial aim had been "to give scant space to new theories and new theologies . . . perhaps *The Baptist* may to some have been thought to have been conservative to an extreme in this direction."[42] If the more liberally-inclined members of the board of publication thought McKay would redress Roberts' conservatism, they must soon have discovered their error. McKay's editorial statements involving social questions differed very little from Roberts'. In Trinier's words, "His editorials were brief, inoffensive paragraphs."[43] In his first months McKay called for purity in politics, and at least once deplored poverty in the midst of plenty, asking Baptists to be "not too discriminating in their charity."[44] By 1905, however, a certain clarification of position can be discerned. Most striking, all references to social issues disappeared from the columns of *The Baptist* — less obvious was a conservative trend in theological statements. Evangelism was now defined simply as the conversion of the individual. Furthermore, McKay stated, "We do not believe that 'New Theology' . . . has any large or lasting place in the minds and affections of our people."[45]

Through the next few years McKay showed great interest in the newly-awakened missionary movements, but not until the closing weeks of 1909 did the editorial column take up again the theme of "practical Christianity." This time, the question involved home missions and particularly recent immigrants into urban areas such as Toronto where forty-five languages were now spoken. "These foreigners may not always be easy to reach with the Gospel, but they are our brethren, and we owe it to them . . . to make strenuous efforts to win them to Christ."[46] This was a theme to which McKay returned several times in subsequent issues, even going so far as to advocate interdenominational cooperation in inner city missions in order to cope with the New Canadian threat to the old Canadian way of life.

Early in 1910 McKay printed an editorial with the allusive title, "Another Gospel?" in which he insisted that the old Gospel of personal salvation is all the world needs to hear. [47] Immediately thereafter he admitted that *The Baptist* had its critics,

and named Elmore Harris as prominent among them![48] Almost
in the same breath the editor announced a forthcoming series of
articles called "Some Fundamentals," and the newspaper noted
the arrival in Toronto of a new pastor, T. T. Shields.[49] It is impossible to discern from the columns of *The Baptist* what were
the sources of tensions, but it must be significant that McKay's
minor crisis coincided with the appearance of *The Fundamentals* and with the height of the attack by Elmore Harris on Mat-
thew's teaching at McMaster University.[50]

During the remainder of 1910, while the Matthews case raged,
and during 1911 and 1912, *The Canadian Baptist* avoided any
social comment that might be interpreted as theologically
liberal, but suddenly in 1913 there was a resurgence of editorial
interest in the Social Gospel. Was it merely coincidence that
Elmore Harris had died at the end of 1911? Under the editorial
title, "Both Individual and Society," McKay commented, "We
heartily agree with the conviction that the Gospel of Christ is a
gospel of a saved society as well as a gospel of saved
individuals."[51] The editorial continued in the same vein with a
quotation from Shailer Matthews that the church must not be
reduced to a social agency.

"Practical Christianity," to judge by various projects
reported in *The Baptist* seemed suddenly to have become
popular, and the trend got a further boost that year when the
Rev. S. Edward Grigg was appointed convention superintendent of social service and evangelism. Grigg announced that in
social service the Good Samaritan is the ideal, and he urged each
congregation to form a social service committee to meet its
neighbourhood needs.[52] Unfortunately, despite letters to the
editor encouraging social service, mission givings did not increase and by the summer of 1914 the Home Mission Board had
to borrow to pay its workers.[53] In an unprecedented fighting
editorial that filled almost a page of *The Canadian Baptist*
McKay asserted, "it is the duty of the Church to preach the
Gospel of the divine love and mercy, and along with it add
simultaneously the Gospel of a better day. Nay, we will go further and say that the line must not be drawn too sharply, that a
full Gospel must satisfy the famine of righteousness and the
hunger for the long-deferred justice of God."[54]

Two days after the publication of this Social Gospel credo,
Germany declared war on Russia. The international chain reac-

tion leading to an Armageddon for western civilization had begun, and polite talk about social justice and the here-and-now Kingdom of God was drowned in the boom of guns.

The story of the place of the Social Gospel in Canadian Baptist life after the First World War, during the years of the Winnipeg strike and the "great depression," and in the two generations since the outbreak of the Second World War, are beyond the scope of this tentative and exploratory paper, but it is a subject that deserves the attention of future historians. As for the years examined here through the columns of *The Canadian Baptist,* certain general conclusions may be offered. Under the editorial guidance of Dadson, Wells and Roberts *The Baptist* displayed an awareness of and sympathy for many of the ideas propounded within the Social Gospel movement. Unlike contemporary Methodist Social Gospellers, Baptist leaders seem not to have espoused any doctrinaire approach to social and moral reform. The recurrent use of the expression "practical Christianity" suggests a greater affinity to the more pragmatic, less idealized, Social Gospel position held and expressed by Canadian Presbyterians.

The sudden removal of Roberts from the editorship and his replacement with the supposedly more conservative McKay must be viewed as another indicator of the deep-seated theological rift that was developing within the Baptist communion at the turn of the century. With considerable success McKay threaded his way through some labyrinth of denominational politics, insisting that the real issue was not individual *versus* social salvation, but individual *and* social salvation as epitomized in the phrase, the "full Gospel." Behind that change in editorial policy undoubtedly lies the turn-of-the-century conflict over higher criticism and modernism.

When all the data is finally assembled and analyzed we will certainly know much more about the ideology of Canadian Baptists, about the ramifications of the modernist-fundamentalist confrontation and about the impact of the Social Gospel on this country's development.

8 The Canadian Baptist *and the Social Gospel,* J. S. Moir

1. The major Canadian Work is Richard Allen, *The Social Passion: Religion and Social Reform in Canada 1914-28* (Toronto: Univ. of Toronto Press, 1971). Among the significant articles are W. H. Magney, "The Methodist Church and the National Gospel," *The Bulletin,* No. 20 (1968), The United Church Archives; G. N. Emery, "The Origin of Canadian Methodist Involvement in the Social Gospel Movement 1890-1914," *The Bulletin,* No. 26 (1977), The United Church Archives; Richard Allen "The Social Gospel as the Religion of Agrarian Revolt" in Ramsey Cook and Carl Berger, eds., *The West and the Nation* (Toronto: McClelland and Stewart, 1976).

2. See, for instance, Brian Fraser, "Theology and the social gospel among Canadian Presbyterians: A case study," *Studies in Religion,* VIII (1), 1979: 35-46; and W. W. Judd, "The Vision and the Dream," *Journal of the Canadian Church History Society,* VII (4), December, 1965.

3. Charles M. Johnston, *McMaster University, Volume One: The Toronto Years* (Toronto: Univ. of Toronto Press, 1976); W. G. Carder, "Controversy in the Baptist Convention of Ontario and Quebec 1908-1928," *Foundations* 16 (1973); 355-376: W. E. Ellis, "Gilboa to Ichabod: Social and Religious Factors in the Fundamentalist-Modernist Schisms Among Canadian Baptists, 1895-1934," *Foundations* 20 (1977): 190-126; C. A. Russell, "Thomas Todhunter Shields, Canadian Fundamentalist," *Ontario History,* LXX (4), December 1978: 263-280. See also Jones H. Farmer, ed., *E. W. Dadson: The Man and His Message* (Toronto: Briggs, 1902), Part I, Chap. VI and Part II, Chap. VII, for an old, brief and uncritical account of Dadson's editorial writings.

4. C. H. Hopkins, *The Rise of the Social Gospel in American Protestantism, 1865-1915* (New Haven: Yale University Press, 1940), especially Part I.

5. H. U. Trinier, *A Century of Service* (Toronto: The Board of Publication, Baptist Convention of Ontario and Quebec, 1954), p. 70.

6. See *The Canadian Baptist* (hereafter cited as CB), 6 March 1879, 22 May 1879, 17 April 1879, 6 January 1881, 18 December 1879, 8 December 1881, and 6 April 1882.

7. *CB,* 4 December 1879.

8. *CB,* 31 January 1884, 11 September 1884.

9. *CB,* 24 November 1887.

10. *CB,* 18 September 1884.

11. *CB,* 26 February 1885, 29 January 1885, 19 February 1885.

12. *CB,* 2 October 1884.

13. *CB,* 12 March 1885.

14. *CB,* 14 May 1885.

15. *CB,* 20 August 1885.

16. *CB,* 11 February 1886, 10 March 1887, *et passim.*

17. *CB,* 25 February 1886.

18. *CB,* 18 March 1886.

19. *CB,* 25 March 1886.

20. *CB,* 8 July 1886.

21. *CB,* 8 July 1886, 5 August, 1886, 7 October 1886.

22. *CB,* 18 June 1888, 16 February 1888.

23. *CB,* 13 January 1887.

24. *CB,* 4 September 1890.

25. *CB,* 21 January 1892.

26. *CB,* 14 July 1892.

27. *CB,* 18 August 1892.

28. *CB,* 3 May 1894.

29. *CB,* 12 July 1894.

30. *CB,* 4 March 1897.

31. *CB,* 21 December 1893.

32. *CB,* 8 March 1894.

33. *CB,* 3 September 1896.

34. *CB,* 14 January 1897.

35. Trinier, *op. cit.,* p. 82.

36. *Ibid.,* p. 85.

37. *CB,* 3 June, 23 October 1902.

38. *CB,* 20 November 1902.

39. *CB,* 11 December 1902, 1 January, 5 February, 12 February 1903.

40. *CB,* 28 January 1904.

41. *CB,* 4 February 1904.

42. *CB,* 28 April 1904, See also Trinier, *op. cit.,* p. 88. regarding the possible desire to have a theologically trained editor.

43. Trinier, *op. cit.,* p. 93.

44. *CB*, 15 December 1904.

45. *CB*, 28 February 1905.

46. *CB*, 25 November 1909.

47. *CB*, 10 January 1910.

48. *CB*, 14 February 1910.

49. *CB*, 24 February, 21 April 1910.

50. See C. M. Johnston, *op. cit.*, p. 110.

51. *CB*, 8 May 1913.

52. *CB*, 5 March 1914.

53. *CB*, 2 July 1914.

54. *CB*, 30 July 1914.

9

Baptists and Radical Politics in Western Canada, (1920-1950)

Walter E. Ellis

Hilda B. Neatby has written that the "hungry thirties" were a harvest time of political revolt in Western Canada.[1] Even more so, the depression decade was a crisis time for popular evangelical theology, the reaping of the tares of a half century of growing disconfirmation of the basic individualism, and laissez-faire doctrines espoused by such a world view. True, Social Gospel exponents first challenged these presuppositions under the impact of urbanization and as a result of their experiences in the industrialized ghettos of New York, Boston, and Chicago. But evangelicalism was forced into cathartic crisis, discredited and ultimately rejected on Frederick Jackson Turner's pristine wilderness, when, in the Canadian west, the sturdy yoemen turned their backs on the myths of progress and mobility when faced with the disillusionment and economic crisis of the "great depression."

The years from 1900 to 1930 witnessed the great migration, the submission of turf to plow, and the growth of cities. It was a time of inherent optimism, despite World War I and numerous mild depressions. Then, suddenly all the plagues of Egypt fell on the Canadian prairies signalled by the 1929 Bay Street crash. For seven succeeding years a relentless sun baked the fields and fizzured the earth with drought. Swarms of locusts darkened the sky and crops that survived ran red with rust. Rivers failed, soil eroded, trees withered. Nature's calamity ushered in economic catastrophy. Debts undertaken during the 1920s when wheat sold as high as $1.05 per bushel became payable with grain prices as low as thirty-four cents a bushel. These visitations heralded the Bennet Buggy, bank foreclosures, evictions, and unemployment. Scarcely had the dust storms abated than the thunder clouds of World War II sounded from Europe. For western farmers and urban workers, for town merchants and city entrepreneurs it was apocalypse now.

Religion has been defined as a system of beliefs and practices by means of which a group of people struggle with the ultimate problems of human life. It is informed by man's ability to imagine "ideal states" which, in turn, provide agendas for political action and signposts for effective social change. Religious influence in Western Canada, though waning, was still a fact of life in the 1930s and the radical political alternatives of Social Credit and the Cooperative Commonwealth Federation won wide support, the former capturing the Alberta legislature of 1935, the latter the Saskatchewan legislature in 1944. Three of their founding leaders were prominent Baptists: Premiers William Aberhart, Ernest C. Manning and Thomas C. Douglas.

At opposite ends of the political spectrum Alberta followed a political agenda informed and undergirded by anthropological pessimism and radical dispensationalism. In contrast, Saskatchewan embraced a democratic socialism informed by an optimistic anthropology, the Social Gospel movement, and theological liberalism. Both radical right and left claimed the inheritance of the black regiment of clergy, who in previous centuries served as interpreters of events, and justifiers of radical political and social change.

The Baptist Heritage

Initially Baptist theology in Western Canada reflected the strong Calvinist influence of the Philadelphia and New Hampshire traditions. In 1884, when the Red River Valley Association of churches was founded, congregations that embraced, in substance, the following doctrines were welcomed:

> The being and Unity of God; the existence of three Equal persons in the Godhead; Divine inspiration of the Old and New

Testaments, as the complete and infallible rule of faith and practice; the depravity and just condemnation of all mankind through
the fall of our first parents; election by grace according to the
fore-knowledge of God; . . . [and] the perseverance of the saints;
the immersion of believers in the name of the Trinity, the only
Christian baptism; The Lord's Supper a privilege of baptized
believers regularly admitted into fellowship and who continue in
good standing in our churches.[2]

Nevertheless, in Eastern Canada pockets of "free-will" and
"open communion" influence still remained and mixed with the
prevailing Calvinism on the frontier. Further, the inherently optimistic spirit of late nineteenth century frontier evangelicalism,
infused with an eminently rational and enlightenment attitude,
reinforced the conviction that what Charles Finney had preached was possible. The advantages of Christian commitment could
be demonstrated, the path of duty outlined, and the pitfalls of
depravity circumvented. Baptists were individualistic
democrats, convinced that the gathered church protected the
voluntary principle, that the workings of God's "moral laws"
in his dealings with nations, classes and individuals were evident; that what a man sowed was what a man reaped, not only
in the life to come, but in this life as well. Hence, the main
stream of Baptist eschatology was post-millennial and readily
embraced the basic concepts of social reform, missionary
endeavour, and the prospect of social evolution toward a more
enlightened, moral, and just society.[3]

For a century this popular attitude (for it was as much attitude as doctrine) prevailed, and such an eschatology provided
the foundation for American ethical and economic theories. For
example, Francis Wayland, the Baptist president of Brown
University, in his *The Elements of Moral Science (1835),* and
The Elements of Political Economy (1840), rationalized Adam
Smith's laissez-faire economics by asserting that the moral order
worked on a system of rewards and punishments as invariable as
"an order of sequence in physics." He explained that in God's
economy man was "adapted to labor" and that "all that existed
of capital, of convenience, of comfort and of intelligence" was
the "work of industry," the rewards God bestowed upon moral
men for obedience to the "law of being."[4]

Six decades later the Baptist theologian Augustus H. Strong
still espoused political and economic doctrines informed by a

universe regulated by law, a social order regulated by divine command, and a free enterprise economic system based on industry and hard work, with charity an appropriate expression of Christian philanthropy for the unfortunate. In short, North American evangelicalism encouraged an inner-worldly asceticism, an inherently post-millennial optimism, an individualistic free enterprise economy, and a liberal political stance. Concurrently, the doctrine of grace addressed the uncontrollable, and proffered the blessed hope of the "resurrection of the body and general judgment; the final happiness of the saints, and the misery of the wicked, alike interminable . . . "⁵ Such was the paradox of evangelicalism. It was at once inner-worldly and other-worldly; at once economically hard-nosed and philanthropic; at once it justified labour but held out the prospect of leisure.

The Western Baptist Tradition

When pioneer Alexander MacDonald arrived in the Canadian prairies in 1883, he was late. Most other denominations had come before him. Succeeding Baptist immigrants did not represent the struggling Ontario yeoman, who a half century before had wrested political and religious independence from a recalcitrant episcopacy and the "family compact." Rather, this new generation of Baptists was a cross-section of upwardly mobile merchants, white-collar workers and professionals intent upon consolidating their foothold at the centre of Canada's social and political establishment. In consequence Baptist influence, apart from limited ethnic pockets, remained confined to urban centres such as Winnipeg, Brandon, Edmonton and Calgary, where the denomination attracted converts already established or aspiring to the benefits of middle class society.

With the passing of Superintendent Alexander Grant in 1897, and for half a century, Baptist leadership, in consequence, reflected the decidedly liberal values and optimistic outlook of their eastern Canadian and American counterparts. Merely to mention the names of A. J. Vining, W. C. Vincent, and J. F. McIntyre; of Superintendent D. B. Harkness who later became executive of the Social Service Council and editor of *The Statesman,* and Peter G. Mode, who moved from Brandon College to the University of Chicago Divinity School, is to illustrate the kind of university-trained executives, editors and educators, many with postgraduate training from the University of Chicago, or Rochester and Crozer seminaries, who led the frontier denomination during its formative period.

Most, like J. N. McLean, who became executive secretary of the Social Service Council of Manitoba, or Dore R. Sharpe, former secretary to Walter Rauschenbusch, who served as pastor, then superintendent in Saskatchewan, shared the Social Gospel passion of the age.[6] The same can be said for succeeding superintendent-editors: C. R. Sayer (1912-15); F. W. Patterson (1918-22), who resigned to accept the presidency of Acadia University; M. L. Orchard (1922-29), who moved to McMaster University, and W. C. Smalley (1929-51). Each of these reflected to varying degrees the prevailing commitment to education, the theology, and values of progressive social Christianity.[7]

Likewise Baptists exhibited decidedly liberal political preferences. In 1905, when Alberta and Saskatchewan became provinces, and in the context of the schools controversy, the *Northwest Baptist* observed that "as far as Baptists are concerned it is probable that nine out of ten have distinct liberal leanings."[8] This was evidenced by the appointment in Alberta of the Hon. G. H. V. Bulyea as lieutenant governor, and by the election of the Hon. A. C. Rutherford as premier. Later J. C. Bowen, a graduate in theology from Brandon was elected Alberta Liberal leader and then appointed lieutenant governor. In British Columbia, in 1918, Premier H. C. Brewster led a reform Liberal government which included J. W. Farris. In Saskatchewan, W. J. Estey, later justice of the Supreme Court, served as attorney general and minister of education in the James Gardiner and W. J. Patterson administrations.

Similarly prairie Baptist educational policy was dominated by a liberal spirit and eastern orientation. From its founding in 1899 under Dr. A. P. McDiarmid, Brandon College epitomized what Peter Mode had warned against — the attempt of a small college in the west to reproduce a New England institution. Staffed as it was by astute, learned and ambitious young men or retirees with eyes turned toward the educational meccas of Toronto, Chicago or Rochester, Baptist institutions committed themselves to break down the narrow denominationalism produced by isolation. Their task was to socialize students who, mellowed by culture, refinement, social convention and ivy-

covered institutions, would create an environment where sectarianism would diminish and ecumenical cooperation and progress would flourish.[9]

Social Christianity, Dispensationalism, and the Founders

Much progress has been made since Alvin W. Gouldner introduced the concept of cosmopolitans and locals to analyse latent social roles. Robert K. Merton noted the close orientation
of locals with their community while cosmopolitans, though living in that community, orient significantly to the "great
society" beyond. Locals tend to relate on the basis of peer
association while cosmopolitans move in a more restricted professional community. Both leadership types are influentials but
"if the local influentials are quantitativists, the cosmopolitans
are qualitativists." When communicating the localite relates on
the basis of sympathetic understanding while the cosmopolitan
functions on a professional-client basis with "some distance
between the advice-giver and the advice-seeker." Merton argues
that localite preachers owe their success to the fact that they
"typically convert news and public issues into personalized
anecdotes." Conversely, cosmopolitan clergy and politicians,
function on a more formal and theoretical basis.[10]

In many respects the typology illumines and explains the
theological and political differences between the clergy leadership in the radical left Cooperative Commonwealth Federation
and the radical right Social Credit movements. Consider first
the biography of J. S. Woodsworth of the CCF.

James S. Woodsworth, born in 1874, was the son of the Rev.
James Woodsworth, who, in 1886, became superintendent of
Methodist Missions in the Northwest. In Brandon, then in Win-
nipeg, James was raised in an atmosphere of middle-class gentility and culture. In 1896 he graduated as senior stick from
Wesley College, Winnipeg, an institution not unlike Brandon
College, and subsequently served under the Methodist Mission
Board. In 1898 Woodsworth moved to Victoria College, Toronto, then on to Oxford the following year. In Britain he became
further acquainted with biblical criticism, the theology of Hans
H. Wendt, a student of Albrecht Ritchl, and with the plight of
the London slum workers. Like Harry Emerson Fosdick and so
many others, Woodsworth capped his middle-class education
with "the grand tour."

In July 1900 Woodsworth returned to Brandon and was ordained. But he was troubled by the dichotomy between the doctrines of Methodism and their Jack of "progressivism" on economic and social issues; also by his failure to attain an expected "twice-born" religious experience. In April 1907 he submitted his resignation because his religious experience "had not been what among Methodists [was] considered normal," and because his attitude to the discipline was "un-Methodistical."[11]

The Methodists found nothing in his doctrinal beliefs to warrant separation, encouraged him to remain and, having accorded him intellectual freedom, appointed him superintendent of All Peoples' Mission in Winnipeg. In succeeding years his activities included editing *The Christian Guardian* and leadership roles in The People's Forum Movement, the League of Social Workers, and the Canadian Welfare League. He directed the Bureau of Social Research, advocated pacifism, pioneeered cooperatives in Gibsons, British Columbia, always with the growing recognition that "the organized church had become a great institution with institutional aims and ambitions," an institution controlled by "men of wealth" and no longer a practical vehicle for "a radical program of social reform." In consequence, in 1918, he finally resigned from the ministry.[12]

Woodsworth became organizer for the Non-Partisan League of Alberta, a precursor of the United Farmers movement, then worked for the Federated Labour Party. He returned to Winnipeg in 1919 to assist in the Winnipeg general strike, to found the Labour Church, and in 1921, to organize the Independent Labour Party.

During the 1920s Woodsworth became convinced that the solutions of American populism, the initiative, referendum, recall, trust-busting and tariff reductions were insufficient. The liberal goal of a self-actualizing individual required that "democracy be broadened out from the political to the economic field."[13] At hand were radical alternatives, the Cooperative Commonwealth model of the progressive Social Gospel, the Fabian principles of British Socialism, the Marxist dialectic and the insights of modern sociology and political theory.

Woodsworth concluded that a uniquely Canadian adaptation

of socialism was possible, and when depression struck these principles gave birth to the founding of the Cooperative Commonwealth Federation in Calgary in 1932, and were incorporated in the Regina Manifesto the following year. The Manifesto read:

> The CCF is a federation of organizations whose purpose is the establishment in Canada of a Cooperative Commonwealth in which the principle regulating production, distribution, and exchange will be the supplying of human needs and not the making of profits.
>
> We aim to replace the present capitalist system, with its inherent injustice and inhumanity, by a social order from which the domination and exploitation of one class by another will be eliminated, in which economic planning will supersede unregulated private enterprise, and competition, and in which genuine democratic self-government, based upon economic equality will be possible . . . . When private profit is the main stimulus to economic effort, our society oscillates between periods of feverish prosperity in which the main benefits go to speculators and profiteers, and of catastrophic depression, in which the common man's normal state of insecurity and hardship is accentuated. We believe that these evils can be removed only by a planned economy in which our natural resources and principal means of production are owned, controlled and operated by the people.

Individuality would not be crushed. Rather more leisure and freedom from want would make for a richer individual life for every citizen. [14]

The biography of the "twice-born" localite, William Aberhart, founder of Social Credit, is a study in contrasts. William Aberhart was born in 1878 near Edmondville, Ontario, the fourth of seven children of William and Louise Aberhart. Limited resources confined his education to Seaforth Collegiate, Chatham Business College, and Hamilton Normal School. In 1901 he received his certification and taught near Wingham, then moved to Brantford. An early marriage, followed by the birth of two daughters, dictated that his education was interrupted. Nevertheless he persisted, and in 1911 received his Bachelor of Arts degree by correspondence from Queen's University, but without success in mastering the biblical languages. [15]

Brantford was the major centre of Niagara Prophetic Conference influence in Canada. Pre-millenarian and dispensational in outlook the conference offered a radical challenge to post-millennialism, teaching the gradual apostasy of the church, the imminent Second Coming of Christ, usually preceded by the rapture of the church; in short, a pessimistic apocalypticism that posited salvation through divine intervention outside of, or as a culmination of, the historical process. It was under the influence of Dr. William Nicol of Zion Presbyterian Church that Aberhart converted to such views.[16]

Dispensationalism, like liberalism and the Social Gospel, was a transdenominational movement, and Aberhart moved freely in circles that included such prominent Baptists as Andrew Imrie, A. A. Cameron, and John Shenstone. He met Elmore Harris, dispensationalist president of the Toronto Bible Institute, consulting editor of the Scofield Bible, pastor of Walmer Road Baptist Church, and author of the 1908 accusations of modernism directed against Dr. I. G. Matthews of McMaster University. Probably through Harris' influence he was allowed to conduct evangelistic services in 1909 at the Massey-Harris shops in Brantford.[17]

Aberhart's frustration with the religious establishment came early. In 1910 Zion Presbyterian Church declined to assist elder Aberhart to attend Knox College, Toronto, to study for the ministry. Hence, when he was offered the position of principal of Alexandra High School in Calgary he moved west. Aberhart joined Grace Presbyterian Church and two years later, Wesley Methodist Church, where he served with the future United Farmers premier of Alberta, J. E. Brownlee. In 1912 he founded the West End Bible Class and in 1915, commenced regular supply at Westbourne Baptist Church, a struggling mission founded and controlled by trustees of the prestigious First Baptist Church. In succeeding years, his Thursday Bible Class, precurser to the Calgary Prophetic Bible Conference, flourished, and Westbourne prospered, much to the chagrin of those of the Baptist establishment who disapproved of his popular style, his hermeneutics, and his dispensational fundamentalism. In 1919, under the influence of former Calgary mayor William Underwood, Westbourne's absentee trustees warned that the church must "either force Aberhart and his class out of the church or they would receive no further support."[18]

Mainline Baptists had good reason to distrust Aberhart. In succeeding years his theology would become increasingly strident and unorthodox. He was not immersed until 1921; then under neo-Pentecostal influence, he espoused such questionable beliefs as baptism in the name of Jesus only, the inerrancy of the King James Bible, a church order distinguished by dual membership, with Aberhart functioning as "prophet;" and the belief that the seven letters to churches in Revelation referred to seven apostate future denominations.[19]

Aberhart participated in the fundamentalist-modernist controversies of the 1920s. In 1923 faculty members of Brandon College, especially Dr. H. L. MacNeill, were charged with modernism. Aberhart joined the attack and moved to extricate the deed of the debt-free Westbourne congregation from the Baptist Union. In 1924 he established "Baptist" control of the Calgary Prophetic Bible Conference. Next he opposed formation of the United Church of Canada because he "feared that the end result would be an apostate church."[20] In 1925 he founded the Calgary Bible Institute, later the Calgary Prophetic Bible Institute, commenced a popular radio ministry and instituted his correspondence Sunday Church School of the Air, the three "locals-type" vehicles that served as springboards for his political success. Both Aberhart's theology and institutions were informed by a populist fundamentalism that believed in the ability of the average person to interpret Scripture and operate churches without benefit of "experts."

Formation of the institute signalled the departure or expulsion of Westbourne Baptist Church from the Baptist Union. In 1927, when William Bell Riley opened the new Prophetic Bible Institute buildings, Westbourne Baptist Church moved in as a tenant. Within two years the congregation split, the older members returning to their church to found a rival Bible institute under Morley Hall and with the assistance of Aberhart's fundamentalist rival, L. E. Maxwell, principal of Prairie Bible Institute. Aberhart subsequently founded his Bible Institute Baptist Church and called from Brantford Dr. Andrew Imrie, a graduate of McMaster and Dallas seminaries, as pastor.

Thus, in two decades the energetic, indefatigable effort of Aberhart had forged an impressive record, albeit in the face of theological contention and ecclesiastical controversy. He not only controlled, he was, the dispensational movement in Calgary. His institute offered localite youth from farm and town biblical training coupled with vocational opportunities. He had mastered radio ministry and adapted correspondence education to religion, all the while serving as principal of Crescent Heights High School. Moreover, his success had been won in the face of roadblocks placed by his social background, by mainline educational institutions and the religious establishment; forged by localite peer associations, the popularization of issues, and broad human contact. The roadblocks confirmed his dispensational doctrines and inherent pessimism, his success was the belief that any man of industry and ability could make it if he was committed to Christ and his moral order.

However, when depression struck, the saints who frequented the institute were not "making it," and this threw Aberhart's classic evangelical presuppositions into question. In the summer of 1932, influenced by Charles Scarborough, he read Maurice Colborne's *Unemployment or War,* and *Economic Nationalism,* popularizations of the Social Credit economic theories of Major C. H. Douglas, and he experienced his "second conversion." In the fall he introduced a course on "The Bible and Modern Economics" at the institute and in February, 1933, published anonymously his yellow pamphlet entitled, "The Douglas System of Economics." By 1935 nearly 3000 Social Credit study groups throughout Alberta were familiar with the explanation that the discrepancy between income and prices was due to money siphoned from the economy by banks, trusts, and financial institutions, and the solution, payment of a social dividend by the government to enable the people to purchase the goods and services they produced.[21]

Discussion of monetary theory had long thrived on the prairies in face of the oppressive influence of eastern financial institutions and corporations. As early as 1908 the Baptist *Western Outlook* lamented that the chartered banks, "though in theory the custodians of the people's wealth, [were] in fact the dictators to the people regarding the ways and means of its distribution."[22] Since 1920 Alberta had been ruled by the United Farmers, a popular agrarian movement, influenced by the theories of group government and social evolution set forth by Henry Wise Wood and F. H. Underhill. Initially, Aberhart attempted to have Social Credit monetary theory adopted by them. Finally, in January 1935, when the scandal-ridden government of Premier R. G. Reed rejected him, Aberhart formed his Alberta Social Credit League, announced that here was an economic system thoroughly Christian in principle, and called the people to put their "faith" in Social Credit.[23]

Aberhart has long served as a whipping boy for Canadian intellectuals. David R. Elliott concludes that "there was no logical connection between Aberhart's theology and his political ideology," and charges that he was motivated by a "desire for power" and an irrational "ecclecticism." According to Elliott, Aberhart embraced a movement steeped in theological liberalism and humanism and preached his "own brand of social gospel" while continuing to hold to a contradictory radical dispensationalism.[24] Thomas E. Flanagan finds only structural similarities between Aberhart's pre-millenarian doctrines and Social Credit, and stresses they both rested on the common element of "faith."[25]

Whether or not men are logical is moot. Certainly in the context of the depression Social Credit must have seemed the most logical of the extant alternatives, given Aberhart's background and theology. Aberhart considered communism and socialism but their association with atheism and liberalism made them unacceptable. The moral scandals engulfing J. E. Brownlee, O. L. McPherson and George Hoadley proved that the United Farmers government was in the hands of "fornicators, grafters, and reprobates concerning the faith," an illustration of the depravity of man.[26] Most westerners agreed that the banks and lending institutions, if not the railways and the *Calgary Tribune* were controlled by "the devil," a sign of the last days.

What was required was an "adjustment" to make the capitalistic system and God's laws of labour and morality work. Social Credit held it could work successfully with three fundamental changes:

> The Government must recover its control over the monetary system; it must issue social credit in the form of a National Dividend (based upon a survey of the real wealth of the nation) to every person; and to prevent the possibility of inflation, it must establish a Just Price for all goods.[27]

The theory fit perfectly into a fundamentalist system. It left doomsday and judgment, and it allowed the classical, ethical and economic theories of evangelicalism to function in the meantime. Explained Aberhart:

> The appeal of God today is for the individual to understand that God's policy is to provide man with a salvation full and free, without money and without price, and *then to offer him future rewards for his individual enterprise in the service of God.* I am convinced that this is the basic principle of a practical economic system. Government credit, such as advocated by Major Douglas, gives to the individual . . . the essentials of physical life, . . . and then offers him additional reward for his individual enterprise.[28]

Scope prevents a detailed examination of the 1935 election campaign — the attempts by Liberals and United Farmers to utilize Major Douglas to discredit Aberhart, the dire warnings of the *Calgary Herald* that "a victory for Social Credit would be the worst calamity that could befall the province," and the charge that Social Credit would "force a regimentation parallel-ed only in Germany, Italy and Russia." The mainline denominations were no help to Aberhart, and after his election both the Anglican and United churches formally condemned his mixture of religion with politics.[29] However, on August 23, 1935 the people spoke and Social Credit swept the field winning 57 of 63 seats. Lamented the *Herald*:

> As the result of almost two years of intensive propaganda, with a hymn as a battle cry and a pulpit as a forum, the new economic gospel fell on receptive ears. It appealed to the discouraged and the discontented, and because of its origin it was believed in by a people wanting to believe.[30]

The Second Generation

If J. S. Woodsworth and William Aberhart dominated the initial phase of radical politics, Thomas C. Douglas, CCF premier of Saskatchewan from 1944 to 1961, and Ernest C. Manning, Social Credit premier of Alberta from 1943 to 1968, dominated the second. Again their personal and spiritual biographies are a study in contrasts.

Douglas was born in 1904 at Falkirk, a socialist area of Scotland, the son of Thomas Douglas and Annie Clement. The elder Douglas migrated to Canada in 1910, but returned with his family in 1914 to enlist. In 1919 they came back to North Winnipeg where, because of limited resources, Tommy left school to work as a printer's apprentice. In 1924 young Douglas enrolled at the Brandon Academy arriving at the height of the "fundamentalist-modernist" controversy. In 1925 he became student-pastor at Austin and matriculated in 1926, having received the governor general's medal for general proficiency. Four years later he earned his bachelor's degree, and received the gold medal for debating, dramatics, and oratory. Upon graduation, Douglas was ordained and moved to his first pastorate, Calvary Baptist Church in Weyburn, Saskatchewan.

Baptist influence in Saskatchewan, and especially at Weyburn had been decidedly liberal due to the influence of superintendents Dore Sharpe, and W. P. Reikie, and pastors like Douglas' predecessor at Weyburn, T. M. Marshall. Douglas majored in economics, and in 1931 following a summer at the University of Chicago where he met Norman Thomas, he founded the Weyburn Association of the Independent Labour Party. In 1933 he completed his master's degree in sociology from McMaster, writing on the impact of retardation on the social patterns and welfare system of Weyburn. The depression was at its height, and faced with the poverty and suffering, Douglas accepted the nomination as Farmer-Labour candidate for the Saskatchewan legislature. Unsuccessful, he ran the following year in the federal election and was elected to the House of Commons to represent Weyburn constituency.[31]

In Ottawa Douglas distinguished himself as an astute debater and tactician. Reelected in 1940, he later resigned to lead the Saskatchewan wing of the CCF in the 1944 provincial election. Douglas had his work cut out for him. Arrayed against him was the powerful Liberal Gardiner machine, now led by Premier W. J. Patterson. Further, in a province of significant Catholic population, the CCF use-hold land and state educational policies had left a burning suspicion. Disaffected Roman Catholics had turned to Social Credit in the 1938 election. Faced with a pastoral letter issued by the archbishop of Regina warning against socialism, Douglas counter-attacked. In 1943 in an important parliamentary address he roasted free enterprise as "the law of the jungle applied to economics." It was every man for himself "as the elephant said when he was dancing among the chickens." It fostered the growth of monopolies and poverty, and enabled "a small handful of bankers" to control the economic system.

Quoting Norman Thomas, Douglas defined socialism as that "form of society in which the means of production, distribution and exchange are socially owned and democratically managed in the interests of all the people rather than for the benefit of a few." Said he, "We agree with the statement contained in the encyclical *Quadragesimo Anno*, written by Pope Leo XIII, that 'anything which dominates the life of the community should be owned by the community.' "[32]

Liberal press and politicians mounted the hustings to set forth the spectre of regimentation, confiscation of savings, insurance, and war bonds, and nationalization of farmland. In Europe men were "fighting to defeat dictators, not to start another dictatorship." The Liberal Baptist A. J. Estey charged the socialist Baptist Douglas with preaching "blue-ruin" with his CCF or chaos apocalyptic vision of unemployment, dislocation, and agricultural depression following the armistice.[33] Douglas countered that CCF land and economic policies would "make ready the way for absorption back into civilian life of those now in uniform and engaged in war work." Socialism would return "property to the people," destroy the dictatorship of big business, provide protection against natural catastrophes and sickness, and restore control over their lives to individuals.[34] On June 14 election tallies showed the CCF had won 47 of 55 seats.

L. D. Lovick observes of Douglas:

> He discussed democratic socialism in terms of Christianity and moral and ethical principles. Surely, it was felt, this would lay to rest the demon of "the godless socialists" and remove the label of "Red" that the enemies of democratic socialism had been attaching to the CCF for years. Douglas described socialism in Biblical terms: a socialist believed he was his brother's keeper; Saint Paul had taught that the strong ought to bear the burdens of the weak. Democratic socialism Douglas seemed to be saying, was no more than applied Christianity.[35]

Tommy Douglas was not the only socially mobile young seminarian whose radical political views were forged or strengthened by contact with such Brandon faculty members as Carl H. Lager, Burton Hurd, Harris L. MacNeill, Thomas Dadson, and Cyril F. Richards, or the Winnipeg Social Gospel climate. Contemporaries with Douglas in the late 1920s were Stanley Howard Knowles and Edgar J. Bailey.

Knowles, elected to the House of Commons in 1942 to succeed J. S. Woodsworth, like Douglas had been a printer's apprentice in Winnipeg. In 1930 he received his B. A. degree from Brandon, then due to closure of the seminary division, moved to Winnipeg, where he was employed by First Baptist Church as supervisor of boys' work and religious education. He attended United College and the University of Manitoba, receiving his B.D.from the latter in 1934. In the meantime he had become interim pastor at First Congregational Church and was later ordained a minister of the United Church of Canada. Knowles distinguished himself as a parliamentarian and later as architect in the founding of the New Democratic Party in 1961.

Another member of the "Manitoba group" was Edgar J. Bailey, Welsh immigrant and Yale graduate, who later served as president of the Baptist Federation of Canada (1965-67). Chaplain Bailey returned from the war to Tabernacle Baptist Church in Winnipeg. In 1945 he unsuccessfully contested the Federal Lisgar constituency for the CCF, while Lloyd C. Stinson, eventually ordained in the United Church, contested Winnipeg South Centre. Bailey was offered the leadership of the Manitoba CCF party but declined. In 1955, when he was pastor of the First Baptist Church, Edmonton, he ran under the leadership of Liberal J. Harper Prowse in the only significant election challenge to Social Credit since their 1935 election victory.

The life and education of Ernest C. Manning stands in marked contrast to that of Douglas and the Manitoba group. Manning was born in 1908 at Cardiff, Saskatchewan, the son of farmer George Henry Manning and Elizabeth Dickson. He concluded his secondary education at Rosetown. Manning "became a Christian listening to Aberhart's religious broadcasts." In 1926, the harvest completed, he took the train to Calgary, attended Westbourne Baptist Church and met Aberhart. In October, 1927, he enrolled in the first Prophetic Bible Institute class and went to live in the Aberhart home the following year. During his last year as a student Manning joined the "teaching staff" of the institute, and, in 1930, at the age of twenty-three became business manager and began to share in the regular radio ministry.

As Aberhart's right hand it was natural that Manning should share in the 1933 institute-sponsored provincial tour of R. E. Neighbour, radical American fundamentalist, and participate in the spread of the Social Credit small group movement throughout the province. Nominated to contest a Calgary constituency, he led the polls in the 1935 provincial election. Aberhart rewarded Manning with the portfolio of provincial secretary, later adding the Ministry of Trade and Industry. In June of 1943, upon Aberhart's death, Manning was sworn into office as premier. He led Social Credit into the August election of 1944, tangled over monetary policy with the federal minister of finance, the Baptist J. L. Ilsley, won reelection and continued as premier until his retirement in 1968.[36] Through the long years, Manning remained the faithful voice of the Back to the Bible Hour, and became a household word on numerous stations throughout Canada.

Several other Baptist ministers likewise won election in the 1935 Social Credit landslide. A Swedish Baptist and graduate of Morgan Park Seminary, J. A. Wingblade, was victorious in Wetaskiwin. Ernest G. Hansell, pastor of Westbourne Baptist Church until 1926, later in Camrose, served in the House of Commons and as Social Credit federal organizer. In Ponoka, Mrs. W. W. Rogers, a Prophetic Conference supporter and imported candidate, defeated J. E. Brownlee, while Peter Dawson, a United Church minister, defeated O. L. McPherson in Little Bow.

Since W. E. Mann published *Sect, Cult and Church in Alberta*, most scholarly research has attempted to downplay the relationship between fundamentalism and the Social Credit movement. Elliott argues that Aberhart's entry into politics split the fundamentalists, assuming falsely a monolithic movement prior to the rise of Social Credit. Likewise, Owen A. Anderson argues that thirty percent of Social Credit MLA's were Anglicans or United and only eleven percent members of other religious groups (fundamentalists, Mormons, etc.). Such statistical data requires interpretation, for it does not address the issue of religious latency, nor recognize the amorphous theological mix found in most mainline denominations.[37]

Conclusion

From the 1930s onward the population on the Canadian

prairies was more or less unanimous in its disaffection from the prevailing Canadian corporate, financial, and industrial establishments. Most believed that the "Fifty Big Shots of Canada" with their protectionism and privileges were keeping the prairie populace mere hewers of wood and drawers of water. Why then could they not unite behind a single, radical, political alternative? For many the bitter divisions between the Social Credit and the CCF were lamentable. Commented the *Western Producer*:

> Premiers T. C. Douglas and E. C. Manning are both young men, earnest, hard-working and competent. They are both ministers of the crown; but they share . . . a greater honor in common — they are both ministers of the gospel. Animated by charity and tolerance, fired by a common purpose to advance the cause of humanity in this critical hour, . . . they might without compromise of their convictions, do much to heal the breach which otherwise will spread no one knows how widely.[38]

The answer to the lament is not a monistic one. But any attempt to write the histories of the CCF and Social Credit movements without attention to the divergent theological presuppositions of the leadership will falter. Two could not walk together unless they were agreed. The theology of "doomsday" led necessarily to the *Politics of Doomsday*, and smoldered into classic conservatism. When Manning retired, Alberta prospered, and the imminent return of Christ tarried.[39] In contrast, the vision of the Kingdom of God, though it often verged on humanism, remained firmly rooted in the historical process and proved adaptable to social change. It remains one factor in the idealism and political commitment of the New Democratic Party.

Reinhold Neibuhr once remarked that religion was "a citadel of hope built on the edge of despair." In the midst of depression and war it was the evangelicals who interpreted events and guided the Canadian West into the precarious future. Some marched on the right road to Zion, others on the left in search of the Kingdom of God. They were led by men of faith, some of them Baptist ministers whose belief grounded and informed their actions.

9 Baptists and Radical Politics, W. E. Ellis

1. Hilda B. Neatby, *The Politics of Chaos, Canada in the Thirties* (Toronto: Macmillan, 1972), p. 231.

2. C. C. McLaurin, *Pioneering in Western Canada* (Calgary: Armac Press, 1939), pp. 110-11.

3. Timothy L. Smith, *Revivalism and Social Reform* (New York: Abingdon Press, 1957), pp. 225-36.

4. Francis Wayland, *The Elements of Moral Science* (1835), and *The Elements of Political Economy* (1840) see discussion and selections in W. G. McLoughlin, ed., *The American Evangelicals, 1800-1900* (New York: Torchbooks, 1968), pp. 101-26.

5. McLaurin, *op. cit.*, p. 111.

6. Western Baptists were disproportionally represented in ecumenical and secular social improvement programs. Among these were: The Rev. D. B. Harkness, General Secretary of the Baptist Union (1904-1916), to Social Service Council of Manitoba (1916) and editor of *The Statesman;* Rev. J. N. McLean, Tabernacle Baptist, Winnipeg, to the Social Service Council of Manitoba (1914); Commissioner of Prohibition (1916); Rev. A. M. McDonald, D. D., Alberta Superintendent of the Dept. of Neglected Children, later Executive Secretary of the St. Paul-Minneapolis, Cleveland and Chicago Baptist Associations; Rev. W. P. Reikie, Weyburn, to Superintendent of Saskatchewan Baptist Missions, then Social Secretary of the Saskatchewan Reform League.

7. Geo. F. May observed that progressive social Christianity generally failed to attract conservative and labour support, but made its deepest impression on the ideals of the progressive middle class. A survey of prairie Baptist editorial comment confirms this view. For example, under the editorship of W. C. Vincent in 1903 the *Northwest Baptist* ran surprisingly sympathetic articles explaining the various forms of socialism (*NB*, June 1, 1900, p. 1). In 1909 under the editorship of D. B. Harkness and P. G. Mode the *Western Outlook* advocated nationalization of natural resources and complained that it was "regrettable that everywhere the principle of private ownership seems to prevail in spite of the growing recognition of the injustice to which it leads." (*WO*, July 1, 1909, p. 4). In 1915 the *Western Outlook* under the editorship of J. N. McLean attacked the Federal government for not grappling with unemployment. In 1918 the *Western Baptist* under F. W. Patterson called for Christians to serve in public office (*WB*, July, 1918, p. 2). The following year, though lamenting the "Bolshevist leadership" of the Winnipeg General Strike, the paper noted that "beneath the present struggle was the wide-spread consciousness that the disproportion between income and necessary expenditure [showed] no sign of being overcome," that "the government [seemed] unable to understand and incapable of giving assistance." The unrest represented failure of human society to do justly; a surprisingly liberal response given the hysteria of the times. (*WB*, July, 1919, p. 4). In 1923 M. L. Orchard defended the social gospel as not repudiating the

gospel for the individual, but believing that the teachings of Jesus should permeate and dominate all phases of life. After the fundamentalist-modernist schism editorial comment became muted, but, from 1928-1933, the theme of the Kingdom of God dominated Union and regional programs. (*WB,* July, 1929, p. 4, June, 1932, p. 3). As late as 1939, under W. C. Smalley the "mutual dependence of humanity," "undesirable things about the social order," "modern business life," and "social reform" were themes representative of sermonic and youth program materials (*WB,* March, 1939, p. 13; December, p. 11; January, 1940, p. 13).

8. *Northwest Baptist,* XX, 2, (1905), p. 2.

9. Peter G. Mode, *The Frontier Spirit in American Christianity* (N. Y.: The Macmillan Company, 1923). Dr. Dore R. Sharpe writes: "Brandon College played a large part in developing a forward looking liberal spirit. The first president, Dr. A. P. McDiarmid, was a staunch liberal as was [President F. W.] Sweet [1923, Chicago and Rochester trained]. Dr. [David] Bovington had taught at the old Rochester Seminary, Dr. H. P. Whidden, president of Brandon and before that pastor of the liberal First Church Dayton, Ohio . . . . Brandon had two liberal scholars both trained at the University of Chicago Divinity School — Matthews had been definitely influenced by Rauschenbusch, while Dr. H. L. MacNeil had been tried for heresy while a professor at Brandon. . . . Note: Rev. S. Everton, Dr. A. A. Shaw, Dr. F. W. Sweet, Dr. H. F. Waring, Martin Storgaard, Charles S. Stone, and H. R. McGill were all graduates of Rochester." Letter, Dr. Dores S. Sharpe to Author, Nov. 16, 1961.

10. Alvin W. Gouldner, "Cosmopolitans and Locals: Towards an Analysis of Latent Social Roles," *Administrative Science Quarterly,* 1957, pp. 281-306; also, Robert K. Merton, *Social Theory and Social Structure* (Glencoe, Illinois: The Free Press, 1957), pp. 387-426.

11. Kenneth McNaught, *A Prophet in Politics: A Biography of J. S. Woodsworth* (Toronto: U. of Toronto Press, 1959), pp. 31-2, 34.

12. *Ibid.,* p. 83.

13. *Ibid.,* p. 186.

14. Cited in L. D. Lovick, ed., *Tommy Douglas Speaks* (Lantzville, B. C.: Oolichan Books, 1979), p. 30. Cf. Rosemary Reuther's explanation of the relationship between the Social Gospel and Christian Socialism in her book, *The Radical Kingdom* (New York: Harper and Row, 1970), pp. 82f.

15. For biographies of William Aberhart, see: J. A. Boudreau, *Alberta, Aberhart, and Social Credit* (Toronto: Holt, Rinehart and Winston, 1975); LeRoy Johnson, *Aberhart of Alberta* (Edmonton: Co-op Press, 1970); and L. H. Thomas, ed., *William Aberhart and Social Credit in Alberta* (Toronto: Copp-Clark, 1977); H. J. Schultz, "Portrait of a Premier: William Aberhart," *Canadian Historical Review* 44 (1963): 185f. For his theology, see David Raymond Elliott, "The Dispensational Theology and Political Ideology of William Aberhart" (unpublished M. A. thesis, University of Calgary, 1975), pp. 8-11.

16. H. J. Schultz, "Portrait of a Premier," p. 185.

17. For a history of the impact of pre-millenarianism on Ontario and Quebec Baptists, see R. L. Whan, "Premillenialism in Canadian Baptist History" (unpublished B. D. thesis, McMaster Divinity College, 1945); for the classic attack from mainline Baptists, see Walter Rauschenbusch, "Our Attitude Toward Millenarianism," *The Examiner,* September 24, 1896, and October 1, 1896. The tension between postmillenialists and pre-millenarians appeared among Canadian Baptists as early as 1851-53, when *The Christian Observer* was edited by Rev. James Pyper (pre-Jarvis Street) and Rev. John Inglis (London, Ontario). Rev. Joshua Donovan espoused pre-millenarian views at the Baptist Ministers' Conference at Brantford in 1878. Rev. A. A. Cameron of Brantford, later Ottawa; the Rev. Alexander Grant, Western Baptist superintendent until 1896; the Rev. William Stewart of Toronto Bible Institute; the Rev. Elmore Harris of Walmer Road Baptist Church and President of Toronto Bible Institute (1895); the Rev. J. P. Ross of Jarvis Street, and Mr. John Shenstone of Brantford were among early pre-millenarian, often dispensational exponents.

18. Elliott, *op. cit.,* pp. 51-2.

19. *Ibid.,* pp. 53-6, 63. Rev. H. H. Bingham, later minister of the First Baptist Church, Calgary, asserted: "It was the content of Aberhart's prophetic lectures that alarmed the Baptist Union. They considered his lectures 'pathetic' rather than 'prophetic.' "

20. *Ibid.,* p. 85. In 1925 the controversial Dr. T. T. Shields visited the Calgary Prophetic Bible Institute searching for support. In a letter from H. H. Bingham to McMaster's Chancelor Whidden dated October 13, 1925 (Whidden Papers, Canadian Baptist Archives, hereafter *CBA*), the former exaulted: "Personally, I do not think Dr. Shields after his arrival felt especially comfortable with Aberhart and the Prophetic Conference crowd."

21. John B. Irving, "The Social Credit Movement," *Canadian Journal of Psychology* 1 (1947): 18; see explanation of the famous Social Credit, A plus B theorem.

22. CBA, *Western Outlook,* March, 1908, p. 3. Many members of the United Farmers movement were influenced by liberal theology. Don Kennedy, M. P. for Peace River, had been a ministerial student at Brandon College. Active in Alberta politics were Henry Wise Wood, William Irving, and Percival Baker, all students of theology.

23. Elliott, *op. cit.,* pp. 150-7.

24. *Ibid.,* pp. iii and 148.

25. Thomas E. Flanagan, "Social Credit in Alberta: A Canadian 'Cargo Cult'?" *Archives de Sociologie des Religions* 34 (1972): 47.

26. Elliott, *op. cit.,* p. 154.

27. Irving, *op. cit.,* p. 19.

28. Letter, Aberhart to J. H. Coldwell, Feb. 2, 1933; cited in Elliott, *op. cit.,* p. 141.

29. *The Calgary Herald,* August 14, 1935, p. 4; August 16, 1935, p. 4.

30. *The Calgary Herald,* August 23, 1935, p. 4.

31. D. F. Shackleton, *Tommy Douglas* (Toronto: Macmillan and Stewart, 1975).

32. Lovick, *op. cit.,* pp. 70-77. For a discussion of "The New Politics and Ethnic Revolt: 1929-1938," see Norman Ward and Duff Spafford, eds., *Politics in Saskatchewan* (Don Mills, Ontario: Longmans, 1968), pp. 151-75.

33. "Premier Sees June Election," *The Cooperative Consumer,* April 14, 1944, p. 2. "Mr. Estey denounced the C.C.F. for 'preaching blue ruin' in Saskatchewan. He declared the C.C.F. denounced monopoly but sought to impose on Canada the greatest monopoly the world has known."

34. "New Government Takes Office in July; Premier-elect Outlines Policy," *The Cooperative Consumer,* June 23, 1944, p. 2.

35. L. D. Lovick, *Tommy Douglas Speaks*, p. 21.

36. *The Western Producer,* May 12, 1944, p. 2. Manning declared that "the present financial system 'of which Hon. J. L. Ilsley appears to be the champion,' is vicious, undemocratic and a menace to the future of the nation."

37. W. E. Mann, *Sect, Cult, and Church in Alberta* (Toronto: U. of Toronto Press, 1955); Owen A. Anderson, "The Alberta Social Credit Party, an Empirical Analysis of Membership Characteristics, Participation and Opinions" (unpublished Ph.D. thesis, University of Alberta, Edmonton, 1972).

38. "Wanted A Statesman," editorial, *The Western Producer,* August 17, 1944, p. 6.

39. Erling Jorstad, *The Politics of Doomsday* (Nashville: Abingdon Press, 1970).

10

World Relief, Development and Inter-Church Aid

R. Fred Bullen

A full documentation of Canadian Baptist responses to world needs, at home and abroad, is not available.[1] But many individuals and groups have given to various needs through many channels, and the record of giving *through the Baptist Federation of Canada* indicates that the interest and concern of our people has grown since the Federation came into being in 1943.

In the year 1978, $441,139.74 was given by our churches to which was added $272,455.08 from the Canadian International Development Agency, Alberta Government matching grants and interest, for a total of $860,924.06 contributed to relief and development. In spite of the fact that this represents only an average gift of slightly above $4 per member, the activities and achievements of the Relief and Development Committee can be viewed as an encouraging example of how the Baptist Federation of Canada (BFC) seeks to fulfill the objectives stated in its constitution.

The first meeting of the BFC council was convened in Saint John, New Brunswick, on December 7, 1944. Following a statement by Dr. Watson Kirkconnell, the council adopted a resolution on postwar immigration. It requested the government of Canada to appoint a royal commission to make a careful study of the number and type of immigrants for whom, under postwar conditions, this country could be expected to provide a satisfactory livelihood and who might be assimilated. It was further agreed to appoint a committee to make plans to appeal to Baptist churches for an offering on V-Day for European relief.

On November 23, 1945, Dr. W. C. Smalley reported that the appeal had been included in the Crusade for Christ fund with the goal of $400,000, one third of which would be applied to European relief — ten percent to be channeled through the Canadian Council of churches and ninety percent through the Baptist World Alliance.

On November 6, 1946, Dr. W. O. Lewis, secretary of the Baptist World Alliance, told the BFC council of his five-month tour through Europe where more than 500,000 people from Eastern Europe were in displaced persons camps in Germany. Among them were several thousand Baptists. He said: "They cannot stay where they are. UNRRA cannot provide for them. We should help them to emigrate." Dr. Kirkconnell concluded: "Canadian people have been deaf and blind to those unfortunate and innocent victims of communist tyranny, dying on the doorstep of the world."

A resolution was passed that stated:

> Whereas there are large numbers of refugees and displaced persons, and the resources of Canada are demonstrably able to support a larger population, and whereas Canada's immigration regulations are alien to Christian mercy and justice towards these victims . . . , we petition the Government of Canada to relax its immigration restrictions to permit the prompt and merciful admission of a fair share of refugees and displaced persons.

A special session of the BFC council was held on August 25, 1947, at which a resolution was adopted that expressed appreciation to the prime minister of Canada for steps taken to bring in worthy displaced persons from Europe. The government programme was designed to bring in 2500 to 3000 carefully selected persons per month from the refugee camps in central and western Europe. However, the minutes of the first BFC assembly held on August 23 to 26, 1947, do not include any report on the financial appeal for the Crusade for Christ nor the appeal for European relief.

On November 17, 1948, the council report on world fellowship stated that the three regional Baptist conventions had simultaneously and independently organized European relief funds to aid fellow Baptists in Britain, Europe and Asia. Unspecified numbers of parcels were sent to Britain and Germany. More than $111,000 in cash was contributed to European relief. The report concludes: "There is a growing belief that all our Baptist relief should come under the Federation. A unified appeal on a national basis would inspire a more sympathetic response and would foster fellowship amongst our churches."

Similar relief ministries were continued through 1949. Food parcels were shipped to Britain and Germany. In Western Canada $5,000 was raised to assist displaced persons to come to Canada. The Latvian refugee minister, the Rev. Rudolf Ekstein, arrived from Germany to secure more sponsors for displaced persons. A clothing depot was established at Trinity Baptist Church in Winnipeg, and in other churches to collect clothes and bedding for shipment to Europe. During this period, the BFC received substantial funds from the Baptist World Alliance to assist with the immigration work.

The summary report on contributions for overseas parcels and the rehabilitation fund, for the period from September, 1947, to June, 1950, indicated total gifts of $41,677 from the Maritimes, $180,264 from Ontario and Quebec, and $71,000 from the West.

At the council meeting on October 31, 1951, two appeals were received. The first was a request from the Baptist World Alliance Relief Committee for assistance to Baptist churches in Bremen and Berlin, Germany, with the task of rebuilding their destroyed sanctuaries. The second was a direct appeal from Jamaica for assistance to Baptists who lost eighty-two churches and hundreds of homes in the August hurricane.

At the council meeting on November 5 to 7, 1952, Dr. T. B. McDormand noted that $8,000 was required for a home for "hard core" displaced persons at Dusseldorf, Germany. There was also an appeal from Kenneth Norquist for financial aid to assist new refugees reaching West Germany.

In 1953 Canadian Baptists gave $5,000 toward the reconstruction of the Berlin and Bremen churches. Further help was provided for the victims of the hurricane in Jamaica — $6,000 together with several tons of used clothing. The floods in southern England and the Low Countries early in 1953, called for immediate help. Canadian Baptists contributed $16,000. Dr. William Sturhahn, secretary of the Immigration Service of the Baptist World Alliance Relief Committee, reported that 2900 refugees had been brought to Canada and that 42,000 more were waiting to be released from Berlin.

In 1955, the BFC made a further donation to the BWA immigration programme. Canada received almost 10,000 displaced persons through the BWA programme of aid to Baptist refugees. The financial statement for 1956 indicates an additional $5,300 contributed to the BWA programme, including a home for the aged in Munich.

In 1957, $2,500 was raised for Hungarian relief. A special committee coordinated the work of Baptist port chaplains at Halifax, Saint John, Quebec City and Montreal. These workers continued into the sixties until air travel became the main mode of transportation. Since that time, an inter-church committee, in which Baptists played an important role, has continued to serve newly-arriving immigrants.

In 1960 R. Fred Bullen became general secretary of the BFC. His first participation in the relief ministry was threefold. A world refugee offering was taken in our churches following Easter 1960. A quantity of canned meat valued at $37,500 was received free from the surplus stock held by the Federal Department of Agriculture. At a cost of about $4,000 the meat was shipped to Germany and Hong Kong for relief purposes. Finally, assistance was given to the Warsaw Baptist Church in Poland to complete its building and furnishings. Since that time, other churches in Eastern Europe have received assistance from our relief funds. The present policy is not to exceed ten percent of the annual receipts for such inter-church aid projects.

During the past twenty years there has been an increase in the number of civil disorders in many parts of the world. The flow of refugees has been growing steadily. In 1963 the BFC council passed a resolution that:

> In view of the fact that thousands of refugees are dying from exposure and starvation, our Baptist people be urged, as followers of Christ, to support generously the efforts of the Baptist World

Alliance and other reputable agencies in relieving this distress, whether in Hong Kong or elsewhere.

The BFC committee worked closely with the staff of the Canadian Baptist Overseas Mission Board (CBOMB), and especially Dr. John Keith, in ministering directly to refugees in areas served by CBOMB.

In 1964, the BFC introduced the theme "One Great Hour of Sharing." Church members were challenged to give one hour's wages to the relief fund. In 1966-67 the BFC began to make funds available for development projects overseas. It was recognized that mere "Band-Aid assistance" was insufficient. Tools, seeds, educational materials and even advisers had to be provided in many parts of the world.

In 1967, almost $150,000 was raised by Canadian Baptists, much of which was used for development projects. The minutes for 1970 indicate cooperation with the Mennonite Central Committee, both in relief and development projects, in the Middle East and Vietnam. The Red Cross and the Canadian Council of Churches served as our agents in Nigeria and other needy areas.

In 1969-70 the work of "Brother's Brother" directed by Dr. Robert Hingson became an extension of Canadian Baptist relief ministries. Dr. Hingson was presented with a cheque for $10,000 at the 1970 assembly. Through his use of a jet peace gun he was able to immunize millions of persons and was instrumental in eliminating smallpox in many parts of the world. During the current quintennium, the Baptist World Alliance is committed to raise one million dollars to assist Dr. Hingson in eradicating six childhood diseases in several countries. In 1970 Canadian Baptists provided $66,000 for Dr. Hingson's work.

In 1973 more than $233,000 was raised for relief and development. In the same year, almost $75,000 was designated for refugees from East Pakistan and over $90,000 for similar needs in Bangladesh. Dr. Bruce Neal, chairman of the World Relief and Sharing Committee, reminded the assembly in 1976 that Canadian Baptists had suddenly awakened to a world with its overpowering problems. The media played a leading role in developing our consciousness of world needs. But we are yet to learn what the increasing population of our world will mean to the depletion of our resources. We are beginning to recognize that everyone has a right to the essentials of life such as water, food, shelter and health care.

It would be impossible to summarize even the highlights of the ever-increasing involvement of the BFC in projects of relief and development during the recent years. A few examples must suffice. Late in 1977 a tidal wave and cyclone devastated the Andhra Pradesh region in India. In cooperation with the CBOMB, the Federation requested Dr. and Mrs. Orville Daniel to initiate the necessary emergency measures. Later, the Rev. and Mrs. Kenneth Knight and the Rev. and Mrs. Roger Cann went to India to supervise the erection of cyclone-proof buildings in fifteen villages, and to assist fishermen in the replenishment of their equipment. The rebuilding of homes, schools and churches was supervised by the Rev. Waldo Penner. The response of Canadian Baptists to the appeal for a quarter of a million dollars was most gratifying. Because of the acceptance of the projects by the Indian government, the government of Canada through CIDA contributed an additional $325,000 in 1977-78.

Other funds are being sent through the BWA and its affiliated conventions in more than one hundred countries. Cooperation with the Mennonite Central Committee and Church World Service has also been frequent and efficient.

There is always a great need in some countries for Christian literature and aids to worship. The BWA has assisted Baptists in the Soviet Union, Cuba and elsewhere with Bibles and hymnbooks. As one avenue of our fraternal aid, Canadian Baptists contributed $5,000 last year toward the shipment of 25,000 Bibles to Moscow, and $15,000 for the printing of a children's hymnbook in Hungary. Such projects are included in recognition that man does not live by bread alone and that in the restricted circumstances in many countries, literature constitutes one of the most urgent needs. It has also been the privilege of the BFC office to serve as a liaison for the BWA with our brethren in Cuba. In addition to personal discussions with government officials, we have been able to supply vehicles and other material assistance.

One of the great needs that all churches face at the present time is the necessity of educating and motivating our people to understand the needs of the world. The Western nations account for no more than 20 percent of the world's population yet they control 80 percent of the world's resources and 90 percent of the world's income. In order to inform and motivate Canadian Baptists, the BFC Relief and Development Committee prepares and sends to all churches a packet of information each January. In emergencies, special bulletins are mailed to churches. In partnership with CBOMB, the BFC provides an educational kit for relief and development.

The phrase "change of life-style" has become more than a cliché. It describes the only direction left for Christians who face *fast* changing conditions, and who must practice the *fasting* which God requires of His people (Isaiah 58:5-8). All Christians, especially in the Western world, have been uniquely equipped to participate in ministries of relief, development and fraternal aid. The love of Christ constrains us. The demands of righteousness and justice are upon us. It is not a question of "*can* we?" but "*will* we?"

10   *World Relief and Development, R. F. Bullen*

1. The paper reproduced here is the abbreviated text of an address delivered at the symposium banquet (October 15, 1979) under the title "What Kind of a Fast Does God Require?" The documentation for the reported data is available in the printed reports of the Council and Assemblies of the Baptist Federation of Canada, 1944-1979.

Part Three

Theological Trends

and Conflicts

11

The Modernist Impulse at McMaster University, 1887-1927

Clark H. Pinnock

McMaster University was founded in 1887, at the beginning of the tumultuous struggles between liberalism and fundamentalism in theology which were to disturb Baptist life in North America for at least half a century. The question was raised at regular intervals as to what extent the new university was part of the movement of modernist theology so influential at several Baptist institutions south of the border. The charge that the modernist impulse was indeed influential at McMaster and that this trend ought to be reversed was registered strongly in the 1920s and led to a division in Baptist ranks. As W. Gordon Carder puts it, "The result of this tragic conflict and schism of the 1920s is still very much in the bloodstream of Canadian Baptists."[1]

The question that concerns me in this paper is the extent to which the charge of modernism in the theological posture of the university was justified. I recognize that it is a subject of considerable delicacy at least for those who remained with the denomination and the school after the split in 1927. It was natural for them to defend the institution against its attackers by denying any truth to their accusations. McMaster of the Toronto years is often depicted therefore as conservative theologically, unfairly set upon by some ultra-conservative malcontents. Was that the situation, or was there more substance to the allegations than the McMaster loyalists like to admit?

The question is of more than academic interest for many Baptists. It is an ecumenical issue in that it lies at the heart of what caused a serious division among us which continues to the present. It is also a nagging problem in the life of the Baptist Convention in that the same sort of suspicion about the theological soundness of McMaster is still quite widespread among the churches. Whatever it is that has caused it over the decades is continuing to do its work. Perhaps by probing into the matter it will be possible to see the truth in a clearer light and gain some wisdom for Baptist life today.

The historical material on McMaster and its struggles during the Toronto years has been sifted by a number of capable scholars.[2]

I will not repeat all that they have discovered or pause to document each detail in the narrative when others have done it already. My purpose will be to uncover some fresh lines of evidence and offer an interpretation of the facts already established. I come to my subject sympathetic with the forces of classical theology in their struggle against the innovations brought in by the modernist impulse and am aware of the possible distorting effect of this standpoint upon my conclusions. I invite the reader to judge my work in that light, while asking him or her also to take account of the assumptions others make in investigating the same question.

The Tumultuous Conflict

The battle over theology at McMaster University was a local manifestation of a momentous collision that was occurring across the continent between two very different theological trajectories. It was a tumultuous period in the social and religious history of North America. Traditional evangelicalism was faced with serious challenges from many quarters at once — from changes in the sciences, in industrial society, and in biblical studies. Out of the ferment there arose a new theology which diverged considerably from traditional beliefs but hoped to be able to meet some of the challenges adequately. Its appearance on the scene was met with fierce resistance from entrenched conservative opinion. A battle was shaping up all across church life in North America, affecting Baptist circles in particular, between proponents of the older evangelical convictions and the advocates of theological reconstruction. It is important to view the struggle over McMaster in the context of this wider conflict.

The modernist impulse in theology could be characterised as a new hermeneutic.[3] There was a certain novelty about the way liberal theology went about interpreting the biblical message in the modern context. It was based upon a sort of double commitment: to the biblical faith on the one hand, and to the modern outlook on the other. The intention was to re-interpret the traditional belief structure in the light of the post-enlightenment understanding of reality. By doing so it was hoping to establish the relevance of the gospel on behalf of contemporary man. If only it could be shown that the Christian message was not tied to the outdated framework of the biblical writers it might be possible to make good sense out of their gospel for those nurtured in the context of Western modernity.[4]

Once we recognize what kind of theology the modernist impulse represents it is possible to understand the tremendous commotion that was caused by it. The liberal theologians themselves felt that they were only acting responsibly in the face of changing cultural conditions when they moved in the direction of a fresh re-interpretation of the gospel. They did not see their efforts at all in terms of any betrayal of the truth of God and were hurt when others leveled that very charge at them. At the same time, one must say, the theological method they were employing involved quite a clean break with the time-honoured assumption that the concepts of Christian revelation were normative categories whose truth was binding upon Christian thinkers. Conservative churchmen were therefore outraged by what appeared to be a revolution in theology which had the effect of a complete sell-out of the biblical message. When one considers the enormous difference in outlook between these two mentalities it is easy to understand why any struggle between them is not readily resolved, and why the debate often gets very bitter and unpleasant.

As for theological fundamentalism it is a militant response to religious liberalism, constructed out of the abundant materials supplied by the traditional confessions, including scholastic reformed theology ably propounded at Princeton Theological

Seminary before 1929, and notions forwarded out of the more recent millennial reading of the prophetic Scriptures developed in the last half of the nineteenth century. It has gained a bad reputation on account of factors related to its militancy, but should receive credit for recognizing the threat to classical belief that the modernist impulse actually posed. For it is the opinion of many who are not fundamentalists (e.g., Karl Barth) that without intending to do so theological liberalism accommodated the gospel to modern humanist culture in a way most harmful to the church. Although the fundamentalists were not generally well-educated and conversant with the scholarly issues being raised, they were able to sense a real danger being posed to the apostolic foundations of faith. It is in a way unfortunate that T. T. Shields, to get ahead of my story, did not keep his eyes more steadily upon the theological principles at stake in the controversy with McMaster, but instead allowed himself to be drawn into a struggle of personalities that ultimately defeated him as a force within the denomination. Had he done so, the truth issues involved might eventually have been discussed in the open and even resolved instead of being swept under the rug and hardly acknowledged.

Baptist groups in both Britain and America were substantially affected by liberalizing trends in modern theology of the nineteenth century. Perhaps because of their non-confessional basis and their respect for the freedom of individuals to interpret the Bible for themselves, Baptists were drawn into the controversies surrounding the new theology. The Northern Baptist Convention in particular was host to more than its share of liberal preachers and theologians, some of them expatriate Canadians, as Robert Handy's paper indicates. The University of Chicago, a Baptist school at the turn of the century, was a centre for modernist theology, as well as being a popular school for McMaster graduates wanting to do further studies.[5]

Another way to ask the question of this paper is to enquire after the degree of affinity in spirit and temper that existed between McMaster and its sister institutions in the United States. To do so will require us to take note of the connections and communications between them.

The struggle over McMaster took place in the wider context of a fierce debate over the very nature of the Christian message and mission. Opponents of the university placed it squarely on the modernist side of the debate. Was this a false charge, or had the school strayed from the conservative theological ideals of Senator McMaster?[6]

False Charge or Coverup?

The evidence for ascertaining truth in this matter is not plentiful, for reasons I shall remark upon later. The first fact to note is the presence of William Newton Clarke as professor of New Testament Interpretation at Toronto Baptist College from 1883 to 1887 just prior to the founding of McMaster University in 1887. The reason this is noteworthy is the fact that Clarke was the Schleiermacher of American theology. He embodied in his person the modernist impulse. His books were influential statements of the new liberal theology.[7] One of his most famous students was Harry Emerson Fosdick who expressed great indebtedness to him in his autobiography, *The Living of These Days*. To Clarke theology was rooted in the universal capacity for religion innate in everybody, out of which Christianity and all religions ultimately spring. The test of truth was more the Spirit at work in humanity than any infallible Bible. His influence was to continue at McMaster through such students as George B. Cross who taught there after doing graduate work at the University of Chicago, where he went to teach in 1909.

Clarke's presence at Toronto Baptist College at this early date certainly makes one ask for an explanation. How could the leading modernist theologian have taught there unless there was some sympathy with the directions his thought was taking? According to Clarke himself the college was well aware of where he stood theologically and not worried at all about it:

> After this third pastorate I spent a few years as teacher of New Testament in a Theological Seminary (Toronto Baptist College). Before I accepted the position I had a long talk with the president of the institution, in which I told him all about my point of view with regard to the Scriptures, and the various departures from the usual views in theology to which I had been led. I did not know but he would withdraw the invitation, as he had full opportunity to do; but he was not afraid of me, and I went to the new work . . .[8]

Later in his book, *Sixty Years with the Bible*, Clarke explains his custom of reconstructing the ideas conservative students held about the Bible when they came to him, and notes that they often would resist his efforts most earnestly, a rather good illustration of the messianic character of liberal theology.9

It would seem a modest conclusion to draw from this curious situation that the modernist impulse was not only present at McMaster University from the very first, but actually predated it. One shudders to think what Shields might have done with this fact had he known about it, and it makes one eager to know what Senator McMaster's mind was on the subject, if he was apprised of it. Were the other faculty comfortable with the liberalism of Clarke? From what we have been able to discover the modernist impulse was certainly welcome at McMaster from the very beginning.

The second incident to notice was the debate that took place in the first decade of the twentieth century over the views of Professor Isaac G. Matthews. Both he and his colleague George Cross were students of Clarke and graduates of the University of Chicago. After their termination at McMaster both went to teach at liberal Baptist schools in the United States; Matthews at Crozer and Cross at Chicago. Although the views of Cross were probably more deeply modernistic than those of Matthews, it was the views of the latter which came under direct scrutiny.10 The story has often been told how Elmore Harris, pastor at Walmer Road Baptist Church, made public objection to the negative critical theories about the Old Testament which Matthews was espousing in McMaster classes, and how these charges led to an investigation and then to an aquittal at the convention of 1910, the motion actually being seconded by Shields.

Elmore Harris was certainly a very conservative man, and it might be fair to say that his insinuations were uncalled for were it not for some other factors. For one thing the Toronto Star quoted Matthews to the effect that modernist views in theology were accepted at McMaster and not the cause of controversy there. Obviously an unguarded remark, but one that makes a person wonder what lay behind it.11 The influential thinking of George Cross must have been a part of it. And student reports that there was scarcely a lecture in which Matthews "did not suggest discrepancies, exaggerations, errors and contradictions in the Old Testament" at least confirm that the professor was introducing students to the latest in German critical introduction to the Scriptures.[12]

It is admittedly hard to reconstruct the precise spirit that prevailed at McMaster at this time and we ought not to extract too much from these bits of data. Nevertheless, it seems quite fair to conclude at least that the modernist directions initiated by Clarke twenty-five years earlier were being pursued by his students at McMaster in the later period, and that traditional Baptists were beginning to take note of it.[13] Since Harris usually gets pilloried for raising his voice in protest and rocking the denominational boat, I would like to accord him a little posthumous praise. It requires courage for a pastor to protest when he thinks the educated leadership is going astray theologically, and Harris was a courageous man. It may even be that he was right.

In the years following 1910 Matthews took pains not to abuse his prerogative as a teacher and to present controversial concepts more chastely.[14] In 1919 the debate flared up again, this time as a result of a remarkable editorial in *The Canadian Baptist* (October 2) which though unsigned may have been the work of Matthews who resigned from McMaster that year. It was entitled "The Inspiration and Authority of Scripture" and deserves an award for *faux pas* of the year. It assumed an aggressively liberal stance, expressing great admiration for British Baptists who presumably had ceased to resist the higher critical views on Scripture and were thus far advanced in theological maturity than many Canadian Baptists with their rather crude religious conceptions. The decision to set forth such views was tantamount to waving a red flag in front of a bull so far as traditional Baptists in Ontario were concerned. In the next issue Shields asked why the piece of journalism had not been run as a signed article representing the opinion of one known individual rather than in the form of a policy statement of the denominational paper — surely a very excellent question. The paper did not back down, however, but went on to print another editorial on October 23 citing A. H. Strong and his willingness to recognize certain imperfections in the biblical text.

In the end, of course, the Convention put an end to the impudence of *The Canadian Baptist* and ordered it to get back into line with the conservative theological stance of the churches. The motion passed with a large majority and Shields won a great victory that day. But we are concerned with the meaning of this incident as it concerns the presence of the modernist impulse in the university and the leadership of the denomination that enjoyed a close relationship. What it suggests to me is that the Convention had in its employ educated leaders who were determined to make room in the denomination for the modernist impulse. Their hands were tipped in this strategical blunder. Ordinarily they went about their work in a quieter, less obtrusive way, because of the conservative sentiments of the majority of the people. In this case they showed their colours, and were soundly rebuked, bloody but unbowed.

The next item to note is the granting of an honorary degree to William H. P. Faunce in 1923. Faunce was a prominent Baptist educator, president of Brown University, author of several books, and a missionary statesman. What could be controversial in honouring a fellow Baptist of such distinction? The answer to that question is clarified by citing two further facts about him. The books Faunce wrote place him squarely in the liberal camp theologically, and one of his causes was the spirited defense of Harry E. Fosdick in his controversies with the conservatives in the Northern Baptist Convention.[15] It seemed plain to Shields that the university was deliberately setting out to honour the man and his liberal views. Here again one might ask whether this was merely an act of administrative folly on McMaster's part or whether its significance lay deeper.[16] At the very least it showed how out of touch those who made the decision to give the degree were with the conservative tenor of the churches. But it also makes quite good sense to conjecture that these people who invited Faunce to come were seeking a way to express their basic sympathy with the modernist impulse as it was flourishing in a sister denomination. It would be a way of expressing their concerns, since they lacked the freedom to speak out boldly in the Canadian context. The Convention rebuked the university in 1924 for its lack of discretion in honouring Faunce and insisted that, in future, degrees not be awarded to those whose views were at variance with evangelical principles. It is difficult to avoid the conclusion that the university was at a very different place theologicaly than its constituency.

The last incident I wish to take account of is the coming of L. H. Marshall to McMaster in 1925. Prior to this time Shields had not enjoyed an opponent who could stand up to him in public debate. But Marshall, a refined and educated Englishman, was prepared to take him on, and the results of that collision were defeat for Shields and schism for the denomination.

The basic story has often been told. The university was satisfied about the doctrinal soundness of Marshall, and refused to open the matter again when Shields charged that he was a modernist. Shields then conducted a campaign in the pages of the *Gospel Witness* designed to oust the new professor. Marshall, however, defended himself in public addresses and condemned what he called the bigotry, fanaticism, and obscurantism of his opponents.[17] His appointment to the chair of practical theology was approved and Shields vowed to fight the issues to the end. Eventually it led to Shields leaving the Convention and forming his own group.

Our concern, however, is not with the details of this particular debate, but with the meaning of Marshall's appointment. Shields himself relied upon a couple of letters he received from W. M. Robertson of Liverpool that expressed concern over the alleged modernism of Marshall. Robertson does not seem to have had personal contact with the professor, so Shields' basis for his attacks appears slim.[18] Furthermore, Marshall did not cooperate with Shields by making any obviously liberal pronouncements and thus supporting his charges. It appeared that Marshall was basically sound as the university claimed and that Shields was being unreasonable in his demands. In the end he was drawn out, shamed, and defeated over it. That is about as far as it goes in the interpretations loyal to the university.

Toward the end of his career however, L. H. Marshall published two books that raise a question over his integrity in the battle with Shields. In one, *The Challenge of New Testament Ethics* (1948), for example, Marshall practices a hermeneutic of the liberal idealist type as epitomized in Adolf Harnack's work.[19] Orthodox Christology is downplayed and kingdom eschatology is lacking. Since this viewpoint was more prevalent in the earlier decades of the century than when Marshall published them, I do not think it is unfair to suggest that they represent the views he held when he was at McMaster. If they do, then Marshall was far less than candid when he assured the committee of the university on the matter of his own conservative theology. Or if he was candid with them, they were not candid with anyone else, because the impression was allowed to stand that there was no truth to Shields' allegations about Marshall when in fact there certainly was. In part, the defeat of Shields was achieved through deceit, either on Marshall's part or on the part of those who defended him.

I would not want to say anyone lied about the matter. The sources do not permit that degree of definiteness. But the effect of what was said was very close to being a lie, and I think it is not difficult to explain how it was rationalized. Liberal theologians take traditional beliefs to be ciphers fit for reinterpretation. They can always profess belief in them when the occasion requires it, because of this novel understanding about what profession implies. The moral fault then lies not so much in an act of deliberate falsehood, as in the willingness to let the impression be held that Shields was fanatical for even raising doubts about the orthodoxy of Marshall's theology, an impression that was to be used to get rid of him completely. It is obvious from a biographical note about Marshall that he did stand in the modernist camp and that he saw his role at McMaster one of championing the new theology against a confederacy of prejudice and suspicion.[20]

Shields went down to defeat then, not because his charges about modernism at McMaster had been refuted, but because the public was being deceived about Marshall and because Shields was too eager to do battle with modernism. He fell into the trap of his own militancy, coupled with a dense fog of untruth. As a result the denomination was split, and the truth issues which had been smoldering since the founding of the university were covered over again. The university now enjoyed more freedom than ever to pursue the path it chose without the critical voice of conservative theology to contend with.

Before venturing on to draw together our final conclusions, we need to look back over the evidence and reflect on the reason for it being so scanty. One of the curious things about this subject is that the conservative views are well known, but the evidence that would settle the question of where McMaster stood theologically is not plentiful. Some will suggest that the reason for this is the uncontroversial nature of McMaster's stance as a basically conservative school beset by ultra-conservatives. But this opinion will not stand the test of the evidence we have brought forward. I think the reason lies in the nature of the administration of school and denomination. Although there were public conventions in which ordinary people had a chance to express their views and make decisions, it seems as if the actual power behind what went on at McMaster was in the hands of a much smaller elite group that steered the university in a liberal direction and handled the objections when they surfaced as public relations problems.[21] It has always been fairly easy to do this. Higher education in North America abounds in illustrations of it. Academically-trained individuals have no difficulty expressing their ideas in ways that can slip past almost any objection voiced by the less educated. It was never very difficult for McMaster to defuse the criticisms sent its way. The troubling thing to me is the failure of the university to be open and candid about what was going on there theologically, and the failure of *The Canadian Baptist* to bring out the truth by means of creative investigative reporting. The impression one gets just because the leadership of the university and the denomination remained so secretive and uninformative on this issue is that the charges brought against the school were very nearly right.

Conclusions

I am not satisfied that the evidential picture needed to settle this question is as yet complete. The facts I have been able to uncover are significant and numerous, but leave a great deal unillumined. The main conclusion however seems fairly clear: the modernist impulse was present at McMaster from the first despite the efforts made to deny it. The conservative critics of the university were correct in the substance of their charges, even if not on target in each detail. That is a painful conclusion to come to for any evangelical member of the ongoing Baptist Convention. The feeling of loyalty stands in conflict with the pressure of truth.

In order to understand how it could be that the school would persist in a theological direction so obviously at variance with the expressed sentiments of the majority of Baptists we have to point to the "messianic" character of liberal theology. The modernist impulse is not the *only* theology which is so sure of the truth of its insights and learning that it feels a mandate to convert people to it whether they want it or not, but it *is* such a theology. The regular way it pursued its goal in North America was to gain control of educational institutions and inculcate the new learning in the eager minds of young students. A liberalizing trend can easily be set in motion by such an undercover operation providing the school can be controlled. Should the ethos of the denomination be somewhat conservative, it is obviously wise to work at this program as covertly as possible. Unfortunately in the McMaster case the strategy was often exposed by sharp sighted and vocal opponents who began to catch on to what was happening and took serious exception to it.

Had Shields not been led to defeat for the reasons outlined there were several courses of action open to him. He might well have been able, had Marshall's true colours been known, and his own militancy not worked to his undoing, to bring about a change in the university by democratic means. After all, on several occasions it was proven that Shields had the majority of Baptists with him. It is easy to imagine a situation where the ruling board of the university could have been reconstituted on explicitly evangelical lines and the modernist trends completely reversed. Or failing that, he could have moved to establish an alternative seminary for training ministers in the Convention, as happened several times in the Northern Baptist Convention. In the latter context, Eastern and Northern seminaries were set up in oppositon to the liberal schools, and have gone on to become the largest centres for the training of American Baptist pastors in the United States. The liberal schools like Crozer and Rochester have declined seriously and graduate few pastors for Baptist churches. The recent decision of the Convention to recognize other schools for the training of Baptist ministers in addition to McMaster represents a move in this direction.

A final question has not yet been raised directly. Supposing the modernist impulse was influential at McMaster from the beginning, why should exception be taken to that? Let us drop the pretense that surrounds this issue and ask directly why the presence of it should represent a serious problem. People seldom get to this question because they become stalled at the factual level of whether it was or wasn't there. As far as I am concerned, the factual issue is settled — a significant measure of the modernist impulse was present at the university from the first. But what of it? This more important question never seems to be discussed.

From the liberal standpoint it is perfectly obvious why the

modernist impulse ought to be present at McMaster. Liberal theology is a creative modern approach in the interpretation of the Word for today. Like other efforts to contextualize the gospel in the history of the church, religious liberalism is a noble effort to commend the biblical message to intelligent minds in the twentieth century. Of course it belongs at a first-rate institution such as McMaster strives to be. Coming at the issue from this angle, the conservative attacks on the university must seem very perverse indeed.

But when one looks at the same struggle from the standpoint of classical Christianity and takes note of the decision to demythologize and reinterpret the major theological categories along the lines of humanistic assumptions about the world, the modernist impulse can only appear to be the quintessence of all heresy. Christological error, let us say, affects one very important element of the biblical faith, but liberal theological method affects every aspect of it. The entire body of revealed truth seems to be subject to a process of relativizing and accommodation to the spirit of the times. Certainly the views of Arius, for example, ought to be studied and contrasted with the truth of Scripture and creed, but advocated in an evangelical school? Never.

McMaster was caught in the crossfire between two ideologies, two trajectories in theology that diverge at a very basic point. It may be too much to expect that a denomination made up of all kinds of people, many of them very independently-minded, would be able to process a disagreement of this enormity and fundamental character. It may be that a truce between them and an agreement to work side by side avoiding conflict is the best practical solution, although it hardly satisfies one's concern for truth.

In the last analysis what the conservatives wanted at McMaster was a truly evangelical school, preparing evangelical pastors for the pulpits of the churches. In part McMaster did this, but in part also there were influential elements determined to introduce the modernist impulse most Baptists did not want. Not only did they do this without any democratic warrant, they also tried to deny what they were doing when confronted with it. Their most vocal opponent was overcome in shady circumstances. It was not a glorious moment in the history of Canadian Baptists.

11 *The Modernist Impulse at McMaster University, C. H. Pinnock*

1. W. Gordon Carder, "Controversy in the Baptist Convention of Ontario and Quebec, 1908-1928," *Foundations* 16 (1973): 375.

2. In addition to Carder's article (note 1) there is Charles M. Johnston, *McMaster University. Volume One: The Toronto Years* (Toronto: University of Toronto Press, 1976); John D. E. Dozois, "Dr. T. T. Shields in the Stream of Fundamentalism" (B.D. thesis, McMaster Divinity College, 1963); and Walter E. Ellis, "Gilboa to Ichabod: Social and Religious Factors in the Fundamentalist-Modernist Schisms among Canadian Baptists, 1895-1934," *Foundations* 20 (1977): 109-126.

3. For the use of the term 'modernist impulse' see William R. Hutchison, *The Modernist Impulse in American Theology* (Cambridge, Mass.: Harvard University Press, 1976).

4. See David Tracy, *Blessed Rage for Order: The New Pluralism in Theology* (New York: The Seabury Press, 1975), chapters 1-3.

5. Charles M. Johnston, *op. cit,* p. 93. See also Robert T. Handy, "Influence of Canadians on Baptist Theological Education in the United States," *Foundations* 23 (1980).

6. The articles of faith belonging to the trust deed of the Toronto Baptist College are an epitome of traditional Baptist beliefs and give a good indication of the conservative direction Senator McMaster wanted the school to follow. See Johnston, *op. cit.,* p. 237.

7. See especially his *An Outline of Christian Theology* (New York: Scribner's, first edition 1894, 20th edition 1912).

8. *Sixty Years With the Bible* (New York: Scribner's, 1912), p. 155.

9. *Ibid.,* p. 212-213.

10. Charles M. Johnston, *op. cit.,* p. 96f.

11. H. H. Walsh, *The Christian Church in Canada* (Toronto: Ryerson, 1956), p. 318.

12. Johnston, *op. cit.,* p. 104.

13. Johnston's, Chapter 5, "Strife", is the best background reading to get a feeling for the tone at McMaster.

14. Johnston, *op. cit.,* p. 113.

15. William H. P. Faunce, *What Does Christianity Mean?* (Toronto: Revell, 1912). Harry E. Fosdick, *The Living of These Days* (New York: Harper, 1956), p. 160-183.

16. Johnston, *op. cit.,* p. 180.

17. Cited in Carder, *loc. cit.,* p. 364.

18. C. Allyn Russell, "T. T. Shields, Canadian Fundamentalist," *Ontario History* 70 (1978): 269.

19. London: Macmillan, 1948.

20. See the preface to L. H. Marshall, *Rivals of the Christian Faith* (London: Carey Kingsgate, 1954), pp. 10-13.

21. The paper cited by Ellis (footnote 2) goes into the social differences between the liberals and the conservatives in this struggle and should be extended in this direction.

12

Another Perspective on T. T. Shields and Fundamentalism

Leslie K. Tarr

The 1927 disruption in Canadian Baptist ranks has frequently been explained in terms of the abrasive character and tactics of fundamentalist leader, Dr. T. T. Shields. Citing his written broadsides, which could be vitriolic, critics have frequently avoided facing the real issues of whether there were grounds to his protests and the adequacy of the response of the Baptist establishment to his charges.

Even his most devoted admirers and supporters would have to concede that Shields could indeed be scathing in his statements. That virulent offensive made his opponents' task easier, for they could point to his charges and dismiss them because of their real or alleged "bitter spirit" or "negativism."

But the historian can hardly accept the contention that the rightness or wrongness of a position is determined by the gentility or abrasiveness of the person holding it. By that standard, a convenient answer to any indictment would be to vilify the messenger who, fortunately for those under siege, could be intemperate in tone and tactics.

Equally unsatisfactory and hardly deserving comment is the oft-repeated, unsubstantiated conjecture that Shields had not received an expected call to Spurgeon's Tabernacle and that he, therefore, vented his spleen on the Canadian convention.

What about the serious charges made by T. T. Shields? What about the response of McMaster and the Baptist establishment to his charges? Those two issues are more crucial than the question of Dr. Shields' temperamental traits.

It seems necessary to survey several denominational conventions at which uneasiness surfaced over McMaster's alleged drift. Although that terrain has been well-trodden, I propose to look it over again with special focus on the Baptist establishment's reponse to Shields and his charges. The question of his temperament and that of the justice of his allegations have been treated by others.

Following an examination of the establishment's response to Shields' charges, I propose to note several important respects in which Shields did not conform to the conventional conception of a fundamentalist.

The 1910 Convention

The 1910 convention heard charges that Dr. I. G. Matthews, professor of Hebrew at McMaster, held views that were at variance with the university's evangelical doctrinal stance. Dr. Elmore Harris, founder of Walmer Road Baptist Church and of Toronto Bible College (now Ontario Bible College), was the chief critic of Matthews. Prior to the convention, he had stated his concern in the public press that "the teaching of Professor Matthews was disturbing and destructive of the historicity, truthfulness, and integrity of the Word of God."[1] In that lengthy article, he quoted stenographic notes of lectures delivered by Matthews.

The convention heard the charges and considered them. A compromise resolution was proposed by Dr. John McNeill of Walmer Road Church and seconded by the Rev. T. T. Shields, who that year had become pastor of Jarvis Street Church. The resolution did not deal specifically with Harris's charges, but called on the university to ensure that its teaching be kept in harmony with the Bible.

Shields was later to contend that he had been naive in seconding the resolution. ". . . as a polemicist, I was inexperienced, and therefore too naive, and too easily convinced of the sincerity of all opponents.[2]

The 1919 Convention

Dr. Matthews resigned from the McMaster faculty in the spring of 1919. In May of that year, Shields wrote to the chancellor:

> I am bound to confess that in no other act of my public ministry have I found it so difficult to keep pace with my own conscience, as in refraining from protest against a situation which the resolution I supported was intended, as I supposed, conveniently to remedy, but to the continuance of which situation my own action had rendered me an unwilling accessory.[3]

For the first nine years of his pastorate at Jarvis Street, he contended, he had not been critical of McMaster — although there is evidence that he was uneasy over Matthews' influence.

With the appointment in 1919 of a British evangelical, H. S. Curr, it seemed that harmony was ahead for McMaster and the convention. An editorial in *The Canadian Baptist* of October 2 of that year was to disturb that tranquility. The editorial, "Inspiration and Authority of Scripture," was a criticism of the traditional evangelical view of scriptural inspiration and a call for a more liberal approach by Canadian Baptists. Appearing three weeks prior to the 1919 convention, which was to be held in Ottawa, the editorial roused the Jarvis Street pastor to action. He fired off a letter to the editor of the denominational paper, stating: "I am resolved to avail myself of the first opportunity of testing the attitude of the Denomination toward the position taken in your article."[4]

At the convention, Shields proposed a resolution which expressed the convention's disapproval of the editorial as contrary to the doctrinal position of the Baptist Convention of Ontario and Quebec. The convention overwhelmingly passed the resolution and in the process rejected an amendment which, among other things, deplored controversy.

The 1924 Convention

McMaster University, in 1923, had conferred an honorary doctoral degree on Dr. W. H. P. Faunce, president of Brown University, the pioneer Baptist college in North America. Shields and others objected to the action which, they contended, put McMaster's approval on an outspoken liberal and a pronounced critic of evangelical faith. Through the pages of the *Gospel Witness,* which Shields had established in 1922, the Jarvis Street pastor registered his criticism.

The 1924 convention, held in London, was dominated by that issue. When it became evident that the majority supported Shields, a resolution was passed which stated:

> . . . without implying any reflection upon the Senate, this Convention relies upon the Senate to exercise care that honorary degrees are not conferred upon religious leaders whose theological views are known to be out of harmony with the cardinal principles of evangelical Christianity.[5]

The resolution was moved by Shields and seconded by the chancellor of McMaster.

Eight months prior to the convention, however, the university's board of governors, at a meeting on January 14, had issued a statement, denouncing "the conduct and methods of Dr. Shields."[6]

Again, the establishment's response was to condemn the messenger without answering his charges. That response and the convention's action indicate the establishment's failure to sense the concern that was present in the ranks.

Following the 1924 convention, Shields seemed to relent in his criticism of the university. He commented: "Since that Convention we have felt under obligations to assume that the University would stand uncompromisingly for the fundamentals of the faith."[7]

Within months of his writing that sanguine statement, a controversy was to erupt which tore asunder Baptist ranks. The controversy centered around the university. In the summer of 1925, the board of governors (of which Shields had been a member since 1920) announced the appointment of the Rev. L. H. Marshall to the chair of Practical Theology. Shields and others had received word from England which charged that Marshall, a British Baptist, was a liberal. Shields did not press the allegation, but he strenuously contended that the situation merited further scrutiny and satisfaction.

Shields, who was in California at the time of the board

meeting that was to ratify the appointment, wired an appeal to delay the appointment until Marshall had the opportunity to respond to charges.

Later he appealed in a written submission to the senate meeting:

> My only desire is to safeguard the denomination against the possibility of admitting to the teaching staff of the University one whose views are in variance with the things commonly believed among us; and in order that there be no necessity for any public agitation on the subject, I respectfully ask the Senate to take such steps as will obviate the possibility of a mistake being made in this matter. It would seem to me to be a reasonable suggestion either that Mr. Marshall should come before the Senate, and that permission should be given to all members to question him touching the subjects represented by these letters; or otherwise, that a committee of the Senate should be appointed to interview Mr. Marshall with the same end in view.
>
> In the event of this report of Mr. Marshall's position being proved without foundation, and if from his own lips we learn that he is true to the faith once delivered, it will be my pleasure to do everything in my power to make his ministry in this University a success.[8]

He told the senate meeting:

> . . . I would remind the Senate that we are in a position where this University needs above all other things not only to command the confidence of the denomination, but so to shape its course as to make it abundantly evident that it deserves such confidence. I have said nothing about bringing this matter to the convention as a matter of fact . . .[9]

That plea strikes me, from this vantage point of 55 years, as one that, in the light of the 1919 and the 1924 convention declarations, should have struck a responsive chord in those who had the interests of the denomination at heart.

The senate's response was verbalized by the dean of theology, Dr. Farmer:

> I would like to ask whether the right thing for us would not be now under the present circumstances to wait and let Mr. Marshall do his work here and see whether he does do it right. If he gives

occasion during the course of a year for objection to his teaching or work, it will be time enough to bring up the difficulty. It seems to me the right thing is to go ahead believing he is in harmony with our position.[10]

The often repeated claim that Shields brought Baptist quarrels to the front pages of newspapers overlooks the fact that he pleaded repeatedly *before* Marshall was appointed, that the appointment be delayed until the senate and Marshall's critics posed the criticism to Marshall. Shields correctly observed:

> . . . if Mr. Marshall has been here for a year . . . when we discuss this matter a year hence, it is a personal matter. I do not know Mr. Marshall at all; I know nothing but what I have read in these letters and in *The (Canadian) Baptist*. But is seems to me it would be much easier to deal with the question before he begins than a year hence.[11]

Following Marshall's appointment, the controversy raged in the public and religious press. On both sides, inflammatory language and personal attacks were mounted and highly publicized by the secular press.

The 1926 convention passed a resolution that called on Shields to resign from McMaster's board of governors and notified Jarvis Street Baptist Church that he would not be an acceptable delegate to future conventions.

The 1927 Convention

The 1927 convention, held in Toronto, read out of its ranks Jarvis Street Church and other congregations declared to be out of harmony with the convention's programme.

• • • • •

The above cursory summary and comment lead this observer to several conclusions:

1) The Baptist establishment's response to Shields was to ignore or deal superficially with his charges and label him as a troublemaker.

Even if Shields was abrasive and provocative, does that in itself invalidate his accusations? His closest friends would have to acknowledge that he could be overbearing. That trait would have to be considered in trying to understand the provocative atmosphere in which his opponents had to respond to his charges and *why* they may have reacted as they did. But the rightness or wrongness of his accusations and of their response cannot hinge on that side issue. The persistent attempt to dismiss the disruption of 1927 as the outcome of one man's bad manners must be rejected on historical and logical grounds.

The pattern of sweeping his accusations aside with resolutions deploring controversy or rebuking his tactics emerged at the 1919 convention and was repeated by the university senate prior to the 1924 convention. In both instances, *when the convention was given the opportunity to vote on the issue and not the personality,* the response was resounding support for Shields.

Only when the establishment succeeded in focusing on something apart from the issue — Shields' abrasive manner and public exposure — did it succeed in getting a vote against him. Whenever the vote was on the issue (or what he contended was the issue), however, he was supported by the convention and, in this observer's judgment, by the grassroots of the Canadian Baptist constituency.

2) The Baptist establishment seemed to display an insensitivity toward expressed concern of a significant portion — if not the majority — of its constituency.

After the furor and implied rebuff at the 1924 convention (which dealt with the Faunce episode), one would expect that the university's leadership would have exercised more care in appointing a new professor. Rather there appears to have been an insistence on pushing through the appointment.

The Marshall affair was finally thrust on the convention floor and into newspaper headlines, and Shields was blamed for the whole incident. Overlooked is the fact that *prior* to the public pamphlet warfare, he had pleaded that:

> . . . in order that there be no need for any public agitation on the subject, I respectfully ask the Senate to take such steps as will obviate the possibility that a mistake be made in this matter.[12]

Was his suggestion unreasonable that Marshall appear for interview before the whole senate or a representative committee?

If that had been done, those future headlines might have been avoided.

Even before the Marshall appointment, Shields was calling for the university's responsiveness to the constituency's concern:

> Prevention is better than cure! When once a professor has been appointed, if his position is discovered to be unsound, it is impossible to raise opposition to his teachings without introducing personal considerations. In this article we are not discussing unsound professors but vacant chairs, and dealing with principles in the abstract. It is to avoid the necessity of holding discussions involving persons this article has been written. We respectfully suggest to the Senate and to the Board of Governors that the utmost care should be exercised when considering men to fill the vacancies referred to, to see that they are in cordial agreement with the great doctrines of evangelical Christianity.[13]

3) Shields was not alone in his contention that Marshall was a liberal.

Dr. C. J. Holman, prominent Toronto Baptist lawyer and an executor of the McMaster estate, expressed his concern in a letter to *The Canadian Baptist*.[14]

T. S. Campbell, professor of Greek at McMaster, faculty member for thirty-six years, and a colleague of Marshall, wrote to the same magazine:

> I am convinced too, that Professor L. H. Marshall, whose attractive personality all recognize, is a supporter of modernism. His sermons and personal talks, he has given to the press and others, clearly show that he is a modernist. His appointment must, therefore, be regarded as a decided gain for modernism.[15]

Resolutions from individual congregations and associations expressed concern. Such charges neither prove nor disprove the contention that Marshall was a modernist, but they clearly indicate that Shields was not alone in his conviction.

4) McMaster's defence of Marshall's orthodoxy was hardly conclusive reassurance to anyone in light of the university's

record of defending pronounced liberals even after their liberalism had been demonstrated conclusively.

As late as December, 1924, Dr. McLay, dean of arts, had written of Dr. Cross and Dr. Matthews, two former McMaster professors who had been criticized:

> Dr. Cross, profound thinker, teacher who trained his students to think for themselves, and sincere Christian who exemplified in his life the spirit of his Master, is Professor of Systematic Theology at Rochester. Dr. Matthews, one of our own graduates in Arts and Theology, who became the storm centre of theological controversy, but who, in my opinion, was misjudged, is expounding the Old Testament at Crozier. The churches heard him gladly when he preached to them, for his words were winged with comprehensive knowledge of the Bible, with veneration for its writers as prophets inspired of God, and with unswerving conviction of the moral and spiritual value of their message.[16]

The glowing assessment of Dr. Cross was not shared by Dr. Augustus H. Strong of Rochester. Concerning the appointment of Cross to that school, he wrote:

> It was the entrance of an agnostic, skeptical, and anti-Christian element into its teaching, the results of which will only be evil.[17]

Was it reasonable to ask that Shields and others simply accept assurances that McMaster, after all, knew what was best?

5) Assuming, for the sake of argument, that Marshall was not a liberal, was the appointment of a liberal-in-embryo warranted in the light of the denomination's pronouncements?

Shields himself recognized that there were degrees of liberalism or modernism. He bluntly wrote:

> Of course there are degrees of Modernism, as there are stages in the development of leprosy or any other fatal malady; but the end is always the same.[18]

But the appointment at that sensitive moment of one who, if he was not a confirmed liberal, was certainly not a convincing evangelical and who could be as provocative as Shields, did not alleviate fears among the university's critics.

No reasonable person could expect that the university should have made its destiny subject to the whims of one man who was its critic. To place that interpretation on Shields' crusade and his objections to Marshall, however, is to fail to recognize the ground, depth, and reality of his concern and that of others who were aware of a modernist triumphalism across America.

Three key elements in that controversy appear to have been: First, Dr. Shield's charges that McMaster was drifting from its well-defined evangelical moorings; second, the refusal by the university administration and the denominational establishment to answer his charges and their counter-charge that the problem was in Shield's abrasive conduct; and third, the insensitivity of the university and denominational establishment to the real concerns of its grassroots constituency.

From my perspective, I conclude that Shields was justified in his charges, that his abrasive manner provided a convenient whipping boy for the besieged establishment, and that the establishment, by its persistent insensitivity and refusal to answer his charges, provided adequate justification for his recourse to a more widely-publicized protest.

T. T. Shields as a "Fundamentalist"

The current resurgence of a "neo-fundamentalism" has made the "fundamentalist" label distasteful to many people who would, under normal circumstances, be properly described by that term. However, to many — including otherwise well-informed observers of the contemporary religious scene — the current aberrations and excesses associated with a militant neo-fundamentalism are attributed to anyone who voices an objection to humanistic and liberal trends in the church.

T. T. Shields declared himself to be, and was, a fundamentalist. That statement, however, is apt to raise a stereotype in the minds of many today — a stereotype which, in many regards, could not justly be applied to him.

The Modernist-Fundamentalist Controversy

Shorn of excessive statements on both sides, the modernist-fundamentalist controversy that reached its climax in the decade of the twenties, was a definite confrontation between two differing viewpoints.

The liberal *Christian Century* sensed that great divide and, from its perspective, bluntly stated:

> The differences between Fundamentalism and modernism are not mere surface differences which can be amiably waved aside or disregarded, but they are foundation differences, amounting in their radical dissimilarity almost to the differences between two distinct religions . . . Two world-views, two moral ideals, two sets of personal attitudes have clashed, and it is a case of ostrich-like intelligence blindly to deny and evade the searching and serious character of the issue. Christianity, according to fundamentalism, is one religion. Christianity, according to Modernism, is another religion . . . Christianity is hardly likely to last much longer half-fundamentalist and half-modernist. It is not merely the aggressiveness of fundamentalism that is forcing a choice, it is the inherent nature of the issue itself.[19]

Whether or not one concurs with that analysis, it is evident that on both sides, the confrontation was conceived in those stark terms. Armchair theorists today may wonder at that perception, but, in the context of that era, the issues were viewed in that light.

Men such as J. Gresham Machen, recognized the either/or nature of the issue:

> Do you suppose, gentlemen, that I don't detect faults in many popular defenders of supernatural Christianity? Do you suppose that I do not regret my being called by a term that I greatly dislike, a "Fundamentalist"? Most certainly I do. But in the presence of a great common foe, I have little time to be attacking my brethren who stand with me in defense of the Word of God. I must continue to support an unpopular cause.[20]

Shields was in the thick of the swirling controversy of that time. In that situation, he also unhesitatingly aligned himself with the fundamentalist forces — although, in many regards, he rejected and denounced excesses (or, to use his terms, "vagaries") of the movement. Like Machen, he concluded, however, that in an hour of crisis a choice must be made.

In fairness to Dr. Shields, then, it should be noted that, in certain important areas, he stood apart from major aspects of American fundamentalism. Understanding clearly that he was a confessed fundamentalist, we should note some of those areas of difference.

Eschatology

Many writers have equated extreme millenarian views — including dispensationalism — with fundamentalism. If that equation were accurate, neither Shields nor Machen would qualify as bona fide fundamentalists. Indeed Shields could be as vitriolic in his denunciation of "Scofieldism" as he was in his denunciation of modernism.

In spite of the scorn of other fundamentalists, he introduced, through the *Gospel Witness,* such authors as Philip Mauro to evangelicals everywhere. A careful study would indicate, I believe, that Shields held a modified amillennial view — devoid of the sensational themes of a secret rapture, a restored temple, and literal end-time battles between fleshly armies.

Excesses of Evangelism

Critics of evangelicalism and fundamentalism frequently cite the Elmer Gantry-type excesses of the movement. No critic was as scathing as Shields who denounced charlatanism, flamboyance, exaggerations, and superficial "believism." Indeed, one could more readily make a case that the weight of his sentiments was against mass evangelism of most kinds.

Never have I heard more incisive denunciations of evangelistic head-counting than I heard from Shields. Over the space of twenty-five years, I can fairly hear his solemn cautions against the offensive exaggerations ("economical with the truth" is the phrase I recall) of those in the fundamentalist camp.

Sense of Worship

"Fundamentalist clap-trap" was odious to Shields. Anyone who attended the regular services at Jarvis Street had to be impressed with the sense of worship. Some would contend that it verged on formalism. A generation of students at Toronto Baptist Seminary (which he had founded in 1927) was reminded again and again that a service of worship should be worship. The great hymns of praise and the Psalms were essential, he contended, and he wedded those with the best of gospel songs.

A visitor to Jarvis Street could not soon forget a baptismal service there. The believer who was baptized by Shields sensed, in the dignity of the services, something of the electrifying symbolism of the act.

Expository Preaching

Topical preaching has characterized much of fundamentalism. Shields, however, stressed and preached expository sermons.

W. A. Cameron of Yorkminster Baptist Chruch is reported by a convention minister to have stated that the best biblical preaching to be heard anywhere in the world was to be heard in Jarvis Street when, Cameron added, Shields stuck to biblical preaching and steered clear of polemics. Dr. John R. Mott, great missionary statesman and a vice president of the World Council of Churches, wrote to Shields in the fifties to express appreciation for the sermons Mott read regularly in the *Gospel Witness*.

A professor at Wycliffe College told me that the Anglican college routinely recommended that students go to hear Shields preach in order to sharpen their homiletical skills. Ralph G. Turnbull, in *A History of Preaching*, put that pulpit ministry in perspective:

> Although remembered for his controversial life, Shields was an excellent preacher with the pastor's heart and concern. A gifted speaker, a forceful personality, a decisive expositor, he preached sermons of substance. The Bible to him was the Word of God . . . His mastery of the English tongue gave him a skill and thrust above many in his day. So clear was his thought and expression that the sermons when stenographically reported needed little editing. . . .
>
> Thoroughly Biblical, clearly theological, simply illustrated, and practically presented — this was Shields in his day of influence. No name was better known throughout all Canada by friend and foe alike. Men might disagree with his theology, but no one denied his natural and spiritual gifts as a powerful preacher. He stands as the exponent of evangelical truth in a period of theological and religious controversy.[21]

The public generally, however, has overlooked the week-by-week, year-in and year-out pulpit menu that characterized Jarvis Street for forty-four years and judged the pastor solely on the grounds of his well-publicizied crusades. That is understandable, but it hardly does justice to his full-orbed ministry.

A Personal Assessment

It must be admitted that, with the passage of years, Shields did become more embroiled in disputes with even close associates. In 1948, for instance, he fired W. Gordon Brown, one of his 1927 allies in the dispute with McMaster. Brown had been dean of Toronto Baptist Seminary, the school founded in 1927 and operated by Jarvis Street Baptist Church.

Brown's firing precipitated a rupture in the Union of Regular Baptist Churches of Ontario and Quebec which Shields had led in 1927 after his ouster from the Baptist Convention of Ontario and Quebec. When the Union of Regular Baptist Churches of Ontario and Quebec joined the Fellowship of Independent Baptist Churches of Canada to form the Fellowship of Evangelical Baptist Churches in Canada in 1953, Shields was further isolated. In his last years, his one alliance seemed to be with the International Council of Christian Churches, headed by Carl McIntire.

Critics could suggest that the isolation was the logical outcome in the life of the man who led fundamentalists in the 1927 dispute. They might further see that isolation as demonstration of the validity of the contention that his abrasive manner and divisiveness were sole explanations for the furor that surrounded the Marshall episode. I dissent from that view.

The record of his many conflicts with colleagues is depressing reading for anyone concerned for the evanglical Baptist cause in Canada. But is it not possible that the experience of 1927, the refusal of the establishment to deal seriously with his charges, and the expulsion from the larger Baptist body made him more isolationist, distrustful of others, and wary of inter-church involvements?

The experience of 1927 made him more committed than ever to the fundamentalist posture. Thus, in 1952, three years before his death, he delivered an address to large gatherings in cities across Canada on the subject, "What Makes Me Increasingly a Fighting Fundamentalist."

Like Machen, he was aware of the shortcomings of fundamentalism, but he embraced it in what he conceived to be a life and death confrontation. He could have concurred heartily with Machen when he stated:

> . . . if the disjunction is between "Fundamentalism" and "Modernism", then I am willing to call myself a Fundamentalist of the most pronounced type.[22]

Finally, half a century after the turbulence of 1927, Canadian Baptists still face the question: Did Shields' contention do irreparable damage to the Baptist witness in Ontario and Quebec? Certainly the rupture of that year cut into the ranks of the Baptist Convention of Ontario and Quebec. Also, until this day, the relations between the Fellowship of Evangelical Baptist Churches in Canada and the constituent bodies in the Baptist Federation of Canada are not intimate, although on a personal level, individual pastors and congregations enjoy fellowship. Doubtless the rupture casts its long shadow to this hour.

I think, however, that Shields' protests of that day and the existence today outside the convention of another vigorous, growing Baptist testimony have influenced the evangelical witness within the convention. That observation is admittedly partisan, but I am persuaded that the absence of a protest in 1927 would have diluted the Baptist testimony in Ontario and Quebec.

This symposium, at which we talk across a table rather than across a chasm, is a hopeful development. In an atmosphere of unchallenged assumptions and caricatures, truth is the victim.

Many will dissent with this interpretation of the leader of the denomination's fundamentalist party. My hope, however, is that it will make a contribution to redress an imbalance in the historical perception and depiction of T. T. Shields and to recognize his legitimate place in the Canadian Baptist story.

12   Another Perspective on T. T. Shields, L. K. Tarr

1. "Dr. Harris on the McMaster Case," *The Toronto Daily Star,* November 20, 1909.

2. Leslie K. Tarr, *Shields of Canada* (Grand Rapids: Baker Book House, 1967), p. 64.

3. *Ibid.,* p. 64.

4. *Ibid.,* p. 67.

5. *The Gospel Witness,* November 6, 1924.

6. *The Canadian Baptist,* January 17, 1924.

7. T. T. Shields, *The Gospel Witness,* April 23, 1925.

8. T. T. Shields, *The Gospel Witness,* October 15, 1925, p. 15.

9. T. T. Shields, *The Gospel Witness,* October 29, 1925, p. 11.

10. J. H. Farmer, *The Gospel Witness,* October 29, 1925, p. 11.

11. T. T. Shields, *The Gospel Witness,* October 29, 1925, p. 12.

12. T. T. Shields, *The Gospel Witness,* October 15, 1925, p. 15.

13. T. T. Shields, *The Gospel Witness,* April 23, 1925, pp. 13-14.

14. *The Canadian Baptist,* March 11, 1926 (letter to the editor).

15. *The Canadian Baptist,* March 18, 1926 (letter to the editor).

16. *McMaster Graduate,* December 1924.

17. Augustus H. Strong (unpublished biography); quoted in Ernest Gordon, *Leaven of the Sadducees* (Chicago: Bible Institute Colportage Association, 1926; reprinted by the Church League of America, Wheaton, Ill., 1926).

18. *The Gospel Witness,* May 12, 1927, p. 8.

19. *Christian Century;* quoted in Ned B. Stonehouse, *J. Gresham Machen: A Biographical Memoir* (Grand Rapids: Eerdmans, 1954), p. 366.

20. *Ibid.,* p. 337.

21. Ralph G. Turnbull, *A History of Preaching,* Vol. 3 (Grand Rapids: Baker Book House, 1974), pp. 329-330.

22. Stonehouse, *op. cit.,* p. 428.

13

Baptist Leadership:
Autocratic or Democratic?

John B. Richards

Our title is deliberately intended to be somewhat provocative. It is not meant to imply that only two categories are possible. The terms "autocracy" (rule of the one) and "democracy" (rule of the people) are both capable of various interpretations, and many varieties of organizational structure are possible in the spectrum between these two extremes.

Our topic can be understood in at least two different ways. It can be approached as an investigation into Baptist leadership as it now exists in reality, and as it has been in the past. It can also be interpreted as referring to the Baptist idea of what church leadership should be. I plan to explore briefly both aspects of the subject.

One of the distinctive characteristics of Baptists is their view of the Church. It is surely a truism that Baptists, at least in recent times, describe their polity as "democratic" and the local church as a "democracy." The famous Baptist theologian, Augustus Hopkins Strong, upholds the concept of "democratic and congregational"[1] church government. Stuart Ivison and Fred Rosser identify the "two most important characteristics" of Baptists as "evangelicalism and spiritual democracy."[2]

Today, in Baptist circles and in our society, "democracy" is a common and "good' word. The same cannot be said for "autocracy." Among Baptists, as among Canadians in general, autocracy stands condemned. Baptist writers tend to avoid the very word, even when describing situations which are obviously "autocratic," and offer instead rather unconvincing verbal substitutes.

Characteristically, the word "autocracy" attaches itself to leadership. "Democracy," on the other hand, attaches itself to the body or group. Baptists tend to describe the church, rather than the pastor, as democratic. But every group has some leadership structure. No less can be said of a Baptist institution. Democracy demands democratic leadership. Whatever democracy is, there can surely be no democracy without such leadership.

What then is the nature of this democracy of which we speak? In our use of the term we tend to operate upon the unwarranted assumption that the word is quite unambiguous, when, in fact, the term is open to various interpretations. We should remember that the word "democracy" does not occur in the New Testament. We have borrowed the word from secular sources and need to remind ourselves that the secular world is by no means clear on the question of how democracy should function in practice.

Ancient Athenian democracy, the source of our term, was direct and participatory. Every male citizen was expected to have a part in the *ekklesia* or assembly. Leadership roles were widely distributed. It must be observed, however, that participation was restricted to males only, and that slaves, who comprised the majority of the population, had absolutely no place in the Athenian system. Modern democrats consider the lack of universal suffrage to be the greatest weakness of Greek democracy. Ancient critics, including Plato and Aristotle, questioned the wisdom of the populace as compared to an educated elite and argued that the people could be easily swayed by the oratory of demagogues. It must be admitted that Greek demagogues were astute in doing this very thing, without all the marvels of modern mass media.

In contrast to the Greek model, modern Western democracy is representative and indirect, while the right to vote is extended to the major portion of the adult population, including women. Modern Baptists tend to understand the word "democracy" in terms of the political structures we have, but, when we set up principles for the practice of democracy in our churches, we tend to think in terms of direct participation. The net result is a good deal of confusion and great variation in the way that individual Baptist churches actually function.

One should note that Presbyterians have also described their church polity as "democratic," but, when they use the term, the word is clearly understood to mean representative democracy. Both in theory and in practice Presbyterianism more closely resembles modern political democracy than does our Baptist polity. Baptist democracy is more like the ancient Greek pattern, not simply because the word *ekklesia* is used in the New Testament to describe the church, but because Baptists place great emphasis on the local *ekklesia* and are committed to congregational polity (as contrasted with episcopacy and presbyterianism).

These observations should lead us to be more cautiously perceptive regarding the claims we make with respect to the contribution of Baptists to the development of political democracy. Modern democracy is the end product of many influences. Some years ago Gregory Vlastos, in his provocative little book, *Christian Faith and Democracy*, saw the seeds of democracy in the Old Testament, with its concept of the essential dignity of every man.[3] More recently, John C. Bennett, having observed that the Christian faith has been historically linked to most of the types of political structure,[4] has made these observations:

> Anglo-Saxon democracy owes most to the sectarian tradition which flowered in the seventeenth century and which was the seed-bed of many influences favoring human rights . . . . The extraordinary debates in Cromwell's army expressed most of the convictions on which democratic institutions are based with elemental power behind which we see both a very human struggle for justice and freedom and a devout religious faith. Reinhold Niebuhr points out that while the French Revolution is usually given credit for shattering the "mold of an organic aristocratic civilization," the Cromwellian revolution, more than a century earlier, was the source of the impulses and convictions of democracy in a much wiser form than the French "abstract liberalism." He suggests that the apparent failure of the Cromwellian revolution because of the restoration of the Stuarts has obscured the real continuity between the influence of that revolution and later British democratic achievements . . . .

Archbishop William Temple pays a very significant tribute to the sectarian source of democracy in England when he says that the English people learned democracy in the "dissenting congregations."[5]

Baptists took part in the army debates mentioned above and Baptists were, of course, numbered among the "dissenting congregations." It was typical of the early English Baptists, however, that they did not use the word "democracy" (which was not in common use at the time) nor did they use any equivalent term to describe their concept of church government. The initial preoccupation of English Baptists was the struggle for liberty of conscience and freedom of worship. They were concerned with establishing independence from state control and autonomy of the local churches. They had no immediate concern for precise structure within the local Baptist body. One searches in vain to find in the early Baptist confessions of faith a clear indication of how a church was expected to function. John Smyth, in his *Short Confession,* formulated in 1609 as a basis for his negotiations with the Mennonites, makes only a broad statement of the principle of congregational government. He puts forward the proposition:

> That the church of Christ has power delegated to themselves of announcing the word, administering the sacraments, appointing ministers, disclaiming them, and also excommunicating; but the last appeal is to the brethren or body of the church.[6]

Later doctrinal confessions of the early English Baptists yield little more precise information. Extant church records of the period are hardly more enlightening. Some private and church records of what is now Broadmead Baptist Church, Bristol, are available in printed form. These *Records* date as far back as 1640, a decade or more before the church was clearly identified with the Baptists. They carry us through the years to 1687. Roger Hayden, editor of the *Records,* makes the comment that "During this period doctrine and polity were fluid and the congregation developed its views out of a concern for Scriptural truth."[7] It was an era when tradition was being formulated rather than followed.

When we consider the obverse side of the issue we find a similar lack of precision with respect to leadership roles in the local church. The thirty-sixth article of the London Confession of 1644 states:

> That being thus joyned, every Church has power given them from Christ for their better well-being, to choose to themselves meet persons into the office °of Pastors, Teachers, Elders, Deacons, being qualified according to the Word, as those which Christ has appointed in his Testament, for the feeding, governing, serving, and building up of his Church, and that none other have power to impose them, either these or any other.[8]

This original wording lists four offices in the church. In later editions of the Confession the words "Pastors" and "Teachers" are omitted. It should be noted that the terms "governing" and "serving" are used with no attempt to define these antithetical concepts.

In the eighteenth century the Particular Baptist worthy, Dr. John Gill, offered a constructive treatment of this problem of antithesis. In his *Body of Practical Divinity*, first published in 1770, he developed the theme of the oneness of pastor and people, and the importance of their mutual allegiance to Christ. Some may find him too idealistic, but he is worth reading, and his persistent use of the term "confederation," to describe the act of believers uniting to form a church, should warm Canadian hearts! A certain "devotional tone" permeates Gill's discussion, but, like others of his time, he does not hesitate to dip his pen deeply into controversy, as is evident from the following quote:

> The ordinary officers of the church are pastors and deacons, and these only; though antichrist has introduced a rabble of other officers, the scripture knows nothing of.[9]

True to the Particular Baptist tradition of suspicion with regard to extra-church structures, Gill offers no enlightenment as to what "rabble of officers" might be appropriate to a Baptist association or convention.

As we turn to the American scene we should not be surprised to find that the Baptist attitude toward church government reflects the influences of American political theory. A time-honoured guide used by our churches on this continent has been *The New Directory for Baptist Churches*, the "newness" of which has quite worn away, through numerous printings, since it was first issued in 1894. Edward T. Hiscox, author of the work, makes extensive use of the term "independency" to describe Baptist ecclesiology and stoutly defends his position as follows:

> It is sometimes objected that Baptists are too independent, and that their liberty degenerates into license . . . .

> . . . But liberty and independence are, at the very most, only the occasion, and are in no sense to be made responsible for the evils which perverse and wrong-headed persons perpetrate under the shelter of their name. Church independency has its peculiar liability to misuse and abuse, but it cannot be shown that its difficulties are any more numerous, or any more serious than those to which other forms of Church government are liable. Indeed, if this be the true, the divine plan, then it is the best plan, with the fewest evils and the most advantages. The defects lie not in the plan, but in those who administer the government . . . .[10]

Later, in discussing ministerial authority, Hiscox argues that "A man's right to preach the Gospel, and administer the ordinances comes from God alone; a man's right to do this in any particular Church comes from that Church alone."[11]

Hiscox's guide was thoroughly revised in 1964 and offers the following thoughtful but somewhat ambiguous statement:

> The pastor is placed over the church by both the appointment of God and the free and voluntary act of the church itself . . . .

> As a rule, the pastor who maintains a dignified and consistent Christian and ministerial life, commending himself to the confidence of the people, will receive all the deference he desires . . . . He may attempt too much to enforce his authority. As a preacher of the gospel his authority is of another and a higher kind . . . . True, his words, even in the pulpit, are not beyond question, since they are to be judged by the infallible standard of the Word of God. But in the administration of church affairs he should secure the cooperation of his members, and gain his object by reason and persuasion, rather than attempting to force compliance by authoritative dictation.[12]

It is along these lines that a theory of Baptist "democracy" has developed over the years. In practice, however, one suspects that decision-making among Baptists is a good deal less "democratic" than we may care to admit.

Is it then possible that autocracy exists in our churches? It is here that the historian must tread softly. Clear unequivocal documentation of autocracy is not easy to find. Minute books and records may raise suspicion, but are typically shrouded in a veil of charity. What church clerk would be willing to write "our beloved pastor dominated the Wednesday business meeting in his usual brisk and autocratic style"? A great deal must surely be left unsaid, unless of course, a heated controversy develops within a church. I know of one church, which, during a period of great internal conflict was blessed with a candid and historically-minded clerk. Alas, after a period of years, the minutes were completely rewritten in a new and expurgated edition. The originals were destroyed. Who can tell what historical jewels were lost to posterity?

Even when sources are available they do not necessarily indicate a true picture. For example, a leaflet published in 1922, during the heat of the Fundamentalist-Modernist controversy in British Columbia, was entitled *Jesuit Methods Used by Baptist Union of Western Canada*. The title tells it all with respect to the feeling of the author. The contents do not prove the validity of the charges.[13] In the final analysis any conclusion regarding autocracy involves value judgments. The situation is further complicated by the fact that to be called "autocratic" is not deemed to be a compliment in Baptist circles. Instead, it is regarded as a libel.

That there are authentic examples of Baptist autocracy in both subtle and blatant forms, seems generally to be conceded on all sides. Autocracy is probably the inner temptation of anyone in a leadership position. Democracy is often the hard way toward accomplishment. What Baptist leader has not at times wished for the powers of a pope!

Any attempt to find authentic examples on the Canadian Baptist scene would be almost certain to turn up two outstanding candidates, T. T. Shields and William Aberhart. There is no question, whatever might have been the assessment of his supporters, that Dr. Shields was under constant fire from his opponents. One of these, for example, is quoted in a 1921 newspaper article as having stated, "He has assumed the position of a dictator, the self-appointed Bishop of the Baptist Church of Ontario and Quebec".[14] Regardless of one's conclusions, the career of Dr. Shields offers us an informative case study of the effect of controversy and personal attack upon a leader who is convinced of the rightness of his cause.

With respect to Aberhart, John Irving has given us a quite objective study in his work, *The Social Credit Movement in Alberta*. S. D. Clark, in his foreword to Irving's book, refers to Aberhart as an example of the "charismatic leader."[15] Irving himself describes Aberhart in the following terms:

> The response of the people to Aberhart's leadership was stimulated primarily by that factor which made him unique in the history of Canadian politics, namely, his earlier and continuing career as the founder of a religious movement . . . . His presence and his voice, for example, contributed to inspire in his followers a fanatical and mysterious zeal: they felt that he spoke as one having authority . . . . His resolute and inflexible will combined with his doctrines and his strong personal attraction to give him a power over his followers which verged on dictatorship. He was infinitely resourceful, and once his mind was made up no obstacles could turn him aside from his self-appointed task.[16]

An even more significant source, from a Baptist point of view, is a work by Elmer Towns entitled, *America's Fastest Growing Churches*. Towns analyzes the growth of ten large Baptist churches in the United States. He attributes this growth to the leadership style of each pastor, which he terms "charismatic," and ends with a positive evaluation of such charismatic leadership. In his discussion Towns avoids terms such as "autocratic" or "dictatorial" but the general discussion and the secular illustrations he uses leave little doubt in the reader's mind that he is speaking of a style of leadership that centres on one individual. Napoleon, Hitler, Mussolini, and Fidel Castro are listed as anti-Christian counterparts of the pastors Towns is describing.[17] He freely acknowledges that these pastors are not following the traditional democratic process.[18]

Elmer Towns appears to be presenting an accurate picture of the churches and pastors in question. The great significance of the book, for our purposes, does not relate to its accuracy but rather to the stance of its author. Towns is openly willing to justify and support a nondemocratic leadership style for Baptist pastors.

What arguments can be made for autocracy in Baptist churches? None at all, it would seem, if we believe that something akin to "democracy" is the Divine pattern. The arguments made are entirely pragmatic. They are really arguments to justify *successful* autocracy. In Town's work unsuccessful autocracy is relegated to the category "pseudo-charismatic."[19]

In fairness to Elmer Towns it should be noted that he deals with some of the dangers and limitations of charismatic leadership. He notes that the ministry of the churches under discussion tends to be limited to the disenfranchised in society; that the churches stress autonomy and independence; and that charismatic leaders do not tend to develop leadership in others, thus the church is brought eventually to a "leadership crisis." To these observations it might be added that this style of leadership tends to mold the leader in a way that does not demonstrate "Christlikeness" (Luke 22:25-27). Whether approval of the charismatic leadership style adds anything to the development of a Baptist theology of leadership is an open question.

We have focused our attention primarily on the local church situation. When we examine Baptist structures outside the local church we find that the leadership problem is intensified. Baptists have not been particularly consistent in applying the "congregational" principle to our denominational structures, our educational institutions, or our missionary enterprises. We do not seem to be at all clear, in fact, as to how the congregational principle can be applied in such areas.

The role of the Baptist foreign missionaries is a separate study in itself. Suffice it to say that Baptist missionaries have generally been left free to exercise whatever degree of paternalism that seemed to them to be suitable to the overseas situation. Furthermore, it ought by no means to be assumed that Baptist democracy is easily importable into an authoritarian culture.

To summarize, we may well raise the question: Is our traditional Baptist ecclesiology in jeopardy? It would appear to be, and for a number of reasons.

First of all, its Scriptural basis is being called in question by some scholars, not just outside, but inside Baptist ranks. It is certain that arguments can be made for all three of the traditional forms of church order: congregational, episcopal and presbyterial. New Testament church order is not as undebatable as some Baptists would like it to be. The important question is whether we as Baptists can sustain our position by deductions from what we understand to be the total New Testament pattern, including the priesthood of all believers, the concept of brotherhood, the diversification of gifts, and the believers' church principle.

Secondly, our present democratic structures, though understood to be justified by Scripture, are in a very real sense traditions which have developed over the years, and which have particularly thrived in the American milieu.

In the third place, our secular democratic tradition, which to some degree is both an outgrowth and an undergirding of our Baptist tradition, is now being seriously undermined in the West, and is virtually non-existent in most of the world.

Fourthly, another style of leadership, autocratic in nature, although not so described, is being openly advocated in some Baptist circles and has gained considerable acceptance, particularly among Baptists of fundamentalist and evangelical persuasion, who, in the opinion of many, constitute the "backbone" of the Baptist cause.

Fifthly, Baptists have not been too successful in applying their democratic principles to denominational organizations outside of the local churches, nor have they developed a consistent theology of leadership that embraces all leadership roles, including denominational officials and educators.

Lastly, Baptists are now very vulnerable to influence from outside our tradition. In recent years there has been an upsurge of material in the area of leadership and church structure, much of it written from other than a Baptist viewpoint. At the same time it must be acknowledged that much of this material is thoughtful and stimulating. Leadership courses in Baptist theological institutions tend to be divorced from theological considerations, even though they may be taught under the rubric "practical theology." One may well suspect that the actual presentation is an amalgam, with the essential ingredients of Scripture, experimental ecclesiology, applied psychology, management theory, church growth concepts, and "just plain common sense." The result may not be "Baptistic."

What then are the practical conclusions we can reach? Are we to assume that nothing can be done? Are we to conclude that inconsistency is the price of Baptist freedom? Are we to conclude that our Baptist fate, if not our mission, is to present to the world a theory of democratic church government, and, at the same time, to provide the world with some outstanding examples of administrative structures which, in practice, appear to operate upon principles that are antithetical to the convictions we profess? There must surely be a better way.

Our past history and present situation should indicate to us that we need to give more attention to the formulation of a Baptist theology of leadership and a more concerted effort to reconcile our views on leadership with our views on the church. We should present a coherent view of leadership to students in our theological schools. We need to train our youth, as Aristotle put it, in the "spirit of the constitution." The most fundamental assumption underlying our Baptist ecclesiology is that its nature and functions are understood and espoused by our membership. Without this, we are well on the way to the loss of our Baptist identity.

13 Baptist Leadership, J. B. Richards

1. Augustus H. Strong, *Systematic Theology* (Philadelphia: American Baptist Publication Society, 1909), vol. 3, pp. 904-905.

2. Stuart Ivison and Fred Rosser, *The Baptists in Upper and Lower Canada before 1820* (Toronto: Univ. of Toronto Press, 1963), p. 5.

3. Gregory Vlastos, *Christian Faith and Democracy* (New York: Christian Faith and Democracy 1938), pp. 14-21.

4. John C. Bennett, *Christians and the State* (New York: Scribner's, 1958), p. 146.

5. *Ibid.,* p. 148.

6. W. L. Lumpkin, *Baptist Confessions of Faith* (Philadelphia: Judson Press, 1959), p. 101 (hereafter cited as *Confessions).*

7. Roger Hayden, ed., *The Records of a Church of Christ in Bristol, 1640-1687* (Gateshead, England: Bristol Record Soc., 1974), pp. 47-48.

8. Lumpkin, *Confessions,* p. 166.

9. John Gill, *A Body of Divinity* (Grand Rapids: Baker, 1971, reprint), p. 863.

10. Edward T. Hiscox, *The New Directory for Baptist Churches* (Philadelphia: American Baptist Publication Society, 1894), pp. 150-151.

11. *Ibid.,* p. 295.

12. Frank T. Hoadley, ed., *The Hiscox Guide for Baptist Churches* (Valley Forge: Judson Press, 1964), pp. 61-62.

13. John B. Richards, *Baptists in British Columbia* (Vancouver: Northwest Baptist Theol. College and Seminary, 1977), p. 80.

14. Cited in Leslie K. Tarr, *Shields of Canada* (Grand Rapids: Baker, 1967), p. 80.

15. John A. Irving, *The Social Credit Movement in Alberta* (Toronto: Univ. of Toronto Press, 1959), p. viii.

16. *Ibid.,* pp. 258-259.

17. Elmer L. Towns, *America's Fastest Growing Churches* (Nashville: Impact Books, 1972), p. 196.

18. *Ibid.,* p. 209.

19. *Ibid.,* p. 212.

14

The Struggle For a United Evangelical Baptist Fellowship, 1953-1965

Kenneth R. Davis

Baptist groups outside of the Baptist Federation of Canada constitute about one-third of all Baptist churches in Canada (ca. 600 churches). Because most of these take a theologically separatistic stance, have their roots in the liberal-fundamentalist controversies and schisms of the 1920s, and subsequently have experienced numerous additional splinterings and controversies, they are sometimes characterized as representative of divisive forces in Canadian society and as suffering from some inherent tendency to fragmentation.[1]

It is the purpose of this paper to analyze another side of the story, often neglected, by focusing on the unitive forces behind, and the struggle for, a national fundamentalistic evangelical Baptist Fellowship in Canada.[2]

Since Canadian evangelical Baptist denominations have not been very historically-minded, most of the records of even major past events are limited to tersely recorded minutes totally lacking in commentary.[3] Denominational journals have tended to be promotional with only limited editorial comment. The few written histories are either brief surveys[4] or irenic popularizations.[5] This study has utilized oral history (a series of taped interviews) as a means of obtaining commentary and interpretation otherwise largely unrecorded.[6]

The relative strength of unitive and divisive forces during the decade prior to World War II among evangelical Baptist groups and churches[7] emerging from the liberal-fundamentalist controversy is difficult to determine. Even while a conscious desire for unity was being expressed in the consolidation of existing groups, fragmentation and tensions also continued and increased.

In the west, the Convention of Regular Baptists of British Columbia and the Prairie Regular Baptist Missionary Fellowship were formed in 1927 and 1930 respectively. Various problems, some external but some internal, including schism, kept growth among the B.C. Regulars to a minimum.

Similarly in Ontario, the Union of Regular Baptists was organized in 1927 as a fairly tightly-knit convention but a number of otherwise sympathetic churches either drew back from leaving the Convention of Ontario and Quebec, or left and remained independent, refusing to join the Union because of the continuing contentious spirit of its major figurehead, Dr. T. T. Shields.[8] Actually the formation of the Fellowship of Independent Baptist Churches in Ontario in 1933 reflected both a continued divisiveness (since some of the founding churches had been excluded from the Union) and a desire for union[9] and cooperation. The Independent Fellowship subsequently combined aggressive evangelism and church planting with relatively conflict-free (though loose) ties of fellowship, resulting in extraordinary rapid growth in membership and churches. The Union, however, grew only slowly and continued to be plagued with controversies and loss of churches and pastors.[10]

After World War II there was a significant move toward wider fellowships, and more effective cooperation with other Baptists of like theological convictions, including a greater willingness to set aside minor differences for the sake of unity.

In the west, the B.C. Regular Convention strengthened its ties with the Prairie Regulars by jointly establishing and supporting Northwest Baptist Theological College in Vancouver.[11] But there is no evidence of any desire to extend ties further eastward, even though there was a fraternal awareness of the Union of Regulars in Ontario. Dr. Shields visited British Columbia and Alberta on several occasions, once as a B.C. Convention speaker. A few British Columbia and Alberta pastors were graduates of Toronto Baptist Seminary,[12] and there was a mild interest in the events of 1950-53 leading to the amalgamation of the Union and Independents in Ontario.[13] Even though Reg Hussey and Lorne Matheson, two young people from Central Baptist Church in Victoria, were among those serving under the French Canadian Mission and imprisoned in Quebec, it was apparently of local interest only, and sparked no active denominational involvement. The Rev. P. Teichrob's explanation was that in those days, "distance was a big factor." The mountains affected British Columbia's thinking greatly.[14]

Dr. J. B. Rowell (Central Baptist, Victoria) had considerable contact with T. T. Shields but he, and some other B.C. Regular pastors, had more opportunities for fellowship with the geographically-closer General Association of Regular Baptist Churches (GARB) in Washington state, especially with Dr. R. Powell of Tacoma, Washington.[15] Dr. Powell, the B.C. Convention speaker in 1944, suggested the possibility of organizational ties, and the B.C. Convention's growing aspirations for unity and fellowship turned southward. In 1945 the B.C. Regulars and the Washington Association of the GARB formed the Northwest Baptist Fellowship (later, the International Baptist Fellowship).[16] Its main function and motivation seemed to be the holding of joint pastors' conferences.

The International Fellowship reached its apex of viability in 1949 and then slowly died out. J. Richards suggests eschatological differences as the main reason for its demise.[17] The British Columbia group was too divided on the issue to conform to the narrow and rigid GARB stance and opted for greater openness. To do otherwise would have threatened the unity of the B.C. Convention. The Rev. Teichrob noted that in addition, several of the pastors in the United States, who had initially fostered the International Fellowship, had died or moved away from the border region.[18]

Concomitant with the waning of the GARB courtship, the B.C. Regulars entered into a second and much less happy trial relationship with the American brethren, with the Washington-Oregon Convention of the Southern Baptist Convention.[19] The motivation came now from those who had been least enamoured with the GARB. Moreover, it was less focused on fellowship and more on promoting techniques for growth and stronger Baptistic identity through the use of Baptist literature.[20] The Rev. D. Hills commented that most advocates "weren't concerned about any kind of fellowship [affiliation] *per se* . . . What we were concerned about was learning from them."[21] The consequences were otherwise. A few pastors wanted to seek actual affiliation of their churches (e.g., the Rev. R. McPherson). However, a strong opposition arose to the Washington-Oregon Convention's tendency to a narrow "landmarkism" regarding the ordinances, to the theologically inclusive stance of the Southern Baptist Convention and some of its seminaries (although the Washington-Oregon Convention was quite separatistic and fundamental) and to any kind of dual affiliation by the local churches.[22] Moreover, the membership in many of the churches was less enthusiastic than expected about American Sunday School materials, even though they were Baptistic.[23]

Both southern ventures indicated a growing concern for a larger Baptist unity and cooperation, but neither attempt could command the full support of the B.C. Regulars. To consummate either plan would have led to a schism in British Columbia which no one wanted.

The threat of such a division became a significant factor in turning the B.C. Regulars toward their sister fellowship in eastern Canada.[24] It was obvious to most of the leadership in British Columbia that some alternative was now necessary to fulfill the growing desire for a wider fellowship and a stronger Canadian Baptist identity. Such cooperation would also provide channels for both Home and Foreign Mission projects. A functional pragmatism replaced fellowship as the primary motivation toward unity.

It is significant that these events in British Columbia (1952-55) coincided with the establishment of the Fellowship of Evangelical Baptists in Canada in Ontario in 1953 with its more nationalistic outlook and a more theological openness on eschatology and the ordinances than among parallel groups in the United States. Moreover, the Rev. D. Hills commented of the B.C. Regulars that we were "starting to realize more and more that we were Canadians."[25]

In Ontario the desire for increased evangelical Baptist unity and cooperation developed rapidly after World War II, both for similar and very different reasons:

1) In the Union of Regular Baptists, a weariness with the continuing crises, contentions and divisions became a prime motivator for change.26 Dr. W. H. MacBain noted that "there were a whole series of issues where we were told either you (the Union) back down or else Jarvis Street will pull out." The Jarvis Street Church functioned as a "kind of Santa Claus." MacBain and others began to see the Union as being under the complete control of the Jarvis Street Church. The only permitted journal was *The Gospel Witness,* and the only authorized school was the Toronto Baptist Seminary, both totally controlled by Jarvis Street Church.

MacBain claims to have told Dr. T. T. Shields that it was wrong that even when a majority in a Union board meeting agreed, they often had to yield to Dr. Shields and Jarvis Street.27 Similarly, after thirteen years in the Union and after serving on its board, the Rev. L. Roblin finally took a pastorate with the Independents (in 1942). He summarized his feelings thus: "I was glad to be in the Independent Fellowship because I had so much heart burning back in the Union. Every time Dr. Shields would raise an issue in Toronto it would drive back into my church and it disturbed me continually . . . . I came to the place that I couldn't take it much longer."28 Dr. Jack Scott actually wrote to Dr. Shields on behalf of a number of younger pastors concerning the divisions among Ontario evangelical Baptists saying, "We did not create them and we do not want to perpetuate them."29 Although insisting that there were no formal discussions of it, Dr. MacBain did admit that these strains had caused some of the Union pastors to think fondly of a possible merger with the Independents even prior to Dr. Shields' withdrawal from the Union. He added, "It was so obvious, it had to be in the books."30

2) The Independent Fellowship was itself originally the product of an earlier union of both excluded and sympathetic Union churches with some totally independent Baptist churches.31 There was a small but continual flow of pastors from the Union to the Independents,32 local exchanges of pulpits and sharing of pastors' conferences.33 Furthermore, the Fundamental Baptist Young Peoples Association (FBYPA) and its camp at Muskoka were independent enterprises that received support from churches in both groups (although mostly from the Independents).34

3) The rapid growth of the Independents and concern over the virtual lack of it in the Union also was a major factor in motivating Union pastors toward amalgamation with the Independents.[35] This concern is confirmed by a document that was circulated among the pastors at the time of the split in Toronto Baptist Seminary (1949) and was addressed to Dr. Shields: "Under your leadership we have not grown." Dr. W. G. Brown commented, "unfortunately, it was true."[36]

4) Situations developed where these two Baptist groups "which believed practically the same things" would be working locally "sometimes in cooperation, sometimes in competition" and many pastors in both groups felt that "it was bad testimony."[37]

5) There was a growing sense of oneness in belief and purpose. As the Rev. H. Hindry (of the Union), after coming to serve as pastor in Hespeler (1950) in close proximity to several fellowship churches, put it: "I gradually sensed that we were one . . . (so it would) be wonderful if we came together as one."[38] Dr. J. F. Holliday, editor of the *Fellowship Evangel* and a former president of the Independents, said that he was one hundred percent for merger because "we were standing for the same things."[39] Dr. MacBain noted that "they [the Independents] had a common spirit with us and that we were closer than is often thought." Indeed, the growing awareness of common belief and purpose was likely in the end the strongest motivator to unity. Holliday was convinced that "the future of Baptists in Canada lay with a combined group."[40] Dr. M. Hall, earlier a secretary of the Union but by 1952 secretary of the Independents, was convinced that if the two were joined, both would grow.[41] Scott, in his letter to Dr. Shields, wrote: "There should be a spirit among the churches of evangelical Baptists that we should go out and preach the gospel, build churches, get souls saved, get involved in missions and not spend our time wrangling." He commented further that "that feeling led to the desire to come together and get on with the job."[42]

The story of the immediate events (1951-53) that led to the successful merger of the Independents and the Union of Regular Baptists in the Fellowship of Evangelical Baptists in Canada in 1953; Shields' unpopular split with Dean W. G. Brown, primarily over Brown's attempts to broaden the outreach of

Toronto Baptist Seminary so as to place graduates in churches outside the Union;[43] the establishment of Central Seminary at Forward Baptist Church; the subsequent withdrawal of Dr. Shields from the Union under pressure, and the positive leadership of the two denominational secretaries, Hall of the Independents and J. Armstrong of the Union, has been adequately told elsewhere.[44] Suffice to assert here that what could have been some potentially divisive elements in eschatology, the ordinances and organization, were treated as minor issues and were set aside fairly quickly by an attitude of openness and compromise which is embedded in the resulting constitution and the "Statement of Faith."[45]

The new fellowship of 1953 was a major triumph for evangelical Baptist unity, combining seventy-one churches of the Union and one hundred and twenty-three churches of the Independent Fellowship,[46] without schism. But it was only a preliminary step in a quickly developing desire for a greater, national unity.

National Unity Through a New Convention of Autonomous Regions (1953-58)

Only a few weeks after the historical merger establishing the Fellowship of Evangelical Baptists in Canada (FEBC), its first president, the Rev. W. H. MacBain, wrote: "To be frank and open in our vision, we must say that we cannot hope for less than that every evangelical Baptist church in Canada should be together in a glorious fellowship of churches, dedicated to the same great Baptist distinctives and employing the same methods of operation."[47] These words stimulated editorial comment by the Rev. D. Reed in the *Western Regular Baptist* (January, 1954) in which he explained the organization of the new FEBC and pointed out its goals and beliefs as outlined in MacBains's article. Reed, echoing MacBain, then added that "the hour has come for a united fundamental Baptist testimony across Canada. . . . This editor feels that it is time to turn our eyes toward the East." Reed's editorial also anticipated later developments by suggesting that the goal should be for "one great, Canada-wide, evangelical Baptist Convention."[48]

The articles by MacBain and Reed precipitated an exchange of letters from February 3 to March 2, 1954, between the two men (five letters in total; two from Reed and three from Mac-

Bain), revealing a mutual eagerness to promote an affiliation of the two groups; an awareness of the problem of distance; a feeling of urgency due to Southern Baptist Convention inroads and the resulting, very confused situation in British Columbia; the need for a Canadian alternative before it was too late; a mutual desire for a strong Baptistic stance, especially in developing a missionary programme as the answer to interdenominational inroads, and the need for a combined investigative meeting of the two Canadian groups to clear up mutual misunderstandings. Reed noted that a better understanding of each other was "all that is needed," and he encouraged a wide British Columbia distribution of the FEBC's magazine.[49]

The correspondence was followed by a visit in the Spring to the British Columbia churches by the Rev. N. Pipe and the Rev. R. Guthrie from the east, and finally by a letter from the executive council of the FEBC suggesting the setting up of an investigative meeting of representatives of the three Conventions (B.C. Regulars, Prairie Fellowship and FEBC). The suggestion was acceptable to British Columbia and Alberta, and a meeting convened at Killarney Church, Calgary, in May of 1956.[50]

Concerning the meeting, the Rev. D. Hills reports: "It was a glorious time. The fellowship was very precious." We were together only a day and a half but we "had so much in common" and there was "such unanimity in the things we were discussing . . . . We faced issues . . . [and] were honest with each other" in reference to the problems we were facing.[51] The discussion focused strongly on doctrinal compatibility and not much on the details of any proposed structure for unity, but both Hills and the Rev. J. B. Richards assert that a definite, organized Canada-wide fellowship was the agreed goal.[52] The four representatives from each of the three Conventions[53] prepared a report for their respective Conventions. They recognized the "desirability of a closer cooperation among the churches" of the three Conventions, and recommended the appointment of two representatives from each Convention to form a liaison committee to study the "problems of, and organization necessary for such association" and report back to the Conventions by December 31, 1957.[54] The recommendation was received warmly by each Convention in 1956, and the suggested liaison committee established.

In all three Conventions there existed substantial inclination toward a Canada-wide evangelical Baptist association. In his editorial (January, 1954), Reed had delineated two major motivating factors prevalent among many pastors in the west, namely their disillusionment with southward (U.S.) associations and a concern to strengthen the sense of Baptistic identity. These tended to combine to create a desire for a Canadian Baptist identity.[55]

To these factors must be added a correlated practical concern for the strengthening of the Baptist Missions programme, at home and abroad.[56] It was increasingly imperative to find some way in Baptist Foreign Missions to provide a choice of more than one field for its young people, a choice where the eschatological factor was not determinative (as it was in most American Baptist missionary societies).[57] The desire for Baptistic publications and Sunday School materials which had led to the Southern Baptist Convention contacts, evolved into a desire for Canadian Baptist material, which was impractical for a small Convention to produce. These and other practical concerns, more than direct fellowship, led Hills (on the British Columbia executive council in 1956) to observe concerning their motives, "It would strengthen all our hands if we had some kind of tie, East and West."[58]

In the east, many of the motivations that led to the successful merger of 1953 could be, and were, transferred to a vision for a national evangelical Baptist unity. W. H. MacBain maintained that the FEBC was interested primarily in establishing fellowship churches nationwide, but he also conceded that some kind of formalized cooperation with the Alberta and British Columbia Conventions was "on our mind from the beginning." It was to be a "uniting" fellowship.[59] As in the west, the Baptist Foreign Missionary enterprise became a major force for a larger unity. In 1951, the Pickerings had volunteered to serve under the Japan Regular Baptist Mission of the B.C. Convention. In 1952, the Union began to assist the enterprise and when the FEBC came into existence, the east was soon providing about fifty percent of the support of the Japan mission.

The B.C. Convention then appointed an eastern advisory committee that included MacBain and R. Brackstone.[60] Some leaders in the east also were concerned that the Southern Baptist Convention might move into western Canada. This threat heightened the sense of urgency to provide a Canadian alternative.[61]

Both east and west had similar motives for merger but the imperatives were much less compelling to the east.[62] Perhaps the urgency of the southern threat and the ease of the 1953 eastern merger, caused the eastern proponents of a national merger to hurry, and underestimate the problems. Interestingly, neither the east nor west specifically appealed to any biblical imperative to a visible evangelical unity, although J. Pickford believed "it was really there in the concern for 'testimony' and a 'doctrinal awareness,' " but, he added, "we are far too independent to say much about a compelling interdependence though we are aware of it and believe in it."[63]

By 1956-58, most of the leaders in the three Conventions favoured a trans-Canada fellowship but in the east, especially, it was not at all clear what this fellowship should be like. In the west the motives were largely operational and functional, but in the east many had yet to be convinced of the need for more than a loose fellowship.

The liaison committee's work spanned the period from 1956 to 1959 and fell into three phases:[64] preparation of the first report to the 1957 Conventions on the basic nature of the proposed Canada-wide organization; preparation of the full report with proposed constitutions and by-laws for the 1958 Conventions; and finally, a proposal in 1959 on revised procedures after Ontario failed to adopt the 1958 report.

The first meeting held at Bethany Church in Winnipeg, January 30 and 31, 1957, prepared a minor progress report for the respective executive councils:

1) advocating an organizational framework for the goal of "unlimited cooperation" (as approved by the 1956 Conventions);

2) expressing a continuing conviction (as with the previous investigative committee) that among the three Conventions there were "the same strong convictions about our New Testament position and we were encouraged to move together to formulate a basis for a Canada-wide Baptist organization";

3) suggesting the setting up of a new General (or national) Convention (with executive officers and a council of five decen-

tralized boards to be located in, and representatively dominated by, appropriate regions) meeting every two years with representation from member churches, and the setting up of six regional Conventions within each, and

4) asking their respective executive councils to respond to the general direction they were taking.[65]

On the basis of this first progress report, and even before the liaison committee's second meeting, the B.C. executive council wrote to the province's churches (March, 1957) serving notice that at their convention in June there would be a full discussion of a proposed Canada-wide organization and a motion in principle to enter such a fellowship. Full information about the liaison committee's report was distributed.[66]

The second liaison committee meeting, held in Calgary, May 9 and 10, 1957,[67] reported approval of approach and direction by all three executive councils. At this meeting the following decisions were made: to call the new Convention the "Fellowship of Evangelical Baptist Churches in Canada"; to use the newly incorporated (1956) name of the Eastern Convention (recognizing that this would necessitate a new name for the Eastern Fellowship, and a new regional constitution or constitutions); to use the New Hampshire Confession as the doctrinal basis; and to present the following motion to all three Conventions in 1957 — "That we endorse in principle the recommendations of the Liaison Committee and authorize it to proceed to complete the necessary organizational framework for a Canada-wide Evangelical Baptist Fellowship." This motion received the approval of all three Conventions in 1957.[68]

With what seemed to be solid endorsement by each Convention, the liaison committee met again in November, 1957, and pressed into Phase 2: the preparation of the full draft of the proposed new organizational structure.[69] W. H. MacBain was assigned to standardize and assemble the whole draft for a second and final review at the next meeting. At J. Pickford's request, the committee discussed the "society" plan of operation (the GARB pattern), but rejected it and any idea of proposing any alternative organizational plan. Finally, the committee agreed that if all Conventions accepted the report in 1958, the first General (national) Convention would be scheduled for June, 1959.[70]

The last meeting, to assemble the final report for publication, convened in Winnipeg, January 28 to 30, 1958.[71] Only five members were present. J. Armstrong, a major contributor to the initial pattern, was now off the committee[72] and W. H. MacBain asserts that he became very ill and was unable to be involved in the final revisions of the by-laws and constitutions. Some seemingly small changes from the Phase 1 pattern were made which were much more significant than was initially apparent. The total number of regions was left unspecified so that the new Convention would begin with the present three Conventions as the only regions. The change, according to Armstrong, affected primarily the east, since it meant a shift in the balance of representation on the boards when only three regions were functional. The priority was also changed from establishing the regions first to establishing the General Convention, and the development was not as adequately staged or extended in time as originally intended.[73] MacBain commented that he had some reservations afterwards about these changes.[74] Dual affiliation was also discussed and the committee passed a resolution stating that "it is not in the best interests of the Canada-wide Fellowship."[75]

The final report was finished and ready to go to the Pastors' Conferences in British Columbia, Alberta and Ontario in May and June respectively, and to the three 1958 Conventions, with an accompanying motion for agreement "to participate in the Canada-wide Convention" to be called the Fellowship of Evangelical Baptist Churches in Canada, "meeting in Convention in Winnipeg in June 1959." The implementation of the Home Misson and Publications Boards was to be deferred until the following convention in 1961. The full report was dated April, 1958, and distributed that spring.[76]

There seemed to be every reason for optimism. By March, the British Columbia executive had endorsed the final report and sent out notice of motion to the churches. Neither Pastors' Conference, west or east, gave indication of any ground swell of negative reaction.[77] All previous official reactions, even in Ontario, by the executive councils and conventions, polled in both 1956 and 1957, had been overwhelmingly positive toward what the committee apparently thought was still essentially the same report.[78]

The report was presented to the B.C. Convention by its executive as the preferred affiliation over anything in the "southern direction" and as fulfilling the goals of a Canadian Evangelical Baptist organization best suited to promote Canada-wide evangelism and world missions. It was approved overwhelmingly (by a vote of 51-15).[79] However, another motion, also accepted, stated that British Columbia action was not intended to prejudice the responses of the other Conventions and that British Columbia was prepared "to wait a reasonable period to permit our sister Conventions to resolve their own peculiar problems."[80] The latter motion may have implied an awareness of potential problems in the east. The Prairie Fellowship subsequently approved the report, unanimously.

The first major negative turn of events occurred when W. H. MacBain presented the report to the executive council of the FEBC (Ontario). It divided, and could not agree to present it to the October convention with its full endorsement. It was too late to make any significant changes. The council allowed the liaison committee representative to go ahead and present it to the convention without executive comment. MacBain later perceived this "going ahead" as a mistake,[81] but at the time, success still seemed probable.

The Ontario Fellowship met in convention at Dovercourt Church in Toronto in October, 1958. J. H. Watt, president, was in the chair.[82] At the morning session, the report was presented and explained in detail by MacBain. It seemed to be received warmly. But, commented MacBain, in the afternoon session which was allotted for extensive discussion, "it fell apart" for several reasons:

1) The convention became aware that the executive council was divided. For many this came as a surprise.

2) A major attack was mounted by the highly respected J. Scott of Forward Baptist, Toronto, and to a lesser extent by the president-elect, L. Roblin.

3) Defensive explanations by MacBain, and a warning by the president, J. Watt (suggesting an analogous situation to an experience of Israel) that "if we turn back now, we will wander in the wilderness for forty years," failed, especially in the face of the threat of possible schism. Scott asserted that his church

would not be prepared to support the proposed organizational structure.[83]

Neither the sense of urgency motivating the west nor the commitment to this particular kind of functional organization was strong enough in the east to risk even the possibility of minor divisions. The report (and its motion to set up the National Convention) was never voted on, nor were its details discussed specifically. Rather, the whole was referred back to the executive council for review, with a comment assuring a continued desire for Canada-wide evangelical Baptist cooperation and fellowship.[84] Apparently everyone, or almost everyone, wanted some kind of organized affiliation, but the east lacked a consensus about what kind it should be. The following review of the negative arguments indicates the division.

The opposition by President-elect Roblin revived some of the sublimated tensions of the merger of 1953. He was concerned to protect the independency of the local church and conversely was suspicious of any convention format designed for united action. He preferred a looser type designed for fellowship. He referred to some from the old "Independent Fellowship" (e.g., N. Pipe and J. Scott) as being "opposed to so much of this machinery," whereas the "Union" men "pushed it," and noted that the eastern representatives on the liaison committee (Armstrong, MacBain and Hindry) were all ex-Union men. However, Roblin asserted unequivocally that he and his supporters also "wanted fellowship across Canada with these groups."[85]

Interestingly, Scott perceived his own objections as not at all directed against the organizational concept *per se*, but rather against its procedures and timing. He objected to the principle of going at it from the top down rather than beginning with a loose cooperation while setting up the associations and regions. Similarly, he believed that the formation of a national Foreign Mission Board was "not yet needed" and home missions did not ever need a national "board" since it was primarily a regional and associational responsibility. The whole was too soon and too costly.[86] MacBain mentioned that Scott was also opposed to any board for educational institutions, perhaps, as W. G. Brown pointed out,[87] because the Independents had made it a "condition" of union in 1953 that Central Baptist Seminary not be a FEBC school *per se*. J. F. Holliday, a strong supporter of Union in 1953, also opposed the report for virtually the same reasons as Scott.[88]

One of the principal architects of Phase 1 of the report, J. Armstrong, also approved of the delay of action. Nevertheless, he remained "very strongly in favour of unity" organized on "the original Liaison concept" (as set out in Phase 1). He perceived the report as basically sound and only needing adjustments. His primary concern was over the report's omission of the original concept of six regional Conventions[89] and therefore the proportions of the representation to the boards were thrown out of line.[90]

In retrospect MacBain suggested that the only objection that went beyond procedure and timing was that "there were some (pastors) . . . who had associations with American Foreign Missionary societies and felt that they [the societies] were going to be sidetracked in their approach to our churches . . . (and) that a Canadian national set of Baptist Boards should now be given a privileged position in the churches."[91]

In summary, those responsible for referring the report back to the executive committee did so because:

1) They thought the organization was too premature, too big for current needs, and had too much machinery.

2) The procedure for implementation was backwards; that is, the Associations and Regional Conventions should come first, then the National Convention in a planned evolution under the aegis of a functioning committee for current and developing Canada-wide cooperation.

3) If set up as presented, the representation on the boards was thrown out of balance from the original liaison pattern in a way unacceptable to the east.

4) The Educational Institutions Board was not necessary and not favoured by many in the east.

5) A few objected to the convention board pattern in favour of a looser federation and independent societies.

6) Though not suggested by any of those interviewed (and found only in J. Watt's book, *The Fellowship Story*), that since the FEBC was nationally incorporated, and had already some

affiliated churches on the Prairies, why not just have the other groups absorbed into it?

Clearly there were few against the liaison report *per se.* Rather, most objected to its procedures and timing. But this was apparently not too clear at the time either to the liaison committee or the executive council of the FEBC to whom it had been referred.[92] Though Watt's interpretation of the convention, as in favour of using the FEBC to bring about unity by persuading the others to join (the principle of absorption), has not been substantiated as a dominant view in the convention itself, it seemed to have become the policy of the new secretary-treasurer in the east, M. Hall, as events will indicate. The trauma of what happened was so strong that Roblin, president of the FEBC for 1958-59, commented on the virtual paralysis of the men involved[93] and MacBain admitted that his reaction was to pull back and opt for a simpler *modus operandi.*[94]

Since the Eastern Executive could not agree after several meetings on a revised version of the report to present to the 1959 Convention, it opted to ask the liaison committee to reconvene.[95] When the liaison committee met again in Edmonton, September 15-17, 1959, it entered the third and final phase of its work with three of the four representatives from Ontario entirely new to the task.[96] The eastern representatives explained their Convention's refusal to endorse the report in 1958 and the executive's unwillingness to place it again before the Ontario Convention in 1959 for immediate implementation, as follows: It could be divisive in the east. Specifically, the executive's representatives said there was dissatisfaction with the New Hampshire Confession as the doctrinal basis, with the staging for implementation, and with organizing a national convention prior to the regional ones.[97]

Roblin (president of the FEBC) recommended setting up some temporary agency to implement some form of cooperation. "This," he stated, "would not mean the abandonment of the Liaison Report to which all agreed in principle, but a deferment, to enable the East to prepare itself for implementation." He agreed that the report should continue as a guide to the development of the Canada-wide organization as the need arose through expansion.[98]

The committee proceeded to recommend a lengthy motion to the three Conventions, the gist of which was as follows: the acceptance of their slightly revised version of the FEBC Statement of Faith as the doctrinal basis for the national organization; the acceptance of the liaison report, subject to major revisions if and as necessary, as the basic plan for building the national organization; the appointment of representatives from each Convention to a trans-Canada committee to recommend and implement (along with the executive councils) areas for immediate cooperation. It also recommended to the proposed Canada-wide committee that cooperation be undertaken in the areas of home missions, publications and evangelism. [99]

These recommendations were approved by the three Conventions in 1959 and 1960 (with British Columbia recommending to the east that Foreign Missions be added to the trans-Canada committee's cooperative efforts) [100] leading to the formation of the Trans-Canada Committee (TCC).

Unity by Cooperation, Absorption or Federation? (1960-65)

The next five years of the struggle for a national fellowship was a period of remarkable progress in spite of some variation and confusion regarding the means for its attainment. The TCC came into existence to explore, expand and implement (in conjunction with the executive councils) various kinds of practical cooperative effort but also (as implied in the minutes of the liaison committee) to gradually develop the now-delayed national organization, since that "approved" responsibility was not delegated to anyone else after the liaison committee was disbanded. [101]

The actions of the first meeting of the TCC (1961) [102] indicated that it took seriously its responsibility to implement the principles of the liaison report by stages. The committee noted that the east had already invited a representative from British Columbia to sit on the French-Canada Committee, and British Columbia had invited representatives from Ontario and Quebec to its Japan Mission Committee. The TCC then requested the east to add one representative from Alberta to the French Board. To distinguish united (national) activities from the FEBC (Ontario) which clearly it wanted to do, the TCC urged the use (by all Conventions) of the name, "The Trans-Canada

Fellowship of Evangelical Churches" (TCF) for the former. It approved sending to all churches a revision of the organizational chart of the liaison report emphasizing the importance and representational significance of developing the six Regional Conventions.[103] Also, British Columbia was urged to begin thinking about how to reorganize the Japan Mission Committee so as to become the Foreign Mission Board of the TCF. It urged *The Fellowship Baptist* to become a national voice for the TCF. Finally, the TCF itself began to study the need for national evangelical Baptist publications.[104] In all, the committee made twelve recommendations to the executives of the three Conventions and several were directly related to the implementation of the liaison report.

At the second meeting (1962),[105] reports were received from each Convention noting that, except for two minor sub-points, all recommendations had been approved. The committee then proceeded to recommend that the Prairie Fellowship begin negotiations with the east (the FEBC) "with a view to it becoming a Regional Convention in accordance with the terms of the liaison committee's report."[106]

The Prairie Fellowship responded positively. J. Armstrong drew up a lengthy "brief" to present to the east's executive council in October, 1962. In the "brief" he warned that "a Canada-wide organization which is merely an expansion of the present evangelical Baptist Fellowship (FEBC) would merely enlarge the problem already existing, i.e., we would continue to work everything from a central office." He emphasized that the Prairie request was for admission to the FEBC as an "autonomous" Regional Convention and that this overture was in response to the TCC's request and was part of the implementation of the liaison report which had been approved by the FEBC in 1959. If approved, he noted, the present FEBC churches in Alberta and Saskatchewan would become an effective part of the new Regional Convention, to the benefit of both.[107]

The Prairie Fellowship's subsequent report to the TCC indicates that the Eastern Executive Council's response was not very warm; their request was stalled and referred back to the TCC.

Nevertheless, at its third meeting (1963),[108] the TCC continued to promote the development of a trans-Canada organization on the liaison report's pattern. It urged the Prairie Fellowship to persist in negotiations with the east; recommended to the three executive councils the setting up of a trans-Canada pastors' conference for May, 1964 in Winnipeg, and in partial conformity with the liaison's pattern, urged British Columbia to turn its Japan Mission Committee into a board of the B.C. Convention.[109]

However, the pattern of national development (in accordance with the liaison committee's plan) by the TCC had begun to run into conflict with the alternative vision of the expansion of, and absorption into, the FEBC, especially over the merger of the Prairie Fellowship. In October of 1963, the Prairie Fellowship ceased to exist. It was admitted into the FEBC but not as a regional convention. It was absorbed. Its churches were received individually into the FEBC.

Armstrong was especially disturbed and dismayed. He described the unforeseen turn of events as something at the last minute "manoeuvered by M. Hall (secretary-treasurer of the FEBC) so we would not be recognized as a Convention within a Convention" though the Alberta Convention had endorsed only joining as a body.[110] W. Tomkins commented that the Alberta Fellowship was small; it was further hurt by losses to the Southern Baptist Convention, and needed the help that only the east could provide. Once committed to merger, it was too late to turn back when the terms were changed.[111] MacBain's comment was: "I don't know how that happened."[112]

It would seem, however, that in spite of Armstrong's presence on the TCC from 1961-1963, and his explanatory letter of March 16, 1961, in which he pressed for regional development, it never promoted the one essential thing for the federation concept, namely the development of additional regional conventions in Ontario. Meanwhile the FEBC had been expanding both eastward and westward, and had already begun to move to forming its own boards by setting up Christian Education, Home Missions and French Canada boards in 1961 and its Foreign Mission Board by 1963. M. Hall and H. Hindry,[113] and perhaps others on the Eastern Executive, apparently now espoused the principle of national unity by absorption and the expansion of the FEBC. In that period of 1961-63, the east was working at the development of its boards and associations, but it was not regionalizing itself.

The Reed file contains a recorded meeting of the B.C. Executive with Dr. E. S. Kerr from the Eastern Executive (March 9, 1964) concerning the demise of the Prairie Fellowship. British Columbia posed the question (among others), "On what basis does the East entertain the TCF — one Convention consisting of regional Conventions or, one Convention which we join (as the Prairies did)?" Dr. Kerr answered, "Let's be frank. It didn't turn out as the Prairies had expected."[114]

The B.C. Executive indicated that it was feeling pressure (and the Kerr interview confirms it) to follow Alberta into being absorbed into the FEBC and to lose its convention status. A crisis of vision and structure was developing that, as Pickford warned the east, could lead to British Columbia turning away from the TCF and from an all-Canada unity to seek again a unity elsewhere. A TCC made up of only two very unequal conventions was not very workable.

Would the desire for national unity be equal to overcoming this crisis? The fourth and final meeting of the TCC (1964)[115] sought to redeem the situation and the original liaison vision somewhat, with three recommendations:

1) that the FEBC "give consideration to the making of provision in their Constitution for the inclusion of the Convention of Regular Baptist Churches of B.C. into their membership."

2) that the churches take under advisement the setting up of one Board of Foreign Missions for the TCF, combining the FEBC Board and the Japan Mission of British Columbia.

3) that a TCF Pastors' Conference be set up for May 11-13, 1965 in Winnipeg.[116]

The president of the FEBC, G. Searle, continued to mend fences by writing (on behalf of the Eastern Executive and in response to the TCC) to J. Pickford (October 6, 1964) that the Eastern Executive was prepared to adjust By-Law III of the FEBC to permit the B.C. Convention to merge "as a group: if it applied 'as a group' " and he urged a meeting of the two executives to work out differences and details relating to such a merger and to the proposal for one Foreign Mission Board. The Reed file contains a recorded transcript of a subsequent telephone conference of the two executives in which the east admitted it was facing up to the constitutional implications for the first time; which it did not do for the merger of the Prairie Fellowship. Many other issues were also clarified.[117] Clearly the east was now prepared to make major adjustments to save Canadian evangelical Baptist unity.

At an Eastern Executive Committee meeting on December 8 and 9, 1964, attended also by Pickford and W. Charlton from British Columbia, a report on negotiations for merger was drawn up that included:

1) a further amendment of By-Law III of the FEBC to allow for the application by and admission of "Conventions and groups";

2) a statement that the B.C. Convention was to be "perpetuated as an autonomous Convention" responsible for local activities and cooperation with the FEBC in areas of national concern, including Foreign Missions,[118] and

3) an agreement to set up a TCF Pastors' Conference for May 18 to 20, 1965, and to call a Special Convention of the FEBC to coincide with the B.C. Convention on June 16 and 17, 1965, to ratify a merger, with the formal reception of the British Columbia churches into the FEBC scheduled for its regular convention in October of 1965.[119]

And so it happened. The forces for evangelical Baptist unity did prevail. The FEBC became a national fellowship consisting of one Regional Convention in British Columbia; a partially functioning (constitutionally undefined) regional set-up in Alberta; a French group; and all the other churches under its direct supervision. The TCC now ceased to function.

In spite of many crises and shifts in the process, and some continuing loose ends and unfinished business constitutionally, by 1965 evangelical Baptists had achieved a national fellowship roughly conforming to the principles of the original liaison report, without division; indeed, without the loss of, or a split in a single church. Would it hold together?

It has, to date (1979), even though tensions over structure remain. Events of 1965 did not constitute a complete victory over the principle of absorption (with its concomitant tendency to a powerful, highly centralized super-convention) but rather provided an uneasy, inconsistent compromise that has continued. Regional groupings, although much weaker now than originally intended, are developing, but not full-scale regional conventions. The boards are now largely centralized at the national level. Neverthless, as W. Tompkins commented: "If carrying out the Great Commission in an evangelical Baptist way isn't sufficient to hold us together, nothing is."120

The establishment of a Canada-wide Fellowship of Evangelical Baptist Churches was a significant ecumenical achievement by fundamentalistic evangelical Baptists in Canada.

14 The Struggle for a United Evangelical Baptist Fellowship, K. R. Davis

1. For a discussion of evangelical disunity see J. M. Kik, *Ecumenism and the Evangelical* (Philadelphia: Presbyterian and Reformed Publishing Co., 1958), pp. 132-141.

2. "Evangelical" is used here to identify various groups of Canadian Baptists committed exclusively to an evangelical theological position.

3. One exception is the events surrounding Dr. T. T. Shields who used *The Gospel Witness* extensively to provide commentary.

4. L. K. Tarr, *This Dominion His Dominion* (Willowdale: The Fellowship of Evangelical Baptist Churches, 1968) and C. A. Tipp, *Ten Years of Fellowship, 1953-63* (n.p.: The Trans-Canada Fellowship of Evangelical Baptist Churches, 1963).

5. J. H. Watt, *The Fellowship Story* (n.p.: The Fellowship of Evangelical Baptist Churches, 1978).

6. Interviews:

Tape IA	— Rev. D. Hills, President of the Regular Baptists of B. C. (1957-9).
Tape IB	— Rev. J. H. Pickford, on the Liaison Committee (1956-9).
Tape IIA	— Rev. P. Teichrob, President of the Regular Baptists of B. C. (1965-7).
Tape IIB	— Rev. J. B. Richards, author of *Baptists in B.C.* (1977), historian.
Tape IIIA	— Rev. W. Tompkins, on the Liaison Committee (1956-9).
Tape IV	— Rev. H. Hindry, on the Liaison Committee (1957-9).
Tape V	— Rev. L. Roblin, on the Liaison Committee (1959) and President of F.E.B.C. (1958-9).
Tape VI	— Rev. J. Scott, first President of Central Baptist Seminary and spokesman at the 1958 Convention of F.E.B.C.
Tape VII	— Rev. W. H. MacBain, first President of F.E.B.C. (1953) and on the Liaison Committee (1956-8).
Tape VIIIA	— Rev. W. G. Brown, Dean of Toronto Baptist Seminary and Central Baptist Seminary.
Tape VIIIB	— Rev. J. R. Armstrong, on Liaison Committee (1956-7) and Trans-Canada Committee (1961-3).
Tape IX	— Rev. J. F. Holliday, Editor of the *The Fellowship Evangel* and Chairman of the Trans-Canada Committee (1961).
Tape X	— Rev. H. Buchner, Union, Independent and Fellowship pastor.

(Tapes to be located in the Fellowship Historical Library, Central Baptist Seminary, Toronto.)

7. The Convention of Regular Baptist Churches of British Columbia, The Regular Baptist Missionary Fellowship of the Prairie Provinces, The Union of Regular Baptist Churches of Ontario and Quebec, and The Fellowship of Independent Baptist Churches.

8. J. Holliday (Tape IX) tells how Shields' continued personal attacks on evangelical pastors in the Old Convention (e.g., Rev. J. McNeill and Rev. Green of Castlefield Baptist) generated such a negative reaction that 25 of his supporting pastors met with him asking him to cease, and major on church building and growth instead — without avail.

9. Holliday, Tape IX, and Watt, *The Fellowship Story*, pp. 32-34.

10. Cf. Buchner, Tape X, and Roblin, Tape V.

11. J. B. Richards, *The Baptists of British Columbia* (Vancouver: Northwest Baptist Theological College, 1977), p. 113.

12. D. Hills mentioned Revs. E. Apps, D. Harvey and J. Duncan (Tape IA).

13. Teichrob, Tape IIA.

14. Richards, Tape IIB and Teichrob, Tape IIA.

15. Richards, Tape IIB and *Baptists of B.C.*, p. 114.

16. *Ibid.*

17. *Ibid.* Teichrob (Tape IIA) and Hills (Tape IA) agree with Richards.

18. Teichrob (Tape IIA) mentions Revs. R. Powell, F. Johnson and M. Lang.

19. For details see Richards, *Baptists of B.C.*, pp. 114-116.

20. Richards, Tape IIB.

21. Hills, Tape IA. Richards agrees (Tape IIB) that the strongest initial promoters, such as Revs. H. Phillips and G. Dawes, never intended a full union with the S.B.C. nor even dual affiliation.

22. Richards, Tape IIB. Teichrob (Tape IIA) says: "These frightened us off" more than the "bigness" of the S.B.C.

23. Richards, Tape IIB.

24. Hills, Tape IA.

25. *Ibid.*

26. Watt (*The Fellowship Story*, pp. 38-41) suggests a decade of relative quiet until 1948 but Brown (Tape VIIIA) and MacBain (Tape VII) assert that there was continuous dissension, and Hindry (Tape IV) comments of Watt, MacBain and himself: "We felt that we could not go on fighting and squabbling." Shields' breaks with M. Hall (Secretary of the Union) and Brown (Dean of T.B.S.) were only the last straws.

27. MacBain, Tape VII.

28. Roblin, Tape V.

29. Scott, Tape VI.

30. MacBain, Tape VII.

31. Armstrong, Tape VIIIB.

32. Revs. H. Buchner, L. Roblin and M. Hall are examples; the latter was General Secretary of the Union in 1946, of the Independents in 1952-53 and of the United F.E.B.C. in 1953-54 and 1957-63.

33. Hindry, Tape IV.

34. Holliday, Tape IX.

35. Roblin, Tape V. Roblin also noted that the Union found that Shields generated so much public opposition that it made Home Mission advance very difficult.

36. Brown, Tape VIIIA.

37. MacBain, Tape VII.

38. Hindry, Tape IV.

39. Holliday, Tape IX.

40. *Ibid.*

41. Brown, Tape VIIIA.

42. Scott, Tape VI.

43. Brown, Tape VIIIA.

44. Cf. L. Tarr, *This Dominion His Dominion,* pp. 97-99 and J. Watt, *The Fellowship Story,* pp. 42-43.

45. They agreed not to opt for any specific pattern of eschatological details, to specify the proper order of the ordinances but say nothing about open or closed communion, and to call the whole merger a Fellowship rather than a Convention. MacBain commented: "We were determined that we should not put anything in the Statement of Faith that would jeopardize our fellowship together." (Tape VII)

46. *The Fellowship Baptist Historical Issue* (May, 1960), p. 22.

47. W. H. MacBain, "Evangelical Baptists, Whither Bound?" *The Fellowship Baptist* (November, 1953), p. 2.

48. *The Western Regular Baptist* (January, 1954), p. 2.

49. "Letters" in D. Reed's *Liaison Committee File* in the B.C. Regular's Executive Office, Northwest Baptist Theological College, Vancouver, B.C.

50. Cf. the Preamble to the Liaison Report of April 1958 (in Reed, *Liaison File*.) But Watt, *The Fellowship Story,* p. 90 dates the meeting as June 1956.

51. Hills, Tape IA.

52. Hills, Tape IA and Richards, Tape IIB.

53. Representatives: from B.C., Revs. H. Phillips, D. Hills, J. Richards, J. Pickford; from Alberta, Revs. W. Tompkins, G. Reeves, J. MacKay; from Ontario, W.H. MacBain, J. R. Armstrong, J. Boyd, W. N. Charlton.

54. L. Tarr prints the full report in *This Dominion His Dominion*, p. 202.

55. *The Western Regular Baptist* (January, 1954), p. 2. Similarly, J. Pickford (Tape IB) comments on the strong sense of need to stand for Baptist principles and doctrines "not in an isolated way" and to make sure that as evangelical Baptists "we had a national voice and a national identity."

56. Pickford, Tape IB and Richards, Tape IIB.

57. Richards, Tape IIB.

58. Hills, Tape IA.

59. Brown, Tape VIIIA and MacBain, Tape VII. Roblin (Tape V) flatly denies that any idea of a "national Convention" was there from the beginning, rather only a vision of F.E.B.C. expansion nationally.

60. MacBain, Tape VII. Cf., also Tarr, *This Dominion*, pp. 162-3.

61. J. Armstrong (Tape VIIIB) comments that MacBains' trip to the West in 1955 (as the speaker for the B.C. Convention) convinced him of the urgency of responding to the S.B.C. threat and he reported to the East that either we reach out the hand of fellowship or we're going to lose these churches. Armstrong also found the same tense situation in Alberta when he moved to Edmonton in 1957. Not all in the East were convinced, however. Holliday (Tape IX) admits a "chance" of an S.B.C. takeover but was quite doubtful of it happening.

62. As Armstrong comments (Tape VIIIB): "They [the West] needed it and Ontario didn't really need it."

63. Pickford, Tape IB.

64. There were 6 meetings: 2 in phase 1, 3 in phase 2, and 1 in phase 3. Meeting 1: W. H. MacBain, J. R. Armstrong (East), L. G. Baker, J. H. Pickford (B.C.), W. C. Tompkins (Alberta).

65. Cf., Reed's *Liaison File*.

66. *Ibid.*

67. *Ibid.* Membership was mostly the same as in Meeting 1: MacBain and Armstrong (East), Baker and Pickford (B.C.), Tompkins and D. G. Milligan (Alberta).

68. Cf. The Preamble to the Liaison Report (April, 1958) in Reed's *Liaison File* and in J. Armstrong's *T.C.C. File,* including the representative's reports to the next Liaison Committee meeting (November 25-27, 1957).

69. Cf. the Minutes of Meeting 3, at Edmonton, November 25-27, 1957 (Armstrong's *T.C.C. File*). H. Hindry now replaced J. Armstrong, who had been much involved in setting up the phase 1 report.

70. *Ibid.*

71. *Ibid.* Present were MacBain, Hindry, Tompkins, Baker and Pickford.

72. MacBain, Tape VII.

73. Armstrong, Tape VIIIB.

74. MacBain, Tape VII.

75. Partly in response to concern expressed in a letter to the B.C. Executives by the Deacons of Ruth Morton Church, January 1958 (in Reed's *Liaison File* — also the Executive's response) and partly in response to overtures made by the Baptist Federation of Canada (Cf. reply in *The Fellowship Baptist*, May 1960, p. 11).

76. A copy is in both Reed's *Liaison File* and Armstrong's *T.C.C. File*.

77. Cf. the Liaison Committee "Minutes" (Reed's *Liaison File)*. The Liaison Committee did meet with the B.C./Alta. Pastors' Conference, May 12-16, 1958 and some were at the Ontario Pastors' Conference in June.

78. It was presented to the B.C. Convention as having "no change in nature or direction" from the earlier, smaller version of 1957 (Reed's *Liaison File*).

79. *Ibid.*

80. *Ibid.*

81. MacBain, Tape VII.

82. No extensive report or analysis of this crucial Convention has ever been written.

83. MacBain, Tape VII. This sequence of events is largely derived from Mac-Bain who referred to them as "indelibly fixed in my mind".

84. Tarr, *This Dominion,* p. 150; Watt, *Fellowship Story,* p. 91; *The Fellowship Annual Report* (1958-9), p. 4.

85. Commented Roblin (Tape V): "We saw the machine boys taking over". MacBain (Tape VII) rejected the suggestion that the division of opinion in 1958 was on Union vs. Independents lines. Hindry, previously a Union pastor on the Liaison Committee, at least in hindsight was not fully supportive of the Report (Tape IV) and Armstrong, also a Union pastor, favoured sending it back to the Executive (Tape VIIIB). J. Scott (Tape VI) did not see himself as identified with Roblin's rejection of the Convention set-up *per se* and said Roblin spoke only for a minority.

86. Scott, Tape VI.

87. MacBain, Tape VII.

88. Holliday, Tape IX.

89. As Secretary-Treasurer in Ontario (1954-7), Armstrong was already convinced that Ontario was too big to administer, and needed dividing (Armstrong, Tape VIIIB).

90. Armstrong does not say how the existing Regions were to be held together and function while others were developed, perhaps a Trans-Canada Committee not unlike what was proposed later.

91. MacBain, Tape VII. When Ontario, shortly after, set up its own Foreign Missions Board, L. Roblin's response was that 1958 had now "come in by the back door" which suggests that his type of opposition to the 1958 Report had nothing to do with Canada wide unity.

92. Tarr (*This Dominion,* p. 150) interprets the referral and the Convention's intention as "delay," until the Regions were set up; whereas Watt (*The Fellowship Story,* p. 91) interprets the mood as a rejection in favour of an absorption by the F.E.B.C. "if the other bodies could be persuaded to enter in."

93. Roblin (Tape V) referred to it as "a sit down strike."

94. MacBain, Tape VII.

95. Cf., *The Fellowship Yearbook* (1958-9), p. 4.

96. It was an expanded committee of 10: J. Pickford, L. Baker, S. Mikolaski (B.C.); J. Armstrong, W. Tompkins, G. Richardson (Alberta); L. Roblin, N. Pipe, W. Charlton, H. Hindry (Ontario).

97. "Minutes" in Armstrong's *T.C.C. File* and Reed's *Liaison File.*

98. Armstrong's *T.C.C. File.*

99. *Ibid.*

100. *Ibid.* Cf. also Watt, *The Fellowship Story,* p. 93, and Tarr, *This Dominion,* p. 150.

101. Cf. the Minutes of the Feb. 20-21, 1961 meeting and Armstrong's letter to all the churches (March 16, 1961) in Armstrong's *T.C.C. File.*

102. Meeting in Vancouver, Feb. 20-21, 1961 with two representatives from each Convention, J. H. Holliday as Chairman and J. R. Armstrong as Secretary.

103. Cf. "Minutes" and Armstrong's letter (March 16, 1961) and organizational chart, in Armstrong's *T.C.C. File.*

104. "Minutes" in Armstrong's *T.C.C. File.*

105. At Edmonton and Lloydminster, Saskatchewan, March 5-8, 1962. Cf. minutes in Armstrong's *T.C.C. File.*

106. T.C.C. Minutes, 2nd meeting, in Armstrong's *T.C.C. File.*

107. A copy of the "Brief" is in the Reed *Liaison File.*

108. Meeting at Vancouver, June 15-17, 1963; Cf. "Minutes" in Reed's *Liaison File.*

109. Representation on the Board was designed to accommodate the reality of initially operating with only three Regions. Therefore the Liaison Report was adjusted to five members from B.C., two from the East, and one from Alberta.

110. Armstrong, Tape VIIIB.

111. Tompkins, Tape IIIB.

112. MacBain, Tape VIIB.

113. Armstrong, Tape VIIIB and Hindry, Tape IV.

114. Reed, *Liaison File.*

115. Meeting in Victoria, B.C., June 15-18, 1964 but without representation from the now non-existent Prairie Fellowship (in Reed's *Liaison File*).

116. *Ibid.*

117. Cf. transcript of the recorded conversations (in Reed's *Liaison File*).

118. Comments P. Teichrob (Tape IIA): "We did not want to lose any of our churches." It was a "strategy" to keep the B.C. Convention intact.

119. "Minutes" and the Report (in Reed's *Liaison File*).

120. Tompkins, Tape IIIB. Teichrob adds (Tape IIA): "I think it [merger] was a marvellous thing . . . I am convinced we made the right decision."

15

National Survey of Baptist Ministers

James A. Beverley

What is the self-identity of Baptist leaders in Canada?
What are the theological views of pastors, educators and admistrators?
How do they view their role in relation to family and finances?
How do pastors spend their leisure time?
What is their position on the charismatic movement?
What are their hobbies?

These, and a host of other questions, 84 in all, were sent to all ordained ministers of the main Baptist groups in Canada. A total of 1466 questionnaires were sent out in the form of a National Survey of Baptist Leaders. This chapter presents a preliminary report on some of the findings and conclusions from that survey.[1]

The questionnaire, mailed in May and June of 1979, was divided into five sections: Personal Data; Educational Data and Evaluation; Attitudes to Ministry; Doctrinal and Theological Questions, and Other Matters.

No attempt was, or will be, made to identify the respondents. The rationale for the survey was its potential as a tool for understanding the identity of Canadian Baptists and for guiding different areas of Baptist work.

Despite the nine-page length and scope of the questionnaire, the percentage of return was high, as the following table illustrates:

Table 1: Response to Survey

Convention or Group	Questionnaires Sent	Returned	Percentage
United Baptist Convention of the Atlantic Provinces (hereafter UBCAP)	349	157	45%
Baptist Convention of Ontario and Quebec (hereafter BCOQ)	322	143	44%
Baptist Union of Western Canada (hereafter BUWC)	141	61	43%
Fellowship of Evangelical Baptist Churches (hereafter FEBC)	420	130	31%
North American Baptist Conference (hereafter NABC)	114	35	33%
Other Baptist Groups[2]	120	47	39%
Totals	1466	573	40%

Because of the ease of tabulating most of the doctrinal and theological questions, the focus of this paper will be in that direction with brief attention to some others matters. Further information will be forthcoming as time permits extended analysis of the more open-ended questions.

First, the Baptist leaders were asked to rate their training for ministry. The vast majority responded, "good" or "excellent." Only five of 150 responses in the UBCAP said their training was "very inadequate." Only one out of 61 did so in the responses from the BUWC.

Second, responses to a question about pastoral relationships reveal that a significant number of pastors have poor contacts with fellow Baptist ministers. Dissatisfaction ranged from 15 percent in the NABC to a full third in the UBCAP.

Third, it was seen that Baptist ministers have an extremely high view of the impact of their sermons upon the congregation. In the NABC, 85 percent of pastors ascribed top value to preaching, as did 98 percent of the respondants from the FEBC.

Another conclusion reached from answers to the survey is that Baptist leaders gave the impression of being hard workers. They were asked to total the number of hours they spent in different areas of pastoral work. Information is available in two categories from the UBCAP response. Here, the lowest average time spent on sermons is three hours per week, the highest, thirty, and the overall average, fourteen hours. In regard to total work-hours per week, the average is about fifty-four, with the lowest about thirty. The highest is a staggering 112 hours, which is either a typographical error or there is a pastor who manages to avoid everything but eight hours of sleep a night along with his pastoral work!

Finally, Baptist leaders in all the various groups are certain that they have had many encounters with God. The options were:

a) no personal experience of God;

b) very difficult to know God personally;

c) have had many encounters with God.

Most chose the last option, ranging from 92.4 percent in the FEBC to 95 percent in the BCOQ.

There is much more to offer the reader by way of information on doctrinal aspects of the survey. The following tables give the percentage analysis of responses from the five largest Baptist groups in Canada. The options given here reproduce the wording as it appeared in the questionnaire.

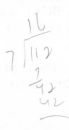

Table 2: The Deity of Christ

Options: Jesus was (is)

a) God incarnate in flesh, fully God, fully man; the Son of God eternal with the Father and the Holy Spirit
b) the only begotten Son of God, pre-existent with the Father, but created by the Father
c) a son of God in the same sense as all men; Jesus had, however, a unique and total commitment to the will of our Father
d) Jesus was a great moral and spiritual teacher; no more, no less

Response:

Groups/ Options	a)	b)	c)	d)
UBCAP	97.4%	1.3%	1.3%	—
BCOQ	95.6	2.2	2.2	—
BUWC	95.0	1.7	3.3	—
FEBC	100.0	—	—	—
NABC	100.0	—	—	—

Table 3: The Virgin Birth of Christ

Options:

a) Jesus had both a human mother and a human father in the same sense as all men
b) the doctrine of the Virgin Birth is simply an early church way of expressing the uniqueness of Jesus; there is no room for dogmatism as to its actual historical reliability
c) Jesus was conceived of the Holy Ghost, born of the Virgin Mary

Response:

Groups/ Options	a)	b)	c)
UBCAP	.64%	5.1%	93.6%
BCOQ	.75	9.7	89.6
BUWC	—	5.0	95.0
FEBC	—	—	100.0
NABC	—	—	100.0

Table 4: Exclusiveness of Christ as Saviour

Options: The deeply committed Hindu, Buddhist, etc., who has not accepted Christ (even though hearing of Him) will be:

a) lost, because only through Christ will men be saved
b) excused, on the basis of his commitment to his own religion
c) I do not know what will happen

Response:

Groups/ Options	a)	b)	c)
UBCAP	84.0%	1.0%	15.0%
BCOQ	62.0	1.0	37.0
BUWC	67.0	2.0	31.0
FEBC	100.0	—	—
NABC	91.4	—	8.6

Table 5: Authority and Reliability of Bible

Options: The Bible

a) is the Word of God written; inerrant and infallible on all matters in the original autographs
b) is the Word of God written; infallible on all matters of faith and practice, with some errors on matters of history, science, etc.
c) is God's Word but it is not infallible even on religious matters
d) is God's Word with the words of man mixed in . . . it is the task of the preacher and theologian to separate the two

Response:

Groups/ Options	a)	b)	c)	d)
UBCAP	79.0%	13.0%	1.0%	7.0%
BCOQ	61.0	27.0	2.0	10.0
BUWC	59.0	32.0	7.0	2.0
FEBC	99.2	.8	—	—
NABC	78.8	21.2	—	—

Table 6: Historical-Critical Issues

Options: *On issues like the Documentary Hypothesis, Unity of Isaiah,*
dating of Daniel, historicity of Jonah and the whale:

a) I think too much time has been spent in battles over such matters; they are not that significant!
b) Issues like these have rightly split the church in the past and we must continue to hold the line against the historical-critical position
c) Issues like these are important and sometimes decisive but we should not wage heresy trials on such lines

Response:

Groups/ Options	a)	b)	c)	
UBCAP	26.0%	25.0%	49.0%	
BCOQ	36.0	12.0	50.0	(2% different answers)
BUWC	38.0	5.0	57.0	
FEBC	10.0	75.0	15.0	
NABC	31.0	19.0	50.0	

Table 7: Fate of the Unsaved

Options:

a) They will be sent to Hell where they will suffer eternal punishment
b) they will be judged for their sin, punished, and then annihilated; I do not believe in eternal punishment
c) eventually Hell will be empty and all of mankind will be in God's presence in the redeemed heaven and earth
d) I refuse to think along the above theological lines

Response:

Groups/ Options	a)	b)	c)	d)
UBCAP	90.0%	5.0%	—%	5.0%
BCOQ	73.0	8.0	.8	18.0
BUWC	89.0	2.0	—	9.0
FEBC	100.0	—	—	—
NABC	94.0	6.0	—	—

Table 8: Prophetic Outlook

Options:

a) I hold to a postmillennial position
b) I hold to an amillennial position
c) I hold to a dispensational, premillennial position
d) I hold to historic premillennialism, non-dispensational
e) I know the Lord will return but I'm not inclined to any specific position
f) I am skeptical about the New Testament picture of Christ's return

Response:

Groups/ Options	a)	b)	c)	d)	e)	f)
UBCAP	1.3%	11.2%	28.3%	17.8%	39.5%	2.0%
BCOQ	—	13.2	8.8	18.4	55.2	4.4
BUWC	—	15.1	1.9	34.0	47.2	1.9
FEBC	.7	14.3	38.9	29.4	16.7	—
NABC	2.9	17.7	26.5	20.6	32.4	—

Table 9: Membership in Baptist Churches

Options:

a) Membership in a local Baptist church should be open *only* to immersed believers
b) should be open to any Christian who wants to join the Baptist church, regardless of mode of baptism or when it was administered (i.e., infant baptism)
c) membership should be open to any Christian who will undergo or has undergone believer's baptism (regardless of mode of baptism)

Response:

Groups/ Options	a)	b)	c)
UBCAP	73.0%	12.0%	15.0%
BCOQ	40.0	20.0	40.0
BUWC	33.0	7.0	60.0
FEBC	92.0	2.0	6.0
NABC	69.0	11.0	20.0

Table 10: Canadian Council of Churches
Options:

a) my convention/association should belong
b) my convention/association should not belong

Response:

Groups/Options	a)	b)	
UBCAP	27.0%	73.0%	
BCOQ	56.0	40.0	(4% different answers)
BUWC	46.0	54.0	
FEBC	—	100.0	
NABC	19.0	81.0	

Table 11: Charismatic Movement
Options:

a) It is, by and large, of the Devil. I am against it
b) I believe the movement is of God, although I recognize serious weaknesses
c) I am unsure about it, but I tend to be negative toward it
d) I am unsure about it, but I tend to be positive toward it

Response:

Groups/Options	a)	b)	c)	d)
UBCAP	21.0%	48.0%	25.0%	6.0%
BCOQ	3.0	72.0	17.0	8.0
BUWC	4.0	83.0	9.0	4.0
FEBC	63.0	16.0	18.0	3.0
NABC	9.0	65.0	20.0	6.0

Table 12: Ordination of Women

Options:

a) I do not believe the New Testament allows it; I am against it
b) the New Testament allows for it; I am for it
c) the New Testament seems to be against it, but I am for it

Response:

Groups/ Options	a)	b)	c)
UBCAP	53.0%	40.0%	7.0%
BCOQ	28.0	60.0	12.0
BUWC	19.0	77.0	4.0
FEBC	96.8	3.2	—
NABC	78.0	18.0	4.0

The main purpose of this report was to provide the basic data from the questionnaire but not to interpret the material. The following comments are added as preliminary observations on the profile of Canadian Baptist ministers.

It is evident that Baptist leaders, generally speaking, are "conservative" in theology.[3] This does not mean that there is total uniformity or that Canadian Baptists, as a whole, are characterized by varying degrees of fundamentalism. However, the survey results indicate that the vast majority of Baptist ministers hold to traditional, orthodox formulations of Christian faith. This applies particularly to their views on the authority of the Bible, the person of Christ, and the nature of salvation.

Baptist insistence on the right of every believer to interpret the message of the Bible for himself (herself) makes theological consensus a difficult goal to achieve. Some might even dismiss it as undesirable, and take pride in doctrinal diversity within their particular church group.

Nevertheless, the survey leads one to the conclusion that at the present time, Baptist emphasis on religious liberty is not precluding an impressive level of agreement on basic theological issues. In view of such evidence, the obstacles that stand in the way of closer fellowship and cooperation among Baptists in Canada must be identified as primarily non-theological.[4]

15 *National Survey of Baptist Ministers,*
J. A. Beverley

1. I wish to thank the following persons for their assistance with the distibution and analysis of the survey questionnaires: George Beverley, Bob Beverley, Cindy Beverley, and most of all, my wife Gloria.

2. For information on different Baptist groups in Canada, see the latest edition of the *Yearbook of American and Canadian Churches,* ed. by Constant H. Jacquet, Jr. (Nashville: Abingdon Press).

3. For a comparison of our survey data with those on ministers with more liberal theological views, see Rodney Stark & Charles Glock, *American Piety: The Nature of Religious Commitment* (Berkeley-Los Angeles-London: Univ. of California Press, 1970).

4. The author will welcome correspondence with the readers about the survey and the interpretation of its data. For address, see Appendix I (Contributors).

BAPTISTS IN CANADA 1760-1980
International Symposium

Sponsored by

Acadia Divinity College

in co-operation with
The Baptist Federation of Canada and
Baptist Historical Committee of the United Baptist Convention
of the Atlantic Provinces

The Symposium includes the 1979 Hayward Lectures
presented as four public lectures in the evening sessions.

October 15-18, 1979

Wolfville, Nova Scotia

Appendix I

Contributors

James A. Beverley, Lecturer, Atlantic Baptist College, Box 1004, Moncton, New Brunswick E1C 8P4

R. Fred Bullen, General Secretary-Treasurer, Baptist Federation of Canada, Box 1298, Brantford, Ontario N3T 5T6

W. Gordon Carder, Minister, United Church, Honeywood, Ontario L0N 1H0 (formerly at Andhra Christian Theological College, Hyderabad, India)

Kenneth R. Davis, Associate Professor, Department of History, University of Waterloo, Waterloo, Ontario N2L 3G1

Paul R. Dekar, Associate Professor of Christian History, McMaster Divinity College, Hamilton, Ontario L8S 4K1

Walter E. Ellis, Minister, Westmount Baptist Church, 411 Roslyn Ave., Westmount, P.Q. H3Y 2T6 (formerly First Baptist Church, Tacoma, Washington, U.S.A.)

Edward B. Link, Professor of Church History, North American Baptist College, 23rd Avenue & 115th St., R.R. 3, South Edmonton, Alberta T6H 4N7

Samuel J. Mikolaski, President, Atlantic Baptist College, Box 1004, Moncton, New Brunswick E1C 8P4 (formerly Principal, Baptist Leadership Training School, Calgary, Alberta)

John S. Moir, Professor of History, Scarborough College, University of Toronto; res., 167 Main St. North, Markham, Ontario L3P 1Y2

Clark H. Pinnock, Professor of Systematic Theology, McMaster Divinity College, Hamilton, Ontario L8S 4K1

John B. Richards, Professor of Church History, Northwest Baptist Theological College and Seminary, 3358 S.E. Marine Drive, Vancouver, British Columbia V5S 2H6

Leslie K. Tarr, Editor, *Faith Today*, and Professor, Central Baptist Seminary; res., 15 Sun Ave., Scarborough, Ontario M1R 3T9

W. Nelson Thomson, Pasteur, Église baptiste de St. Constant; res., 730 Croissant Picard, Brossard, P.Q. J4W 1S5

Robert S. Wilson, Dean and Professor of History, Atlantic Baptist, College, Box 1004, Moncton, New Brunswick E1C 8P4

Jarold K. Zeman, President, Baptist Federation of Canada, and Professor of Church History, Acadia Divinity College, Wolfville, Nova Scotia B0P 1X0

Appendix II

Symposium Papers Published Elsewhere

Other papers presented at the symposium "Baptists in Canada 1760-1980" at Acadia Divinity College, Wolfville, Nova Scotia, October 15-18, 1979, have appeared in the following publications and are available from the respective publishers, or from the Baptist Resource Centre, 217 St. George Street, Toronto, Ontario, M5R 2M2. (Tel. 416-922-5163)

A. *Repent and Believe: The Baptist Experience in Maritime Canada.* Ed. Barry M. Moody. (Lancelot Press Ltd., P.O. Box 425, Hantsport, Nova Scotia, B0P 1P0). 1980. $6.95.

Contents

1. *From New Light to Baptist: Harris Harding and the Second Great Awakening in Nova Scotia.* George A. Rawlyk
2. *Church Covenants and Church Discipline among Baptists in the Maritime Provinces, 1778-1878.* Charles W. Deweese
3. *The Role of the African United Baptist Association in the Development of Indigenous Afro-Canadians in Nova Scotia, 1782-1978.* Savanah E. Williams
4. *Without Intervention of Prophet, Priest or King.* Esther Clark Wright
5. *"Joseph Howe is Their Devil": Controversies among Regular Baptists in Halifax, 1827-1868.* Philip G. A. Allwood
6. *The Maritime Baptists and Higher Education in the Early Nineteenth Century.* Barry M. Moody
7. *The New Brunswick Baptist Seminary, 1836-1895.* Allison A. Trites
8. *Alice Shaw and her Grand Pre Seminary: A Story of Female Education.* James D. Davison
9. *The Union of the Regular and the Free Will Baptists of the Maritimes, 1905 and 1906.* Frank H. Sinnott

B. *Baptist History and Heritage*, Vol. XV, No. 2 (April 1980). (127 Ninth Ave. N., Nashville, TN 37234). $1.50.

Contents
1. *Highlights of the Relationships of Southern Baptists with Canadian Baptists.* A. Ronald Tonks
2. *Formative Influences on Baptists in British Columbia, 1876-1918.* Gordon H. Pousett
3. **Prominent Church Covenants of Maritime Baptists, 1778-1878.* Charles W. Deweese

*Not presented at the symposium.

C. *Foundations,* Vol. 23, No. 1 (January-March 1980). (18 Putnam Road, Arlington, MA 02174). $3.00

Contents
1. *The Fellowship of Believers and the Nature of Belief.* Russell F. Aldwinckle
2. *The Interrelationships of Baptists in Canada and the U. S. A.* Winthrop S. Hudson
3. *Influence of Canadians on Baptist Theological Education in the United States.* Robert T. Handy
4. *The Era of the "Great Preacher" among Canadian Baptists: A Comparative Study of W. A. Cameron, John J. MacNeill and T. T. Shields as Preachers.* G. Gerald Harrop
5. *Canadian Baptist Ecumenical Relationships.* I. Judson Levy
6. *Many Confessions, One Creed.* James R. C. Perkin

D. The paper on "Trends in Canadian Baptist Evangelism Since World War II" by Thomas B. McDormand appeared in *Expect a Difference: The Report Volume of the Baptist Federation of Canada 1976-1979,* edited by R. F. Bullen. It is available from Baptist Federation of Canada, P.O. Box 1298, Brantford, Ontario N3T 5T6.

E. The paper on "Thomas Todhunter Shields, Canadian Fundamentalist" by C. Allyn Russell appeared in *Ontario History,* Vol. 70 (1978): 263-280.